DEVELOPMENTS IN MODERN HISTORIOGRAPHY

Also by Henry Kozicki

TENNYSON AND CLIO
History in the Major Poems

THE WRITING OF HISTORY
Literary Form and Historical Understanding (*co-editor*)

*WESTERN AND RUSSIAN HISTORIOGRAPHY
Recent Views (*editor*)

Also published by Macmillan

Developments in Modern Historiography

Edited by

Henry Kozicki
Professor Emeritus of English and Linguistics
Indiana University–Purdue University

With an Introduction by
Sidney Monas

© Henry Kozicki 1993

First edition 1993
Reprinted 1998

Published by
MACMILLAN PRESS LTD
Houndmills, Basingstoke, Hampshire RG21 6XS
and London
Companies and representatives
throughout the world

ISBN 0–333–58597–6 hardcover
ISBN 0–333–74826–3 paperback

A catalogue record for this book is available
from the British Library.

Copy-edited and typeset by Grahame & Grahame Editorial, Brighton

This book is printed on paper suitable for recycling and
made from fully managed and sustained forest sources.

10   9   8   7   6   5   4   3   2   1
07   06   05   04   03   02   01   00   99   98

Printed and bound in Great Britain by
Antony Rowe Ltd, Chippenham, Wiltshire

Contents

A Note on Transliteration from Cyrillic

There is no completely satisfactory system of transliteration. The phonetic (or, as some like to call it, "fanatic") system is precise and economical, but to the uninitiated reader, seeing *Cexov* on the page for *Chekhov* or *Tolstoj* for *Tolstoy* can be a mildly unsettling experience. In this collection, we have used, consistently in the notes, the Library of Congress system, used in most libraries in the English-speaking world. In the text, we have modified it somewhat by omitting the Cyrillic soft sign (') and hard sign (") and by using the adjectival name-ending -sky instead of -skii. Thus, we would have Dostoevskii in the notes and Dostoevsky in the text, but wish to assure you, gentle reader, that he remains the same person. In the case of familiar spellings of familiar names, we have retained them in the text: thus, Tolstoy, and not Tolstoi. In the case of Russians who have published extensively in English, we have retained their own preferred spelling of their names: thus, Yanov, and not Ianov. In the Library of Congress system, it should perhaps be added that both the soft e (pronounced "yeh") and the hard e (pronounced "eh") are transcribed by "e". In the notes, we have tried to follow the Library of Congress system consistently.

Notes on the Contributors

Leon J. Goldstein is a Professor of Philosophy in, and a former chairman of, the Department of Philosophy at the State University of New York at Binghamton. Since 1979, he has been an editor of the journal *International Studies in Philosophy*. He has published some fifty articles and over 100 reviews on a variety of subjects. His books include *Historical Knowing* (1976) and (with Lucy S. Dawidowicz) *Politics in a Pluralistic Democracy* (1963; 1974). A work-in-progress is a book, *Conceptual Tension*.

Georg G. Iggers is a Distinguished Professor of History at the State University of New York at Buffalo. He has held many posts abroad, most recently as a visiting scholar at the Technische Hochschule Darmstadt. He is the author of *The Cult of Authority: The Political Philosophy of the Saint-Simonians* (1958; 2nd edn 1970); *The German Conception of History: The National Tradition from Herder to the Present* (1968; rev. edn 1983; German and Hungarian translations); and *New Directions in European Historiography* (1975; rev. edn 1984; German, Italian, Danish, Korean, Japanese, and Chinese translations). He has edited or co-edited *The Doctrine of Saint-Simon* (1958; rev. edn 1972); *Leopold von Ranke The Theory and Practice of History* (1973); *International Handbook of Historical Studies* (1978; Chinese translation); *Leopold von Ranke: The Shaping of the Historical Discipline* (1990); *Marxist Historiography in Transformation: East German Social History in the 1980s* (1991; German version, *Ein anderer historische Blick: Beispiele ostdeutscher Sozialgeschichte* [1991]). He has published many journal articles in the U.S.A. and Europe.

Gerald N. Izenberg is an Associate Professor in the Department of History of Washington University, a Co-Director of its Literature and History Program, and a Faculty Member of the St. Louis Psychoanalytic Institute. His book, *The Existentialist Critique of Freud* (1976), his articles and papers, and his contributions to collections, are in the general field of psycho history. He has also published *Impossible Individuality: Romanticism, Revolution and the Origin of Modern Selfhood, 1787–1802* (1992).

Michael A. Kissell was a Professor of Philosophy at the University of Leningrad 1972–1985, and is now the Chief Research-Associate of the Institute of Philosophy of the Academy of Sciences of the USSR, in Moscow. He has been a Visiting Professor at the University of Moscow, Wroclav University in Poland, and Turku University in Finland. He has published more than 100 articles. His nine books are on Hegel, Sartre, Vico, and various philosophical subjects. His most recent books are *Hegel and the Modern World* (Leningrad, 1982), and *The French Enlightenment and the Revolution* (Moscow, 1989). He is also a co-editor of, and author of the introductory essay to, the Russian translation of R. G. Collingwood's *The Idea of History*.

Eero Loone is a Professor and Head of the Department of Philosophy and Political Science at Tartu University in Estonia. He is also a Board Member of the Institute of Philosophy, Sociology, and Law in the Estonian Academy of Sciences. Among his recent works are the articles "Philosophic Questions about Historical Research" and "The Classical Theory of Verstehen and Methodogoical Choices in Historical Research," in the *Acta et commentationes Universitatis Tartuensis*: no. 599 (1982) and no. 731 (1986), respectively; and the books *An Introduction to the Marxist Philosophy of Society* (Tallinn, 1989), and *Soviet Marxism and Analytic Philosophies of History* trans. Brian Pearce, foreword Ernest Gellner (London: Verso, 1990); originally published in Russian (1980).

Arthur Marwick is a Professor of History at the Open University, in England. He has been a Visiting Scholar at the Hoover Institution, and the Director of L'École des Hautes Études En Sciences Sociales in Paris. His main publications are *The Deluge: British Society and the First World War* (1965); *The Nature of History* (1970), rev. editions 1981, 1989; *War, Peace and Social Change in the Twentieth Century: A Comparative Study of Britain, France, Germany, Russia and the United States* (1974); *Class: Image and Reality in Britain, France and the USA Since 1930* (1980), 2nd edn 1990; *British Society Since 1945* (1982), rev. editions 1989, 1990; and *Beauty in History: Society and Personal Appearance c. 1500 to the Present* (1988); he has edited *Total War and Social Change* (1988) and *The Arts, Literature and Society* (1990).

Sidney Monas is a Professor with a joint appointment in the Department of History and the Department of Slavic Languages at the University of Texas at Austin; he is a former chairman of the latter. He has been a visiting professor at the Hebrew University in Jerusalem and St. Antony's College at Oxford. He has translated and edited many works from the Slavic and especially the Russian language, in particular the works of Dostoevsky. He has served on the editorial boards of many journals in his fields; currently he is the editor of *Slavic Review*.

Andrus Park (formerly Andrus Pork) is a Professor of Philosophy at Tartu State University, and currently a Member of the Presidium, and Acting General Scientific Secretary, of the Estonian Academy of Sciences. He has been a Research Fellow at institutions in London and the U.S. He has published over 70 works in Estonian, Russian, and English. Among recent articles in English are "Assessing Relative Causal Importance in History" and "Critical Philosophy of History in Soviet Thought" in *History and Theory* 24 (1985) and 27 (1988), respectively; and "The Role of Examples in Social Explanation" in *Philosophy of the Social Sciences* 19 (1989). Among recent books in English are *Epistemological Independence and Explanation in the Social Sciences* (Tallinn, 1986), *Some Aspects of Relative Causal Importance in History* (Tallinn, 1986), and *History, Explanation and Typology* (Tallinn,1987).

Theodore K. Rabb is a Professor of History at Princeton University, having taught as well at Stanford, Northwestern, Harvard, and Johns Hopkins Universities. He has been an editor of *The Journal of Interdisciplinary History* since its foundation in 1970, and has held offices in various national organizations, including the American Historical Association and the Social Science History Association. He has published numerous articles and reviews. Among the books he has written or edited are *The Struggle for Stability in Early Modern Europe* (1975), *The Origins of Modern Nations* (1981), *The New History: The 1980s and Beyond* (1982), *Population and Economy* (1986), *Art and History: Images and Their Meaning* (1988), and *The Origin and Prevention of Major Wars* (1988). His book *Sir Edwin Sandys (1561–1629): A Life and Times* is forthcoming. He is currently involved in preparing for the Public Broadcasting Systen a multi-part television series on Renaissance history.

Richard T. Vann is a Professor of History and Letters, and the Director of the Center for the Humanities, at Wesleyan University. He has been Visiting Amundson Professor and Visiting Mellon Professor at the University of Pittsburgh. He is the Executive Editor of *History and Theory*. He has published more than 40 articles and review essays, among the most recent of which is the article "Louis Mink's Linguistic Turn" in *History and Theory* 26 (1987), and chapters in two forthcoming collections. Among his recent books are: (co-edited) *History of the Family and Kinship: A Select International Bibliography* (1980), and *Friends in Life and Death: The British and Irish Quakers in the Demographic Transition, 1655–1723* (forthcoming).

Preface

Henry Kozicki

This collection of original articles, within its limits, follows such broadly-based examinations of developments in historiography as the *International Handbook of Historical Studies: Contemporary Research and Theory*, edited by Georg G. Iggers and Harold T. Parker (Greenwood Press, 1979), and *The Past Before Us: Contemporary Historical Writing in the United States*, edited by Michael Kammen (Cornell University Press, 1980). These volumes, dealing with the work of the 1970s, were informed by a sense of rapid transformations in the discipline – new approaches, new areas of inquiry, new standpoints – which were welcomed as rich diversity, heuristic divergencies, and cosmopolitan pluralism. The authors in the present collection, examining the work of the 1980s, find that these changes have not brought satisfactory results. They argue that traditional practices, reassessed and properly understood, constitute the scientific grounding of the discipline.

The first of the volume's two parts contains studies that consider in various ways the objective and the subjective in history. Professor Iggers argues that historical inquiry has always affirmed an objective reality that can be understood rationally, with due account of evidentiary uncertainty and the subjective interests of the historian, notwithstanding the invocation, particularly by social and cultural historians, of theories of textuality that virtually deny referentiality and rationality in historical inquiry. Professor Izenberg demonstrates that current theories of self-sufficient textuality which deny the validity of context are more honored by their practitioners in the breach than in the observance, as in some writings of de Man, Derrida, and LaCapra; on the other hand, an inescapable biographical-psychological context appears when leaving the text, a context that is irreducible to, but fully consonant with, other levels of historical explanation. Professor Rabb examines two overviews of the current state of historiography and finds that both exaggerate the division between scientific objectivity and the modernist perspectives that seem to deny it; in fact, the current situation is much like the condition of science in the sixteenth and seventeenth centuries where methodologies warred with no clear or common purpose yet also shared the cohesiveness implicit in vital, open-ended diversity; historians (and the public) should appreciate a golden age when they are in one. Professor Goldstein faults commentary that focuses upon what historians say and fails to attend to what they actually do, and faults also a failure to understand the nature of scientific thought in history; he argues that we may see in what Charles Tilly *does* a merger of sociology and history that provides a truthful account of the past not in story-telling nor yet in deduction from general laws but scientifically for all that: an account of how things were and why. Professor Kissell uses Marx's *The Eighteenth Brumaire of Louis Bonaparte* as a paradigmatic work, in the Kuhnian sense, to derive the criteria of scientific history, criteria informed by a non-Hegelian dialectic inseparably both object and subject; he argues that every historical event is singular: neither the inevitable result of "iron" laws nor accidental or irrational: real history is more complex than all methodologies applied to it.

The second part is given over to commentary on historical sources, the resources needed to secure them, and the explanations that utilize them. Professor Marwick argues that, while historians are quite aware of the complexity of their subject and its relation to other disciplines, historical writing is based on the suitable utilization of at least thirteen types of sources and documents; in this manner, historians have achieved much understanding of the real past (they do not compose merely self-reflexive, competing discourse-fictions), but can no more be expected to provide an overarching explanation for all of history than scientists do for the whole physical universe. Professor Vann examines the extensive literature on the history of the family, and demonstrates the inadequacies of the statistical sources and the interpretations that underlie thought about the family in terms of Marxist theories of production. He also faults the Freudian psychology, and its data, in theories of patriarchy, property, and repression. There is, in fact, no theory of the family that satisfactorily unifies social and psychological facts; Professor Vann suggests that a combination of Marx and Malthus would be a fruitful line of inquiry. Professor Loone finds a crucial distinction in historical statements that compare matters over time: between quantitative statements involving variables that in themselves are valid across time-frames, and qualitative ones involving essential differences between time-frames; the historian's language should reflect this distinction as the universals and, relatively speaking, the particulars in explanation. Professor Park analyzes six types of causal explanation (summary, description of causes, emerging causes, periodization, the hierarchical typology of causes, and the narrative of causes) in some historical texts of Marx, Engels, and Lenin, and suggests that these types of explanatory strategies appear, as well, in non-Marxist and all historical studies, and thus constitute the basic forms of historical knowing.

This volume demonstrates, in short, that despite current theoretical distractions the historical discipline is soundly based on traditional practices properly understood.

1 Introduction: Contemporary Historiography: Some Kicks in the Old Coffin

Sidney Monas

Critics who feel that the historical profession is in crisis, at an impasse, point to an unseemly number of unresolved controversies, a disarray of methodologies, and a confused relationship to the social sciences and psychology on the one hand and philosophy and literature on the other. There is the failure of cliometry to achieve comprehensive results, and the threat of "narrativity" to remove history from the strictures of scientific method and reducing it to the condition of a merely literary genre. Too, history seems to have lost its popular audience and to have diminished its role in education.

Some of the authors here, like Georg Iggers, seem to feel that there is indeed a crisis. Arthur Marwick implies something of one by the very passion and clamor of his defense of "source-based" history. Richard Vann argues the lack of a recent Marxist historiography of the family. Whether there is or is not a crisis in historical thought is not resolved by these essays, but they do demonstrate an exceptional liveliness of thought, introspection, and criticism in the field of historiography.

To me, the most striking thing about George Iggers' essay, apart from its erudition, generosity, openness to the ideas of a new generation of historians – qualities I have learned to expect from him – is its defensive tone; and behind that tone a sense of embattlement, as of one under siege. At the end, he addresses his fellow historians with an anguished plea in defense of "rationality," as if reason itself were under siege in the profession and in danger of being throttled.

Iggers begins by saying that "a historical text must be understood with reference to the context to which it refers and that this context contains an element of objectivity not fully identical with the subjectivity of the historian and an element of rationality which presumes elements of intersubjectivity in the methods of historical inquiry." And yet, in historical inquiry, how is such a "context" to be established or construed except by means of other texts? Leon Goldstein, in his essay, "A Note

1

on Historical Interpretation," cited in his note 37, points out that what might at first glance seem to be different interpretations of the same event are in fact arguments based on totally different constructions of the presumed event. We are back in the hermeneutic circle. The search for Iggers' "element of objectivity" need not throw rationality overboard, yet the kind of reason required clearly differs from that which can be confirmed by direct experience or experiment.

For Iggers, some definable distinction between "Dichtung" and "Wahrheit" is essential to the survival of reason. Yet Dichtung and Wahrheit have been staring at each other, sitting together and spitting at each other, for many centuries now, and they have tended to become not only "semblables" but mutually dependent. Even Iggers admits the line between them has been crossed innumerable times. One might even take note of Vico's conception that all ratiocination is founded on a basically passional conception of the world – that Wahrheit is a "corrected" but slightly weary Dichtung.

Like most historians, with the notable exception of Simon Schama,[1] Iggers is eager to maintain the distinction between "objectivity" and "free Imagination," which I take to be analogous to Wahrheit and Dichtung. He does say "free" imagination and that does imply a difference from objectivity, which presumably is the product of discipline, restriction, limitation, and not "free" at all. Free imagination is essential to fiction and not a bad thing for history either, providing it does not obliterate the core of objectivity that is essential to the latter.

Yet writers of fiction and poetry tend to speak not of a free but a "disciplined" imagination. Nor do they eschew objectivity or verisimilitude in depiction even when the depicted is another person's dream. Tolstoy did not simply "make up" *War and Peace*, though his "sources" differed from those used by the historians and included his own experience of war. The sardonic tone of Elsa Morante's *History: A Novel* has to do not with the question of objectivity but with the putative subject-matter of history (battles and great men, as opposed to the ordeals of family life) and the non-participative attitude of historians. When Stephen Dedalus in James Joyce's *Ulysses* says, "History is a nightmare from which I am trying to awake," he means the process of history (conceived as "battles and great men"), not, directly, the writing of it. In short, it seems to me that novelists and poets have on the whole shown more respect for history and the writing of it than historians have for "Dichtung."

This is a pity, for if historians were less fearful of turning fictive, more self-conscious about what they wanted to do with words, they could learn a lot, not only from novelists and poets, but also from their critics, who have made the possibilities and limitations of language the direct object of their study for a much longer time. There is no doubt more to history than narrativity and emplotment, as there is also to fiction, yet surely they are as vital to the one as to the other, and not merely in the writing, but in the very conception of a project. Most twentieth-century historians, including those who exult in their story-telling abilities, are still telling nineteenth-century stories. I would take a twentieth-century story to be one that is told like Joyce's *Ulysses*, with a simultaneously layered sense of time, so that Leopold Blum is at once a secularized Irish Jew in the year 1904, Homer's Odysseus, the prophet Elijah, and the wandering Jew of the Middle Ages. To the best of my knowledge, Oswald Spengler alone has attempted to write history in this way.

The "linguistic turn" in historiography was all but inevitable. It had occurred almost everywhere else in the human sciences earlier. This was due to a large extent to the success of the structural linguistics that derived from Saussure, was further developed by Roman Jakobson, and came to Claude Lévi-Strauss and anthropology from Jakobson. The extraordinary success of Noam Chomsky's "transformational grammar" owed something to Jakobson as well. In the 1960s, linguistics was the most dynamic and the most "successful" of the social sciences – in the sense that it produced "covering laws" that could be formulated with mathematical precision. All the human sciences panted hungrily at the heels of modern scientific linguistics. If history proved laggard, it may have been in part because the new linguistics was primarily synchronically oriented and had relatively little interest in historical change. The real impact of linguistics on historiography came later, by way of literary theory and literary criticism with a theoretical bent.

Saussurean linguistics did tend to emphasize the autonomy of language as a symbolic system. In this sense it fed into formalist trends in literary criticism, like the New Criticism in America and the textual exegesis of Gustave Lanson in France. Post-structuralism – "Derridadaism," as one wit called it – pushed the idea of linguistic autonomy to radical and extreme conclusions. The existence of a written text that survived its author by centuries made any conjecture as to the intentions of the author a wild guessing game at best. Authorial intent was not a presence in the text, but an absence. The language of the text became a free play of signifiers, and the game they played was with each other, not with any putative "objective world." Derrida accompanied his campaign of textual liberation with a radical skepticism of the metaphysical assumptions of western philosophy. His primary subjects were not literary but philosophical, though any text was potentially fair game, and almost anything could be "textualized." His close friend and disciple, Paul de Man, even wrote a well known essay on an Archie Bunker sitcom, for example.[2] Deconstructive criticism can be applied to anything; it is rather fun to practice, lends itself adoptably to the support or demolition of almost any ideology, and requires the mastery of a methodology and a vocabulary rather than the command of a great deal of erudition. And the literary mossbacks and mastodons all hate it. So it is no wonder it has been immensely popular and influential among the younger brighter set of teachers of literature. Of course it has itself by now become fairly routinized and there has been a strong reaction against it, not only by the aforementioned mossbacks who claim to fear the moral void, but by the young as well, who begin to find it boring. The historical profession has until quite recently been little touched by it. But because its practitioners there are defensive, cautious, and tend to use it in conjunction with other techniques and to minimize its jargon, it has been effective and useful and I see no reason why it should not continue to be so.

I have no intention here of outlining a history of the "linguistic turn" in historiography. Iggers' own outline of the "crisis" in our historical world – occasioned by the growing awareness over the past two centuries both of the central importance of language to the development of the psyche and at the same time the limitations imposed on that psyche's grasp of the "objective world" by what Nietzsche called "the prison-house of language" – is eloquent and impressive. I will only quibble a little here and there and insert a few details I feel are essential to understanding the present situation.

He begins with Herodotus and Thucydides, claiming for them a dividing line between fact and fiction he clearly wishes their descendants had held to. But Herodotus made no such distinction. He thought the stories people told about themselves at least as significant for understanding them as "what actually happened." True, every so often he adds after one of his stories that he does not really believe it, but this is more the exception than the rule. As for the much sterner Thucydides, he begins his history by saying that, with regard to speeches on important occasions where he had no completely reliable witness, he reported them as "the logic of the situation demanded."

Iggers is perceptive and acute in pointing to a certain relationship between nineteenth-century historical practice and the Bildungsroman, or fictive account of the formation of a mature "sensibility," a word that encompasses perceptions, emotions, ideas, their coherence into an overall outlook, and the way in which, under the impact of events and experience, they change and shape what nevertheless remains a unitary "character." He might have added, however, that not only does the hero's character change in the course of what was usually a fairly lengthy work (and a long time in the writing, too) but often the author's character as well. The seeming coherence is not as well-grounded as Iggers imagines. A little applied "Derridadaism" here might be quite revealing.

For Burckhardt, Iggers writes, though discontinuity plays a major role in history, an epoch nevertheless "has a cohesion and a spirit that can be portrayed." I would add only that for Michel Foucault, too, an "epoch" coheres, has its own identifiable discourse and episteme. In fact, "traces" of Burckhardt's imagination seem to me unmistakable in Foucault's work. The problem for me lies in the fact that Foucault, unlike Burckhardt, feels himself under no conceptual obligation to account for how one epoch becomes another.[3] There is neither development nor evolution in Foucault and, although there are such things as remnants and survivals from one episteme to another, their discourses are as fundamentally impermeable to each other as Spengler's cultures and civilizations.

Surely neither Karl Marx nor Sigmund Freud believed, as Iggers still seems to, that documents could either mean what they say or say what they mean. It is true, however, that both men still believed that in some sense, in spite of "false consciousness" on the one hand and psychic repression and "censorship" on the other, there was a meaning in them, and it could be decoded after all. For my part, I still find such decodings useful, up to a point, and surely one need not be by now either a Marxist or a Freudian to use selectively the systems by which they operate, yet one should bear in mind a certain bleak history of shabby interpretations practiced under the aegis of both systems and not be overconfident.

Iggers' defense of hermeneutics is that, "even if it rejects clearly defined methodological procedure, [it] is not in itself an expression of irrationality but rather an attempt to understand cultural meaning by means of adequate forms of reasoning." He does not oppose an alliance of reason and imagination in pursuit of coherence. "For if no coherence of any kind can be constructed in history or reality, then reason loses its claim to show a path to critical understanding."

But the key word here is "constructed," as Iggers seems not to be aware. Coherence is a construct, and no such construct is absolute or final. Dialogue, the ongoing criticism by "those who are qualified," is always called for. Nor should one forget that congregations of the qualified, the professionals, the professors, develop an institutional momentum of their own, with institutional vested interests that are not always pure distillates of truth-seeking, so that sometimes, and not rarely, the voice of an outsider is needed to tell the Emperor he has no clothes. A little "Derridadaism" is not always out of order.

It should also be pointed out that fiction and poetry are not without their congregations of the qualified – theorists, critics, reviewers, and the literate public (if there still is such a thing) – who have analogous virtues and failings and are subject to the same temptations. And Iggers refers us to Thomas Kuhn, who testifies to the same process as the basic sustenance of science.[4] If we take science, the social sciences (including history) and literature on some sort of continuum, it is clear that the standards of what constitutes a satisfactory coherence vary; yet the process for establishing and maintaining those standards strikes me as not dissimilar.

If Hayden White concludes, as Iggers has it, that "an historical text is in essence nothing more than a literary text," at least he concludes also that it is nothing less. I refuse to accept the notion that a great work of fiction or poetry has no truth value, though its relationship to that rational-imaginative construct Iggers calls "objective reality" might well be, and quite consciously, different. Neither the poet nor the historian is simply at the mercy of the generic possibilities available to him. He contributes to, and to some degree shapes those possibilities. To a large degree, the genre and mode and emplotment he "chooses" is an affair of his temperament and character and is in some sense "there" before he sets pen to paper, or even does his "research." White's point, as I take it, was that the nineteenth-century historians and philosophers of history he deals with were all great erudites and in impressive command of the information available to them. The differences among them were not to be explained in terms of who was right and who was wrong, who plugged in to "objective reality" and who did not, but rather in terms of the differences of temperament and the relationship of temperament to genre, mode, and emplotment. None of them used evidence "improperly."

We cannot live in a world without values and meanings. The trouble is there are so many different ones, and no absolute grounds for any of them. The trouble is that such relativism tends to put value and meaning as such at hazard and presents the temptation of an absolutism at some level known to be false. What Mikhail Bakhtin says of Dostoevsky's characters, that they are "unfinalizable," and that this unfinalizability is sustained by means of dialogue, the "dialogic principle," is true by analogy of the discourses that sustain science, the social sciences, and all the arts.[5] That great history-book-in-the-sky that I suspect Ranke envisioned when all the research was done, critically examined, and written up, will never be completed. The dialogue will go on and perspectives will shift. Without imagination, reason is a snake that swallows its own tail.

With Gerald Izenberg's fine essay, I am in complete sympathy. His aim, stated with admirable clarity at the beginning, is twofold: to argue against ignoring the role of context in interpreting texts significant to intellectual history; and for the importance of the psychological-biographical context, "often indispensable in intellectual history and always irreducible to other levels of explanatory context." At the same time, he distances himself from those who refuse to take the radical-textualist "linguistic turn" seriously. David Hollinger's attempted rebuttal of anticontextualism, while it is not without point, loses something by his admission "that he has not tackled the theoretical objections to context head-on." While it is true that radical-textualism is fundamentally ahistorical, virtually a denial of the need for historical research, Izenberg argues: "For historians to avoid considering certain linguistic theories just because they [historians] couldn't continue to work as they have if the theories were true, is hardly a comfortable position to take for a discipline which prides itself on the rationality of its procedures."

Respectfully, but with a sure and lapidary touch, Izenberg shapes a brief but compelling critique displaying the virtues and limitations of the discourse-oriented work of J. G. A. Pocock and Quentin Skinner and Fredric Jameson's murky idea of a "political unconscious," all of which tend to devalue the importance of the author, his psychology and biography, for an understanding of the work.

Izenberg goes on then, not without a certain respect and admiration, to deconstruct the work of Dominick LaCapra and Paul de Man.

While LaCapra claims to be offering not a substitute for but a necessary supplement to the traditional explanatory practices of historians, his own theoretical commitments push him in a more radical direction. One might well grant that complex texts, as Izenberg puts it, "through their rhetorical and structural devices" – and one might add as well, through a depth of insight gained from the anomalies of personal experience – do something to the historical material they are presumed to represent, "so that they cannot be reduced to mere instances of their sociopolitical and discursive contexts," and yet hold some brief for a knowledge of those contexts in order properly to understand the texts. In going back to those contexts, the virtues of traditional historiography – meticulous research and critical rationality – are fully in order for LaCapra. What could be more sensible? Izenberg points out that LaCapra's critical practice tells another story. He seems to see all efforts by historians to relate particular themes in art or thought of a period to their sociopolitical or cultural milieu as reductive synopsis and illegitimate causal attribution. Izenberg attributes this tendency of LaCapra's not so much to a casual disjuncture between theory and practice, as to "an unintentionally over-rigid distinction between text and context which forces him in practice to a choice that in theory he does not wish to make."

The subtlety and acuity of Izenberg's deconstruction of de Man's notorious reading of Rousseau is fully up to the complex "apologetic" argument and wayward intelligence of the text itself. He even finds in de Man's text, which seems to evade or even deny the idea of Rousseau's moral responsibility, an argument for the possible referentiality of even fiction and poetry, implying that "it could be held to be offering morally accountable portrayals and judgments of the world." He finds in Jacques Derrida's practice, too, a notable exception to the radical logocentrism of which Derrida has often been accused – his "Coming into One's Own," in which he discusses Freud's *Beyond the Pleasure Principle* very much in a biographical-psychological context.[6] Derrida's well-known aphorism that "there is nothing outside the text," for Izenberg, has been widely misunderstood. Deconstructive practice by no means precludes attention to sociopolitical or cultural or biographical context. "The particular contribution of modern literary criticism to intellectual history," Izenberg writes, "has been to alert us to the fact that it is possible to speak of structural, narrative, stylistic, and tropological incoherences, and that tensions in the aesthetic elements of even a discursive text are part of its meaning and argument."

In his exceptionally interesting essay on the disarray of seventeenth-century scientific thinking, Theodore Rabb means for us to take heart – and this in spite of the grim appraisal of our professional situation that he cites from an essay by B. G. Mogilnitsky, "Some Tendencies in the Development of Bourgeois Historical Thought"[7] – an assessment which Rabb seems to accept.

The seventeenth century was after all the age in which the foundations for modern achievements in the exact sciences were laid – the pioneering period of modern science. Yet some of its most prominent figures, as he points out, were at loggerheads with each other, to say nothing of the large admixture of metaphysical thinking that most of them still considered to be an essential part of their work. Rabb suggests that something analogous is true of the study of history in our time. Under the seeming disarray and the conflicts of perspectives that characterize our current historiography, and still unknown to the public at large, a new historiography is coming into being that promises a future science of history, that is laying the ground for such a science in much the way that Galileo and Kepler and Brahe for all their squabbles among themselves prepared the ground for Newton.

I find the afflatus of Rabb's essay immensely appealing, but his argument unconvincing. Let us be a little more rigorous in applying an historical perspective. It isn't a question of "time to catch up." History, after all, is just about as ancient an enterprise as any of the sciences. Aristotelean physics are in a totally different realm of discourse from the physics of Galileo, whereas Thucydides, for all the critical scrutiny he has received, the lacunae, the biases that have been pointed out, is still quite remarkably "one of us." Even in the age of modern warfare, it makes sense to read him; he seems relevant, whereas Aristotelian physics are of specialized academic interest only. I would not say that historical understanding has gained nothing since Thucydides, but it has not "progressed" in the manner of the sciences. I doubt that history will ever be a science in the sense that Rabb anticipates.

Leon Goldstein's paper matches Izenberg's for appositeness and articulation. It takes Mogilnitsky's account of the "desperate" situation of "bourgeois" historiography head-on, and at the same time has some fun with it, suggesting a Straussian reading in which "really to understand what Mogilnitsky is doing is to recognize it as a piece of self-criticism."[8] He goes on to conclude that what Mogilnitsky has to say has in fact nothing to do with bourgeois or any other historiography, since the Russian quotes only what historians say about history and writing history, not in fact what they actually do. Izenberg, in his essay, seems to attach a similar importance to such a distinction. What historians say about historiography may bear little or no relation to their practice, and it is that practice that defines the situation, not what is said about it. This is something of an analogue to D. H. Lawrence's remark about the novel, that one should trust the tale and not the teller.

But Goldstein goes considerably further. He has argued elsewhere at considerable length and here very succinctly that history is not a kind of writing, but a mode of knowing; that the real work of history gets done before anything is written and is fundamentally a communal affair – once again, that congregation of the qualified, dialogue, mutual criticism, etc. He argues as well that while there is a great deal of disagreement as to what science is, most people would agree that history is a discipline that "provides . . . knowledge now about a then we cannot know by acquaintance." How secure that knowledge is, he does not query, and he does point out that the uses to which that knowledge may be put are quite various. By making an extremely sharp distinction between history as a research discipline and the later writing of it, Goldstein walks rather jauntily out of the argument about the "linguistic turn." He seems to understand Hayden White and Dominick LaCapra and David Harlan well enough, yet remains untroubled by their work. In his terms, they are writing "about" history, not "doing" it.[9]

Sticking close to the methods of history as a discipline, he also sees its professional identity as reasonably secure. Because, relatively speaking, history has a secure disciplinary identity, it is free to choose conceptual assistance from other disciplines to aid it in its singular task of describing and understanding the past. And since history is not a theoretical discipline and sociology is primarily that, and since the life of human societies and cultures is the common subject matter of both, it is only natural that the two should enter into a symbiotic relationship. Here, Goldstein distinguishes between an "historical sociologist" who uses historical materials to bolster or "flesh out" a theory, and a "sociological historian" who uses social theory to understand the past. He sees Charles Tilly as an exemplary practitioner of sociological history and as close to "scientific" history as it is possible these days to get.

While I admire Goldstein's polemical skill and the charm of his argument, I believe he evades the arguments of the post-structuralists rather than answering them. What has been written and said "about" history is a powerful factor in the "doing" of it, even if, certainly, it is not the same thing. And he seems to be more certain concerning Tilly's disciplinary identity than Tilly himself. Without subscribing to Mogilnitsky's "dire straits" assessment of our historiography, I do believe the situation is more complicated and problematic than Goldstein makes it out to be.

Louis Napoleon's rise to power in the wake of the revolution of 1848 had an impact on nineteenth-century European thought that sits oddly with the seeming inconsequentiality of the man himself. He became a symbol for the disappointment of democratic hopes and for the dissolution of the previously joined political forces of socialism, liberalism, and nationalism. He inspired eloquent rhetoric in the form of scathing denunciations, not only from Karl Marx, but from Victor Hugo, Pierre Proudhon, Alexander Herzen, and many others.[10] But Marx seems to have set himself the task not merely of denouncing the "little" Napoleon, but explaining him, and explaining him in such a way as to enspirit the temporarily defeated revolutionary movement. Michael Kissell is certainly correct in foregrounding the outstanding quality of Marx's *The Eighteenth Brumaire of Louis Napoleon.*

Is it correct, however, to see as he does its "scientific" qualities as primary and its literary eloquence as merely auxiliary?

I do not see how they can be separated. Marx's intellect is driven by his indignation, and it takes off from the calendrical reference of the title (the French Revolution's adoption of the Roman calendar, and the whole Roman sociopolitical scenario that the Republic of Virtue attempted to enact) to the theme of history and repetition – repetition and difference, repetition and diminution – the burden of the past that lies on the brain of the living like an Alp. Marx does not merely refer to repetition and diminution – he uses the former as a structural device and involves the latter in tropes of pettiness, tinsel, and shoddy artifice. The notions of illusion, insubstantiality, and irresponsibility are carefully structured through striking imagery and skillful repetition; images of the circus, the theater, the casino, the improvised trickery of mountebanks and charlatans, the play of illusion, "dramatize" the nature of the political scene and its volatility, the drama of power reduced to the illusional tricks of a peep show.

Marx's analysis of the incompleteness of capitalist development in France and the role of the deceived peasantry – dreaming back on the land-allotments granted them by the first Napoleon – as powerful factors in the coming to power of the "third," is impressive. Yet how does one shake it loose from the powerful imagery that buttresses it?

One can, if one wishes, see Marx's essay as an anticipation of the French disaster at Sedan. Yet then one must note that many of Napoleon III's "improvisations" lasted a substantially long time. One should also be aware that Marx underestimates the amount of working-class support the "little" Napoleon's presumably pseudo-socialism gathered to itself, and that such wishful underestimation has flawed Marxist analyses of proto-fascist movements since his time.

If it were not for that magnificent deployment of the images of theatricality, repetition, and illusion, who would read the *Eighteenth Brumaire* today?

Arthur Marwick's indignation is directed at those he feels are attacking the viability and usefulness of source-based history. What other kind of history can there be? There can, I suppose, be the writing "about" history that both Izenberg and Goldstein distinguish from "doing" it. Yet such historiosophy would soon become more insubstantial than Napoleon III's circus if it had no referent but itself. Sources are to the writing of history as lived experience is to the novel. Henry James, in one of his prefaces, said that even a lifelong sequestered virgin could write a novel about army life if she had powerful enough imagination. It would be unfair to James to point out that exemplars do not suggest themselves in great profusion. The same for writing history without a rich exposure to the sources.

I cannot imagine a rational attack against "source-based" history, yet I think I do understand what is meant by "a fetishism of documents," which are a particular kind of source. Documents are without a doubt often extremely useful, especially if they are examined critically, with all the tools of contemporary analysis applied to their reading. Certainly, where relevant documents exist, they should not be overlooked. Yet surely Marwick is aware of a fairly strong past tendency in our profession to overvalue them – by tending to privilege those subjects for which orderly documents exist (i.e., powerful, centralized institutions) and also by privileging documents themselves as opposed to other sources. A single document may tell us more than a powerful theory. Or then again, it may not. As Goldstein has pointed out, history is not a theoretical discipline, and some historians, unlike Charles Tilly, have even developed a kind of habitual dislike for theory, to pummel which a document can always be found if one searches. In other words, there is such a thing as a fetishism of documents. It is not a good thing and should not be confused with a respect for them.

A subject of both widespread and intense contemporary interest is the history of the family, for which documentation is scarce and fragmentary, and for which theory is indispensable, to say nothing of links to other disciplines like demography, psychology, sociology, anthropology, and ethnography. Richard Vann, in an exceptionally intriguing essay, makes abundantly clear how uncropped the field still is, in spite of such landmark works since Engels' *Ursprung der Familie*, etc., as those of Philip Ariès, Louis Henry, Lawrence Stone, and a few others. He points out that the promising intellectual framework foreshadowed by Marx and Engels has gone virtually unexploited in what used to be the Soviet Union. He suggests as well that a strong, imaginative linkage with Freud and Freudian theory would be in order. Turning to the Freudians, however, he urges on them the even higher value of Marxist theory.

Not only does Vann's essay touch briefly, lightly, and intelligently on the major problems confronting the historian of the family and explain the need for a theoretical as well as empirical approach to them, in reviewing what has already been done he provides a fascinating account of the flawed but interesting work of that now almost forgotten maverick Freudo-Marxist, Wilhelm Reich.

In his essay, Vann repetitively suggests that the family, whatever it may be – and definitions have not been consistent – is not the domain solely of consciousness and rationality, but that will and desire play a vital role. A rational theory therefore, or for that matter any meaningful study, must be capable of taking the irrational into account.

Eero Loone and Andrus Park were, at the time of writing the essays included here, Soviet citizens. Now the Soviet Union no longer exists. While no doubt not everything has changed in the Baltic states from which these scholars come, there is what Loone would call a "particular qualitative difference." Neither essay is conformist to Soviet strictures even to the degree Mogilnitsky's was, yet both display a seemly generosity towards Marxism as a cogent system of thought with something to offer the intellect, especially of the non-believer.

Perhaps Loone is a little hasty in his dismissal of the "linguistic turn." One can believe that a rhetorical analysis will reveal much about an historian's temperament and character, even the structure of his mind and his spatial-temporal and experiential horizons, without believing that history is "only" rhetoric. Loone's charge of "reductionism" is not entirely just. For the radical deconstructivists, however, any statement about any text has to be reductive, since it can not take into full account the infinitely free play of the signifiers.

Loone's familiarity with western scholarship on the European Middle Ages is gratifying, especially the work of the late Michael Postan, and he is to be thanked for reminding us of that splendid Soviet medievalist, Boris Porshnev.[11]

I would like to end with a few historiographical notes on matters not touched on in any of the essays in this or the "companion" volume published by Macmillan, *Western and Russian Historiography*, or touched on so briefly as to scant what I feel to be their relative importance.

For those historians now moving closer to literature and philosophy the work of Mikhail Bakhtin is of crucial importance. Of course, his book on Rabelais has been known since the late 1960s, and transformed the reading of that author, lifting it out of the realm of specialized scholarship into that of literature. His conception of "carnival" and the "carnivalesque" as articulated in that volume had some considerable impact on historians like Natalie Zeman Davis as well as on anthropologists, and blended rather well with the *Annales* School's interest in the history of public festivals.[12] His book on Dostoevsky, however, seemed pretty much the property of Slavists until the appearance of the Holquist-Emerson translation of his most important essays and the Clark-Holquist biography.[13] Then it became apparent that Bakhtin was not simply a Rabelais or a Dostoevsky scholar but a major philosopher of language who had at least as much to say to all the human sciences, including history, as Derrida – probably more, in fact – and although a difficult and not always a graceful writer, was without the often irritatingly playful and formidable obscurantism of the Algerian rabbi.

His concept of the fundamentally dialogic nature of language is, I think, a happier and more fruitful one for historians than Derrida's infinitely free play of signifiers. About dialogue in fictive prose, Bakhtin is a revelation, as he is about indirect speech, and what he calls quasi-indirect speech, or "the word with a sidelong glance."[14] I think it might turn out to be productively suggestive with regard to what Izenberg and Goldstein in this volume and Lionel Gossman elsewhere have indicated they consider to be the essentially dialogic nature of the historical enterprise. For Bakhtin, dialogue is essentially neither argument nor critique nor dialectic, though it does not preclude them, but a taking up and carrying on of the word.

Another useful concept of Bakhtin's is what he calls the "chronotope," the sense of spatial and temporal horizons and their relationship. It is from the chronotope that the image of man shared by an epoch or expressed in a literary or historical work emerges. Indeed, Bakhtin's work is very rich, profound, undogmatic, and in no way doctrinaire. Unlike Derrida, he outlines no method; like him, he foregrounds literary texts as prime exemplars of a fundamental ambiguity inseparable from language as such. Historians cannot afford not to read him.

Along with Bakhtin, something must be said about the Prague School of linguistics and literary criticism. Arising in the late 1920s and powerfully influenced by Russian Formalism through the presence of Roman Jakobson and (temporarily) Yuri Tynianov, the Prague scholars attempted to find an historical dimension and a social nexus, in a sense to "rescue" the autonomy of the text so dear to the Formalists. Fundamentally structuralist in their outlook, they sought "historic" or contextual structures as well as textual. Since most of their examples were taken from Czech literature little known to the outside world, the work of Jan Mukarovsky, Felix Vodicka, Ladislav Rieger, and especially David Levi has had little impact until recently.[15]

Closely related to the Prague School, and perhaps more distantly to Bakhtin as well, the so-called Tartu-Moscow School of Semiotics (or sign-systems) has concerned itself as much with culture and cultural history as with literary texts, and with music and the visual arts as well. The key figures here have been Yurii Lotman at the University of Tartu and Boris Uspensky at Moscow University. For the last twenty years they have published an irregularly appearing journal called *Works on Sign Systems* (*Trudy po znakovym sistemam*) full of the most interesting "semiotic" essays on the history of European, Asian, and Russian culture, a few of which have recently been translated.[16]

While many historians continue to work within the conceptual framework of national history and many also try to transcend or seriously challenge the conceptual solidity of that framework, a new problem has arisen in our time for the many new nations that have arisen since the end of World War II which have no established historiographic traditions, and few well-preserved documentary sources. The nations of Africa come first to mind, and it is clear that the creation of an African historiography ideologically liberated from but professionally instructed by European professional practice is an outstanding problem of our time.[17] And now that the Soviet Union no longer exists and the world's most highly bureaucratized and ideologically most standardized historical profession has virtually dissolved, problems of temporal and spatial scope, creation of new terms and new periodizations will probably loom up for many historians both there and here more vigorously than problems of epistemology or the ambiguities of language.

Finally, I would like to mention a genre that has close links to both history and literature – that of biography. Rabb's expressed dismay (in his essay) at the bookstore best-seller shelves loaded with grossly conceived accounts of "wars and lechery," violence and garish sex, should be some-what relieved by the frequent presence on those shelves of quite serious, well-researched, sometimes even brilliantly conceived biographies. Public interest in the form is indisputably vigorous, and it is history of a sort.

Nor is it really a return to an anachronistic "great man" or "biographical" theory of history, though no doubt it responds in part to a certain public hunger for vividness of personality occasioned by the contemporary break-down and fragmentation of the self under the impact of modern conditions. The biographical approach is perhaps best exemplified by such older works as Edmund Wilson's *To the Finland Station* and Bertram Wolfe's *Three Who Made a Revolution*. Far from exalting personality as such, these works tend to see and present it as symbolic (i.e., "representative") of broad sociopolitical-historical currents most clearly grasped by demon-strating their dramatic confluence in a personality. Robert Tucker's recent biography of Stalin, Robert Caro's of Lyndon Johnson, tend to follow in that direction.[18]

I do not see the essays in this book as harbingers of Rabb's "age of scientific history," but neither are they the tombstones of Mogilnitsky's "bourgeois history graveyard."

Notes

1. Simon Schama, *Citizens: A Chronicle of the French Revolution* (New York: Knopf, 1989), *The Embarrassment of Riches: An Interpretation of Dutch Culture in the Golden Age* (New York: Knopf, 1987), and especially his most recent tour de force, *Dead Certainties: Unwar-ranted Speculations* (New York: Knopf, 1991).
2. Paul de Man, *Allegories of Reading: Figural Language in Rousseau, Nietzsche, Rilke, and Proust* (New Haven: Yale University Press, 1979), 9–10.
3. Jacob Burckhardt, *The Age of Constantine the Great* (Berkeley: University of California Press, 1983).

4. Thomas S. Kuhn, *The Structure of Scientific Revolutions* (Berkeley: University of Chicago Press, 1970).
5. M. M. Bakhtin, *Problems of Dostoevsky's Poetics* (Minneapolis: University of Minnesota Press, 1982).
6. Jacques Derrida, "Coming Into One's Own," in *Psychoanalysis and the Question of the Text*, ed. Geoffrey Hartmann (Baltimore: Johns Hopkins University Press, 1978).
7. This essay, to which Leon Goldstein (below) also refers, appears, in my translation, in *Western and Russian Historiography: Recent Views*, recently issued by Macmillan; Mogilnitsky's essay appeared originally in *Voprosy istorii* (Moscow, 1987).
8. Leo Strauss, *Persecution and the Art of Writing* (Chicago: University of Chicago Press, 1988).
9. See Leon J. Goldstein, *Historical Knowing* (Austin: University of Texas Press, 1976).
10. Victor Hugo, *Les années funestes, 1850–1870* (Paris, 1941): see also *Oeuvres Complètes*, I, Histoire, vol. 19 (Paris, n.d.); P. J. Proudhon, "Louis Napoleon," in *Oeuvres Complètes*, vol. 9 (Paris, 1936), 172–92; Alexander Herzen, *My Past and Thoughts: The Memoirs of Alexander Herzen*, 4 vols (London, 1968), 2:643–833, 901–12, and *From the Other Shore* (New York: Braziller, 1956).
11. Michael Postan was a prominent contributor to the *Cambridge Medieval History* and a distinguished economic historian, both of the Middle Ages and our own time; Boris Porshnev, *Ocherk politicheskoi ekonomike feodalizma* (Moscow, 1956).
12. M. M. Bakhtin, *Rabelais and His World* (Bloomington: Indiana University Press, 1984).
13. M. M. Bakhtin, *The Dialogic Imagination: Four Essays* (Austin: University of Texas Press, 1981); Katerina Clark and Michael Holquist, *Mikhail Bakhtin* (Cambridge, MA: Harvard University Press, 1984).
14. Sidney Monas, "Mikhail Bakhtin: The Word with a Sidelong Glance," *Encounter* 66.5 (May 1986).
15. *The Prague School: Selected Writings 1929–1946*, ed. Peter Steiner (Austin: University of Texas Press, 1982); see also F. W. Galen, *Historic Structures: The Prague School Project 1928–1946* (Austin: University of Texas Press, 1985).
16. *The Semiotics of Russian Cultural History: Essays*, eds. B. Gasparov and A. S. Nakhimovsky (Ithaca: Cornell University Press, 1985).
17. Caroline Neale, *Writing "Independent" History: African Historiography, 1960–1980* (Westport, CT: Greenwood Press, 1985).
18. Robert C. Tucker, *Stalin as Revolutionary, 1879–1929: A Study in History and Personality* (New York: Norton, 1973), and *Stalin in Power, the Revolution from Above, 1928–1941* (New York: Norton, 1990); Robert A. Caro, *The Path to Power* (New York: Knopf, 1982), *Means of Ascent* (New York: Knopf, 1990), and *The Power Broker: Robert Moses and the Fall of New York* (New York: Knopf, 1974).

Part One
Object and Subject in History

2 Rationality and History

George G. Iggers

I

The past two decades have seen a lively theoretical discussion internationally on how history is to be written and at the same time a conscious reorientation in the writing of history itself. The term "postmodernism" has at times been applied to the new theoretical outlook and the new historiography.[1] The discussion has raised certain very fundamental questions regarding the nature of historical inquiry similar to those which have been asked regarding other forms of intellectual activity. These questions have revolved around the assumptions which have underlain historical writing – and philosophical thought – since the beginning of the Western tradition of secular history. There were two assumptions which were central to this tradition from Herodotus and Thucydides to the very recent past, namely, that there is a distinction, even if not necessarily an absolute dividing line, between fact and fiction, and similarly that there is a difference between rational thought and free imagination, even if the two may intersect.

In dealing with the problems of reality and rationality raised in those segments of recent philosophic thought which have identified themselves as post-modern or deconstructionist,[2] this article proceeds from the assumption, rejected by this thought, that a historical text must be understood with reference to the context to which it refers and that this context contains an element of objectivity not fully identical with the subjectivity of the historian and an element of rationality which presumes elements of intersubjectivity in the methods of historical inquiry.

This crisis of modern historical thought is itself part of a broader crisis of the modern world, a world which was deeply affected by what has been described as the philosophy of the Enlightenment. One notion which was primary to the modern tradition of scientific thought, and which was integrated into the traditions of historical scholarship, was the notion of objectivity and of the possibility of rational inquiry and understanding of objective reality. But this notion underwent several important transformations in the course of the Enlightenment. Its classical Cartesian form saw the dualism of a rationally constructed passive nature counterposed to an active, inquiring rational faculty which could comprehend and control it. Ernst Cassirer in his *Philosophy of the Enlightenment* showed the fundamental transformation which already took place in the eighteenth century of the Cartesian *esprit de système*, which believed that the fundamental problems of existence and reality could be analyzed by abstract reason, into a much more humble *esprit systématique* which marked the empirical approach of the new science, for which science resided in method and hence in a process of questioning and thus not in the construction of systems and the positing of answers. With Hume and Kant, the problematic nature of reality was recognized. Science was thus never a reflection of reality but a construct; but not an abstract construct. The core of scientific reason was contained in scientific method. Notwithstanding the later attempts by philosophers from Friedrich Nietzsche to Gaston Bachelard and Paul Feyerabend to see in science a variation of poetic imagination,[3] the basic ethos of scientific inquiry did not change with the very fundamental reorientations in world view which occurred at the beginning of the twentieth century. In this sense Einstein was as fundamentally convinced as Newton of the meaningfulness and rationality of the scientific enterprise. The mechanistic conception of an objectified universe, which served as the whipping boy of much of anti-scientific thought, represented even in physics merely a fleeting and by no means universal viewpoint. Very soon in the nineteenth century the close relation between science and culture was recognized. Even as avowed a materialist as Karl Marx in the *First Thesis on Feuerbach* recognized the active role of the mind in reconstructing a picture of reality.

The so-called German scientific school of historians from the very beginning operated with a very guarded sense of objectivity. The new historical science which Ranke propagated was based not on systematic empirical inquiry and analytical generalization but on philological and hermeneutical procedures. The source of historical studies was a text, whether a written text in the sense of a document or an artifact in Droysen's sense. Not literal or lexicological analysis but comprehension – Wilhelm von Humboldt's *Einfühlung*, Ranke's *Verstehen* – was at the core of historical science. The whole new critical approach to historical study, not only in Germany but generally in the Western world since the Enlightenment[4] – from the cultural studies of Heyne, Winckelmann, and Wolf, and from Gibbon and Voltaire on – rested on an approach to the past as a means of understanding the subject of historical inquiry not immediately but mediately. Behind this, there of course rested the belief that a source in fact reflected a subject matter of history, which could be studied and understood, even if never understood fully and finally.

The notion that historical understanding, even if always qualified and perspectivistic, was possible was closely interwoven with two other notions which have been radically challenged in recent philosophical thought, the notion that there were subjects of history both in the individual, personal sense and in an interpersonal setting. A historical source, again whether a written documents or an archeological artifact, embodied and communicated meaning which was potentially capable of being understood. The text thus expressed the intentions of the author or the outlook of a social group. This again assumed that the author could express intentionality and meaning. Again the historiography of the nineteenth century did not work with the notion of a constant, unchanging personality. The biographies of the time, such as Dilthey's lives of Schleiermacher or of the young Hegel,[5] parallel the *Bildungsroman* in which the person himself undergoes change. Nevertheless the confidence remains alive that the text reflects the meaning of the author and that the document means what it says.

On a broader collective level, history is seen as continuity, whether this continuity points to progress in the sense of Hegel, Comte, or Marx or to diversity as in Herder or Burckhardt. Even for Burckhardt, for whom discontinuity plays a major role in history, an epoch has a cohesion and a spirit which can be portrayed. Cohesion means that some form of explanation is possible; the causal factors in Ranke's Great Powers, in de Tocqueville's *The Old Regime and the French Revolution,* Marx's *Eighteenth Brumaire of Louis Bonaparte,* or Burckhardt's *Civilization of the Renaissance in Italy* may be very different, but they presume that there is sufficient coherence on the individual or collective level to make historical understanding possible. However, several important caveats appeared in the course of the nineteenth century in respect to the confidence regarding the coherence of the human personality and the historical process; we need only mention the names of Marx and Freud from two very different perspectives. For Marx the relationship between supposed knowledge and power relationships, for Freud that between knowledge and mental state were inseparable – although for both the possibility for rational communication remained, as it did later for Jürgen Habermas.[6] The extent to which historical dialogue was distorted by social, political, and emotional interests below the consciousness of the author became increasingly apparent, yet the recognition of these distortions provided a basis for the restoration of rational discourse.

II

The revolt against the conception of historical truth and with it the belief in the applicability of rational criteria, say scientific or scholarly, to the investigation of the past cannot be viewed as a current in historical thought in a narrow sense but as part of a broad reorientation of modern consciousness under the changing conditions of modern existence. The world which took shape in the late eighteenth century – its origins were much earlier – not only generated the Enlightenment conceptions which were fundamental to the shaping of the new approaches to historical perception but also created a deep sense of uneasiness – which called its own presumptions into question.

It is perhaps a commonplace to say that cognition has never taken place in a vacuum. The whole discussion on the character of history, historical truth, and historical method has taken place in the context of political debate. The first incisive attack on the conception of truth and with it of historical truth comes from Nietzsche, in *The Birth of Tragedy* and in his deconstruction of science in his later writings. This attack is part of a critique of "bourgeois" society which is much more radical, going to the roots, than the contemporary critique by Marx. Marx after all affirms the basic world-view of the bourgeois culture of the nineteenth century, its affirmation of rationality as an instrument of understanding and fashioning the world, its cult of progress not only in the general sense of improvement but in the Condorcean sense of the conquest of nature and the rational ordering of society. The criteria of truth remain, the belief in an objective reality, the possibility of mastering it scientifically, the confidence in the purpose of history in which human existence would find its fulfillment. There is, of course, another much more critical side to Marxist theory, that radically questions the technocratic ethos of bourgeois culture, which remains dormant until the emergence of cultural Marxism in the twentieth century.[7]

In applying the label "right" to Nietzsche's cultural critique, we must nevertheless qualify what is meant by "right" in this context because in many ways the Nietzschean conception of truth and history is radical rather than conservative, radical in the sense that it denies the entire Christian religious and communitarian conception of the traditional conservatives who turned against Enlightenment, liberalism, and capitalism. Nietzsche's refutation of Christianity itself contains an element of Enlightenment rationality. Yet at the core of *The Birth of Tragedy* lies the assertion, taken up again by Heidegger, that the entire philosophical tradition of the West, beginning with Socrates, has been false and rested on the myth that reality could be grasped by means of concepts. The place of logos must yield to the realm of poetry and imagination, reason to ecstasy, balance to chaos. Yet this vision, which conceived itself as aesthetic, and hence as unpolitical, and reviled politics, in fact involved a deeply political passion, the reassertion in the form of Nietzsche's cult of genius of an aristocratic order in which the supposed complacency and vulgarity of bourgeois society with its pursuit of welfare, peace, and broader opportunity for the many would give way to the creative and aesthetic expressions of heroic violence.

The intellectual foundations of the critique of reason and with it of historical reason were well formulated before 1914. They were highly politicized in the aftermath of the war, primarily in Germany, for reasons which had to do with the conditions and traditions under which Germany faced the problems of modernization, but were not restricted to Germany. In different forms, Oswald Spengler, Ernst Jünger, and Carl Schmitt called for a revival of the mythical, the reassertion of violence, a new biologism which involved racial war, and an ambivalent attitude toward technology, which on the one hand sought a return to simpler, pre-industrial forms on life, and on the other hand admired the military potential of modern weaponry and saw in the First World War a heroic, revitalizing experience. *The Myth of the Twentieth Century* by Alfred Rosenberg,[8] which sought to give National Socialism a theoretical foundation, is only a vulgarized expression of what amounted to a broad consensus on the Right. Nor is there a break in Heidegger's well-known Inaugural Address as Rector of the University of Freiburg in 1933, between the basic yearning for a home in an ontic *Sein*, a way (which defies all rational comprehension) out of the homelessness of modern man, and Heidegger's invocation of solidarity with mythical and mystical origins, which German science is to serve.[9]

Yet it is the Left, and in fact a New Left, which in the years after 1945 has taken over many of the arguments of the cultural critics of the Right, including its critique of science, technology, and progress, and has paid its tributes to Nietzsche and Heidegger, although from emancipatory and egalitarian motives diametrically opposed to those of the Right. The seminal attempt to integrate the critique of science and rationality of the German intellectual Right into a Marxist conception of culture came in György Lukács' 1923 collection of essays, *History and Class Consciousness*,[10] criticizing the narrowly economistic understanding of Marx by the Second Internationale. Most interesting for the purposes of this essay is not Lukács' brilliant attempt to show to what extent capitalism has molded not only material life but also consciousness and culture, but his critique of modern science. Drawing on Weberian analyses of capitalism, Lukács sought to show that modern science reflected the world view of capitalism, a reified picture of human reality, which, as Lukács believed even before the 1844 Manuscripts were published, Marx had consistently diagnosed from his early writings on and given most poignant expression to in the famous section on "The Fetishism of Commodities" in the first volume of *Capital*. Max Horkheimer and even more clearly Theodor Adorno distanced themselves from Lukács' messianic dialectics while developing further his ideas on the commodification of culture in a capitalistic society. Horkheimer's residual Marxism led him to a simplified explanation of liberalism as the political concomitant of capitalism. He thus placed much greater blame for the rise of fascism on the "culture industry" represented in its most developed form in the United States than on the heritage of authoritarian attitudes in German political culture. This hostility to the tradition of political liberalism was interwoven in Horkheimer's 1947 *Eclipse of Reason*, and in Horkheimer and Adorno's joint work, *The Dialectics of Enlightenment* (originally published 1944 in Amsterdam), with a critical reassessment of the Enlightenment outlook from which this political tradition originated. It was the Enlightenment now which in its attempt to create a society of free men and women on rational foundations was given a great share of responsibility for the Holocaust. In a strange way, the early Marx and Heidegger were now made to speak a similar language.

This merger of Marx and Heidegger, or Marx and Nietzsche, deeply characterized the philosophic outlook of the New Left which replaced the Old Marxist Left. The cult of progress with its scientific, technological, and cultural implications appeared hollow and destructive. What gave the New Left which emerged after 1945 its impetus was a continued, deep-felt sense of justice, in fact a sense of justice which went far beyond the more narrowly economic conceptions of traditional Marxists and traditional liberals. But the ideals of the past, whether Christian, Enlightened, or Marxist, had in its view proved disastrous for human freedom and dignity. It is this sense of the lack of any element of objective meaning, of any logical grounds for ethics, the Weberian sense of the ethical irrationality of human existence, which led Jean-Paul Sartre, the fighter in the French Resistance, to find important sources in Heidegger's *Being and Time* for his theoretical formulation of the existentialist viewpoint in his *Being and Nothingness*, published in 1956 but written under the German occupation.

Despite the radical critique of the Enlightenment conception of rationality, French thinkers from Sartre and Lévi-Strauss to Foucault and Derrida remained committed to basic ethical, and this includes political and social, values of the Enlightenment, even if they rejected the philosophic foundations upon which this ethics rested. May 1968 symbolizes the transition from the conventional analysis of capitalism by the Left to newer forms which took into account the fundamental transition which had taken place in the world since World War II. Marxism in its traditional forms became irrelevant as a meaningful instrument for the analysis of the modern industrial world, often called now, in my view not quite correctly, post-industrial. It only survived, radically transformed, as a Western Marxism which invoked the concept of alienation of Marx's early writings without considering why Marx repudiated these writings. It was partly out of nostalgia for a revolutionary tradition of the past that broad segments of the left continued to use the language of Marxism while repudiating the political theory of the historical Marxist movements. In the setting of the late twentieth century, a fundamentally different perception emerged among the political Left of what constituted oppression. Notwithstanding their emphatic avowals that the world is ethically irrational, the line of thinkers from Sartre and Beauvoir to Foucault and Derrida is characterized by a deep commitment to social justice and humanity (even if in Sartre's case this may have included a blindness to the oppressive aspects of Stalinism and Maoism). It is this sense of justice which deeply distinguishes the confrontation of nothingness by Sartre and Foucault from that of Nietzsche and Heidegger .

Foucault's great contribution to this discussion has been his redefinition of oppression. The Nietzschean conception of the centrality of power was reinterpreted to give it a radical edge which challenged the social order in the broadest sense. The Marxist conception of power as emanating from a central core of political and economic power was now replaced by the recognition that forms of power and oppression permeate all forms of human relations. The history of the modern world was viewed with, as I shall argue later, an excessive yet well-founded pessimism, which saw Enlightenment as a means to exclude and control all those who did not conform readily to the norms of a society in which the prerequisites of performance dominated. The Left in the streets of Paris, Berlin, or Berkeley in 1968 had little to do with the traditional left, as the inability of students and workers to cooperate in Paris and elsewhere showed. The calls for racial equality, equality of the sexes, the end of the Viet Nam war, the recognition of alternative life styles rested on a radically pessimistic view not only of the capitalist but also of the industrialized world, including the socialist countries in which political repression and industrial and ecological irresponsibility were even less checked than in the capitalist countries. The fear of nuclear destruction which hung over Europe in the 1950s and 1960s gave way to an even more real fear of environmental catastrophe. While the developed countries achieved increasing affluence, accompanied to be sure by new forms of poverty and degradation in the American cities and gradually also elsewhere, a great deal of the formerly colonized or semi-colonized world fought an increasingly hopeless struggle against deprivation, sickness, and violence.

Despite the utopianism of segments of the protest movements in the 1960s, there was little room left for any utopian hope.

III

Yet from the perspective of this article with its focus on the role of historical thought in historical writing, we are less concerned with the destructive aspects of rationality in modern civilization, than with the critique of rational means of inquiry, although the two are very closely related. For if no coherence of any kind can be constructed in history or reality, then reason loses its claim to show a path to critical under- standing. "Reason," of course, has very different meanings. The critics of modern civilization, from Weber to Horkheimer and Foucault, have been primarily concerned with what has been called instrumental reason. Yet Horkheimer in his essay on "Critical and Traditional Theory"[11] in the 1930s still recognized a normative side to reason. The core of the Hegelian notion of science, which Lukács and Horkheimer accepted, was that all items of knowledge have to be seen in a broad historical, cultural context. This, of course, involved a much more complex kind of reasoning which in the tradition of hermeneutics involved qualitative perceptions and the interrelationship of an abstract reasoning process and creative, empathetic imagination. Hermeneutics, even if it rejects clearly defined methodological procedure, is not in itself an expression of irrationality but rather an attempt to understand cultural meaning by means of adequate forms of reasoning.[12] For the Horkheimer of the 1930s, the world was still accessible to rational inquiry.

However, with the collapse of a sense of meaning, the possibility of rational inquiry is also eliminated. If history has no structure or reality, then any sort of approach which seeks to understand historical reality "rationally" is, of course, senseless.[13] And with it is the distinction between *Dichtung* and *Wahrheit* (poetry and truth), history and myth, while never absolute, is now completely abolished.

Often, structuralism and post-structuralism were distinguished as two stages of recent thought in which the dissolution of a concept of reality, objectivity, and personality was completed. Moving away from the concep- tion of hard, measurable artifacts of thought, a new generation of cultural anthropologists increasingly likened a culture to a literary text, a web of meaning, which had to be decoded. A culture was seen as a language, with its grammar and syntax, which determined human behavior rather than being determined by it. Yet for Clifford Geertz, Marshall Sahlins, and Pierre Bourdieu, there was still very much of a whole world, or rather a set of whole worlds, of cultures which had to be understood and could be understood even if they required means which burst the imagination of traditional social science.[14]

For Foucault and Jacques Derrida this residue of coherence disintegrated. Derrida does not introduce a new note when he argues that the text never exactly means what it says or says what it means. Marx and Freud had argued the same. But what Derrida suggests is that the text has no discernible meaning because there is no reality apart from language and language no longer has a structure. Saussure's relationship between signifiers and their signified is broken; words circulate freely. An archeology of knowledge in Foucault's sense is no longer possible, because there is no longer meaning to be uncovered, because there are no longer authors, integrated personalities which can convey intentions capable of rational understanding. The reader of Derrida is confronted by an apparent contradiction, the destruction of the claim of reason as a tool of knowledge through the cold and incisive application of logical arguments to destroy the claims of reason. Yet particularly historians, who have been close to the recent concern with language, have frequently stressed the extent to which women and men "make their own history" in response to oppressive conditions, political, economic, social, cultural, and sexual,[15] an idea which is in contradiction with the determinism suggested by structuralism and the dissolution of meaning and personality assumed by deconstrution.

IV

How has this philosophic reorientation expressed itself in the theory of historical knowledge? It has become common to speak of a "linguistic turn."[16] Insofar as this means that history cannot operate without language and that to an extent language shapes historical knowledge, there can be no argument. Nor can there be with the centrality of language not only in historical writing but also in historical consciousness. The pioneering work of Quentin Skinner and J. G. A. Pocock in the history of modern political thought moves away from the reconstruction of the abstract ideas held by a select number of great individuals to the attempt to see these ideas as part of the discourse of a broad group of educated persons.[17] Civic humanism is less an ideology than a common vocabulary. Yet Skinner or Pocock have never argued that this discourse can be reduced to a linguistic game. As against the textualism of the post-structuralists, for whom the text has an existence apart from its authors, the intentions of the authors remain

fundamental for Pocock and Skinner. There is a great distance between
the recognition, which has in fact accompanied the emergence of critical
historical research practices since the middle of the eighteenth century, that
all history reflects the subjectivity and the perspective of the historian and
the radical hermeneuticist position that the historian is totally bound by
his prejudices or pre-judgments (*Vorurteil*)[18] In a fundamental way, the
problem of history is not that different from that of science, even natural
science. As Thomas Kuhn; has argued in *The Structure of Scientific
Revolution*, an historical and cultural element enters into scientific work
too. Yet what distinguishes science from imaginative fiction for Kuhn is
the presence of a dialogue carried on by a community of scholars who
speak a common language, but not an arbitrarily chosen language. And
a similar dialogue, much less exact, much more evasive, but nevertheless
governed by principles of rational discourse, also governs the work of the
historians.

The new emphasis on history as a form of literature is related to the
reduction of history to language. Within the tradition of professional
historical scholarship in the late nineteenth and into the twentieth century
there arose an insistence on the strict separation of scholarly, scientific,
and literary discourse. Hayden White is thus quite right in insisting that
every historical text is also a literary text and that as such it is governed
by literary criteria. But White goes beyond this to then conclude that a
historical text is in essence nothing more than a literary text, a poetical
creation as deeply involved in the imagination as the novel. The history
the historian writes is determined ultimately not by any reference to his
subject of study but by literary decisions, by the limited choices permitted
by such literary determinants as "emplotment" and "choice of tropes,"
to follow White's highly formalized terminology which paradoxically,
as that of other post-modernists, adopts the jargonized language of the
professionalized sciences which it calls into question.

This attempt to explore the "linguistic grounds" of historical texts as
a deep "verbal structure"[19] which underlies the historical evidence has
direct relevance for the role of evidence in historical investigation. From
Thucydides on, the proper – i.e., critical – use of evidence formed the basis
for a truthful historical narrative and the purpose of a historical narrative
was broadly, even if not universally, held to be truthful narrative. Now
we are very well aware that history has often had a different purpose as a
means of establishing a sense of ethnic, religious, or political identity and
heritage in very different civilizations from ancient Babylonia or Hellas
or traditional Black Africa to the national and ideological legends of the
nineteenth and twentieth centuries. Yet a distinction, perhaps too rigid,

has been maintained, particularly since the Enlightenment, between history and what has come to be called mythistory. Donald Kelley in a recent provocative article sought to establish the history and the legitimacy of the latter.[20] Most historians, including cultural historians, nevertheless remain committed to an evidential base as a requisite of meaningful historical writing. The recent debate between Robert Finlay and Natalie Davis on Davis' use of evidence raises the question to what extent the historian may imaginatively go beyond the literal sources.[21] Doubtless the layers of truth are deeper and the operations of reason more intricate than traditional historiography assumed. The symbolism inherent in fiction, mores, and folk beliefs may, and probably do, contain greater keys to the understanding of societies and cultures than do accounts of the Venetian ambassadors which Ranke took so seriously without a critical analysis of the distortions which entered into them.[22] But cultural anthropology too involves method, in the sense of controlled strategies of research, and operates within a scholarly community of discourse. Yet one may wonder to what extent critical research in history will be possible if, as F. R. Ankersmit confidently observes, the "metaphorical dimension in historiography is more powerful than the literal or factual dimensions. . . . There is reason to assume that our relation to the past and our insight into it will in future be of a metaphorical nature rather than a literal one" (152).

V

There is a German saying that food is never eaten as hot as it is cooked, and I believe that this is also the case with the new cultural history which identifies itself with the conception of reality and the understanding of post-modern philosophy. Post-modern philosophy in itself has not been committed to any particular political and social outlook. In a sense it has belonged to a new right as well as a new left and the intellectual forebears it invokes, whether Heidegger or Paul de Man, hardly reflect the emancipatory concerns of many of the new historians who seek to write in the vein of the new philosophy. What they share is a deep distrust against what has appeared to them as the ideology of a technologized culture, identified in earlier language – e.g., in Horkheimer or Adorno – with liberalism or capitalism. And intellectual schemes and strategies which even remotely suggest modes of social scientific thinking have encountered suspicion in so far as they seemed to be part of this technologized outlook.

Philosophers from Nietzsche to Foucault and Derrida have seen hidden or not so hidden instruments of power in technology, science, and logical thought. A fundamental shift took place between the older historiography, exemplified by traditions of historical writing and political thought from Thucydides and Aristotle to Ranke and Hegel – but also very definitely including Nietzsche and Heidegger, for whom power and hierarchy were beneficial and creative of culture – and the new philosophy and historiography for whom power was exploitative and destructive of human potentialities. For despite its deep sense of the ethical absurdity of the world and its insistence on the lack of coherence in history, society, and personality, the new cultural history proceeded from ethical and political values which were deeply rooted in the Enlightenment. In saying this, I am fully aware of the deep contradictions inherent in Enlightenment conceptions of the social and political order between the formal equality and liberty it piously proclaimed and the distinctions of status and power which it was willing to justify in practice. In a sense, we must deconstruct the hostility of the new cultural historians to the Enlightenment conceptions of a rational social order to unearth the deeper level of their thought hidden between their explicit formulations.

From the viewpoint of the new historiography, two traditions of historical writing became unacceptable, the kind of history practiced by the majority of professionally trained historians from the beginnings of Ranke's seminars until very recently, and the newer traditions of history oriented in social science. In both cases, the critical attitude of the new historians rests on political values. In the eyes of the new historians, traditional professional historiography involved political bias not only in the choice of subject matter but also in its restricted use of sources, the concentration on the centers of political power, the construction of narratives in which the powerful appear as the main agents of history, and the reliance on documents written by the powerful.

By the 1970s or 1980s, the main competitor of the new cultural history was, however, not the older professional history with its specific kind of political narrative, even if the latter experienced a limited revival, but rather history oriented in social science. The place devoted to cultural factors differed within the social-science traditions. We can establish a spectrum ranging from a position which emphasized such material factors as the economy, biology, climate, demography, and social strata defined by quantifiable variables, to one which stressed much more strongly cultural factors. At the one end of the spectrum stood the logical, positivistic conception of a "covering law"-model proposed by Carl Hempel and Karl Popper which stressed the unity of logical inquiry in all areas of knowledge,[23] and at the other end Clifford Geertz' "Thick Description" (3–30). Yet in a very important way the new cultural history, with its stress on culture and its skepticism in regard to theory, profited a great deal from social-science approaches to history. The work of the *Annales* historians – which now spans almost a century since the early regional studies of Lucien Febvre before World War I on the Franche Comté during the Reformation[24] – shifted the focus from the central institutions of political and economic power to society and culture viewed (in part) apart from these.

Somewhere in the work of the new, structurally-oriented historians in the 1970s, transition takes place to a new cultural history which questions the social-scientific assumptions of this older history but benefits from it immensely. Lawrence Stone in his now-famous 1979 article on the revival of history noted that "the movement to narrative by the 'new historians' marks the the end of an era: the end of the attempt to produce a coherent scientific explanation of change in the past." In many ways, the new narrative history builds methodologically on the structural analysis of the social history in the *Annales* tradition. It expands the concern with the lives "of the poor and obscure" but now with a greater emphasis on life as it is experienced and felt by individual human beings, with personalities of their own, rather than with these people as collective groups. If historians have given up the search for "coherent scientific explanations," they have, however, not given up a related concern, namely, that of analyzing societies and cultures by other means, which nevertheless still aim at understanding a historical past, by "tell[ing] the story of a person, a trial, or a dramatic episode, not for its own sake, but in order to throw light upone the internal workings of a past culture and society."[25] Nor have they broken with traditional modes of scholarly inquiry in critically dealing with sources, which primarily remain written sources, although their interest now shifts from price data and hard demographic information, to documents such as court proceedings, diaries, letters, but also records of oral history, which reflect human opinion, behavior, and emotions.

The new work reflects both the "linguistic turn" and the skepticism regarding grand theory which this turn implies.[26] The primary focus is still on collective behavior. The quantifiable series in French studies of changing *mentalités* in the 1970s now yielded to narrative sources, particularly records of criminal and inquisitional proceedings which were often available. Again the French – and the Anglo-American historians dealing with France from the sixteenth to the nineteenth century – were innovators in bringing the new cultural approach into the study of political history. They thus replaced with this approach Georges Lefebvre's Marxist analysis of the French Revolution in terms of conflicting class interests, analysis which had provided the basis for a Marxist approach which dominated French studies of the Revolution for a quarter of a century after

1945. Nevertheless, even these studies introduced a concern for culture and consciousness, as in Lefebvre's exploration of the collective psychology which shaped the "Great Fear" in the French countryside in 1789,[27] and Albert Soboul's examination of the political ideas and social values which gave coherence to a Sansculottes movement recruited from very diverse social groups.[28] François Furet's reconsideration of the political and ideological factors which made the French Revolution possible constituted not only a frontal attack against the Marxist affirmation in the 1970s and 1980s of the French Revolution as an unqualifiedly progressive event of history but also an attack against an economic interpretation of history.[29] Yet in a sense, Furet still represented a transitional step to new approaches, deeply effected by the turn to culture seen through symbol and language. In the 1970s, Maurice Agulhon and Mona Ozouf were already dealing with the consolidation of a republican tradition in nineteenth-century France by studying the symbols of the Republic, as reflected for example in its festivals and its songs.[30] There is a marked break between Charles Tilly and Edward Shorter's statistical study in the early 1970s of strikes and violence in nineteenth- and early twentieth-century Europe, and Michelle Perrot's history of French strikes embedding the political and economic issue in a much broader setting of popular behavior.[31] Robert Darnton's *Great Cat Massacre* represents an attempt to make sense of the symbolic actions through which the deep structure, the basic code of a culture expresses itself.[32] The past thus becomes a text to be interpreted very much in the sense of a literary text which, in the conception of post-modern theory, contains an autonomy and inner structure of its own, even if filled with contradictory and alternative meanings. Saussure's linguistics, with its belief that language shapes reality rather than the reverse, lays the foundation for such inquiries into the history of *mentalités* as Lucien Febvre's 1942 study of unbelief in the age of Rabelais,[33] seen not in terms of ideas but of the "mental work-tool" (*outillage mental*) provided by language. Yet if these approaches to popular culture have at times tended to submerge individuals in deeply-buried structures of consciousness which control them rather than are controlled by them, other writings, such as those of E. P. Thompson, Herbert Gutman, and Carlo Ginzburg, have stressed the role of conscious, intentional behavior.[34]

The historians as usual have been less explicit about the theoretical assumptions which guided them than have the philosophers. Works like those of E. P. Thompson and Carlo Ginzburg show to what extent the stress on culture can be combined with an awareness of the forces of transition operating in modern societies. It is no accident that some of the historians who have retained the link between culture and society have viewed themselves as Marxists. One cannot speak of one Marxist tradition of historical writing because Marxist approaches to history have been so multifaceted and contradictory, even in the historical writing of Karl Marx himself. We have observed above the narrow scientism of much of official Marxist historiography, both in the Social Democratic tradition before 1914 and in that of Marxism-Leninism after 1917. On the other hand, Marxist theorists, beginning with György Lukács and Antonio Gramsci, made important contributions to the critique of the scientistic and economistic approach – which Marxism had taken over from the general intellectual climate of the nineteenth century – and to the new emphasis on culture.

The dividing line between Marxist and non-Marxist approaches to history, which seemed so important before the 1960s, became increasingly irrelevant in the New Left. Despite the continued use of Marxist rhetoric by segments of the New Left, the understanding of what constituted exploitation and oppression now extended to areas of everyday life and culture – which had been excluded in the more narrowly economic critique of modern society by the established Marxist movements – and included segments of humanity, women, ethnic and racial minorities, as well as the socially marginalized groups which had been neglected not only in the main stream of historical writing but in Marxist historiography as well. The non-Western societies, too, now were viewed from a very different perspective, no longer, as even Marx and particularly Engels had seen them, in terms of the imperial policies of the West – policies which were to enable them to enter the world of modern economic development and civilization – but as cultures with their own history and character. This broadening of historical interest had to bring about a fundamental reorientation in methodological approaches and strategies of knowledge which with the new emphasis on experience in turn had to lead beyond the narrow confines of the old conception of scientific inquiry and of rationality.

VI

This essay, in its plea for rationality and Enlightenment, is not intended as a rejection of the new kind of history but rather as a critical examination of the theoretical assumptions which this history has frequently invoked in support of its practice. There is a fundamental contradiction between the radical rejection of rationality (admittedly with the use of rational arguments) by deconstructionists and the attempts by the new cultural historians to recapture the life and experience of real human beings

in the past. The new cultural history which we have described above
in very fundamental ways continues Enlightenment themes which were
repudiated by the radical critics of modern civilization such as Nietzsche,
Spengler, and Heidegger who demanded the restoration of hierarchical,
authoritarian structures. It continues to operate, not necessarily explicitly
but fundamentally, with the conception that individuals are to be taken
seriously, that notwithstanding Foucault and especially Derrida's critique
they are capable of expressing, either verbally or in terms of their behavior,
intentions which endow them with a high degree of integrity and autonomy
so that they deserve to be understood and ultimately can be understood. In
the final analysis for Thompson, or Ginzburg, or Hans Medick,[35] the text
is not a text consisting of signifiers which circulate freely but reflects a
reality which goes beyond the words and symbols which constitute it,
even if this reality can only be reconstructed through the mediation of
subjectivity and culture. This reality to be sure is not an object in the
sense either of classical materialism or of Michel Foucault's *Archeology
of Knowledge* but represents a reality with a human face. The very stress
on the central role of culture in history and the understanding of culture as
a system of meanings and values contradicts the idea of a world in which
there are no meanings.

   In practice, the new cultural history involves not a rejection but an
expansion of scientific rationality. The human, the social, and the natural
world from the perspective of the late-twentieth century appear immeas-
urably more complex and opaque than they did to the authors of the
Encyclopédie. Post-modernist philosophy and literary theory have created
a new orthodoxy which has faced remarkably few challenges although
it contradicts so profoundly the world of actual experience and value
from which modern cultural historians proceed. In fact until now no
post-modernist history has appeared which in any ways parallels post-
modernist theoretical discussions. Rationality, the attempt to understand
the world which confronts us by means of reason and understanding,
can take on very different forms. The past century and a half, since the
emergence of history as a professional discipline, has seen the extension of
sources and of the means of interpreting these sources, which would have
dumbfounded the imagination of a Ranke but which nevertheless constitute
an expansion of rationality.

   As practicing historians today recognize, the concepts and methods of
the historians oriented to social science and to culture by no means exclude
each other. The interesting work being done in such areas as working-class
and women's history increasingly focuses on the examination of the experiences of men and women in settings of social structures and social change.

Even Carlo Ginzburg's *The Cheese and the Worms*, which is often cited as a prime work of the new cultural history, is profoundly aware of the new political and economic forces in which Ginzburg sees the sources of the destruction of the peasant culture. Almost all of the new cultural historians have been aware of these changes. Robert Darnton similarly in *The Great Cat Massacre* portrays the journeymen printers' reaction to their masters in terms of the interplay of artisanal culture with the powerful forces of emergent capitalism. Ginzburg and Darnton dispense entirely with the empirical instrumentarium of the social sciences and instead seek to recapture the deeper structures of a culture contained in the records embodied in the written testimony of the miller and the recollections of the journeyman. David Sabean attempted something similar in the utilization of court cases involving religious deviation in his *Power in the Blood*, but then showed in his in-depth study of the Suabian village of Neckerhausen over several generations how computer techniques applied to material conditions and to legal relations can contribute to an understanding of a popular culture, which yet requires anthropological interpretation as well.[36] The stress on the great impersonal forces in the shaping of human institutions and life which marked the historical perceptions of classical Marxism, analytical social science, and *Annales* structural history have increasingly given way in recent studies to a recognition of the role of cultural factors, including language and rhetoric, in influencing political and economic change rather than in being influenced by them.

We can agree that the idea of progress, as it was conceived by Condorcet is dead and with it a dominant version of the grand narrative. The tremendous arrogance which for a broad current of nineteenth-century opinion, from Ranke and Hegel to Marx and Spencer, identified the history of the world with that of the West, has been chastened. Yet it is hardly true that history is without any discernible directions. A theory of modernization may well be justified as a heuristic device if it refrains from blindly identifying modernization with capitalism, as prophets like Walt Rostow are prone to do,[37] or, in not entirely different ways, as those of a technocratic Marxism have done with social and civilizational progress. In this sense the questions raised by modern social historians on the transformation of modern societies both in the economically highly developed countries and those of the so-called Third World need to be combined with those raised by cultural historians on the impact of these changes on the experiences of human beings. To proclaim that history has no structure, as Foucault or Derrida do, is to bury one's head in the sand. The absence of any over arching direction in history, as conceived by the great theologians and philosophers of history, does not

mean that there are no forces at work in modern societies which require
rational analysis and call for conceptions of historical and social change.
Foucault's whole cultural critique implies, notwithstanding his assertion to
the contrary, that history, or at least modern history, has a direction, one
against which he struggles. In this sense interpretations of the history of
the modern Western world, whether those of de Tocqueville or of Max
Weber, or Alfred Weber, appear not as pure speculations or fictions but
as conceptual constructs in the attempt to gain a rational understanding
of the world in which we live. It is a characteristic feature of modern
and post-modernist theories or visions, including those of Heidegger and
Foucault, that they assume that there are forces involving scientification
and technicalization which they reject but nevertheless see as the driving
forces of modernity.

Certainly no interpretation even of limited historical subject matter,
much less so of larger processes, can claim finality. But history, like
every intellectual discipline, is an ongoing process guided by certain
criteria of what constitutes reasonable communication. And this takes
us to the core of Enlightenment values. The obvious limits of reason do
not need to lead to the repudiation of the rational tradition of the West,
suggested by the critique popular since Nietzsche and Heidegger, of a
supposed logocentrism. The tradition of Western philosophy since Socrates
needs to be critically reexamined from the viewpoint of the political and
technical manipulation of nature and human beings which it implied. Max
Horkheimer and Theodor Adorno were right in pointing at the elements of
a myth of reason in the Enlightenment by which an emancipatory ideology
led to its opposite. The products of an instrumental rationality in science,
technology, and political and cultural control contributed to the horrors of
the twentieth century. Yet there is no substitute in a civilized community
for rational inquiry even if reason in today's world has burst the limits of
conventional logic.

The contradictions of the modern world seen from the viewpoint of the
dignity of human beings are apparent and these contradictions call into
question the very conception of a civilized community. But the process of
modernization, which in many ways has been the heir of the Enlightenment,
has not been all evil. The future is by no means certain; nuclear and
ecological destruction and genocides are all very real possibilities. The
Enlightenment need not only mean the use of instrumental rationality in its
scientific and technological forms to create more perfect forms of control
and domination; it also included a serious call for emancipation from the
tyrannies of the past – from despotism, disease, poverty, and ignorance
– to pave the way for a world in which man would be freed from the

tutelage which had been accepted in all previous civilizations, Western and non-Western, as natural or God-given. The tradition of cultural criticism from Nietzsche and Heidegger to Horkheimer and Foucault, which itself has roots in the Enlightenment, has offered important correctives to an Enlightenment unaware of its inherent contradictions. A chastened idea of the Enlightenment, and with it, as its essential constituent part, a chastened rationalism, still have meaning today. The modernist and post-modernist critique of Enlightenment has often overlooked the extent to which the Enlightenment conception of man and society aimed at creating the conditions under which human beings would be able through their critical faculties to make reasonable decisions about their lives. The alienated reason they chastised, which sees the expansion of rational control as the aim of human activities, is foreign to the Enlightenment as understood not only by Lessing or Kant, Voltaire or Paine, but also by Condorcet for whom progress serves human beings rather than the reverse. Not as a philosophy of history but as an ethical task, the idea of progress conceived by the Enlightenment retains validity. Reason continues to have a task in creating a reasonable world in which human beings can finally live under conditions which they have been denied too long in societies in which gender, ethnicity, class, and caste determined status and expectations in life. The new cultural history has made important contributions in finally throwing light on those who in the Brechtian image have until now not been seen because they lived in the dark. In doing so, this history, often in despite itself, has shared in the Enlightenment conceptions of reason and human dignity.

Notes

1.   See, for example, F. R. Ankersmit, "Historiography and Postmodernism," *History and Theory* 28 (1989):137–53.

2.   Allan Megill, *Prophets of Extremity: Nietzsche, Heidegger, Foucault, Derrida* (Berkeley, 1985).

3.   See Friedrich Nietzsche, "On Truth and Lie in an Extra-Moral Sense" (1873) in *The Portable Nietzsche*, ed. Walter Kaufmann (Hammondsworth, 1959), 42–47; Gaston Bachelard, *The New Scientific Spirit* (Boston, 1984); and Paul Feyerabend, *Against Method*, rev. edn (London, 1988).

4.   See Hans-Erich Bödeker *et al.*, *Aufklärung und Geschichte: Studien zur deutschen Geschichtswissenschaft im 18. Jahrhundert* (Göttingen, 1986); Peter Hanns Reill, *The German Enlightenment and the Rise of Historicism* (Berkeley, 1975).

5.   Wilhelm Dilthey, *Leben Schleiermachers* (Berlin, 1922–26); *Die Jugendgeschichte Hegels* (Berlin, 1905).

6.   Jürgen Habermas, *The Theory of Communicative Action* 2 vols (Boston, 1984–87).

7.   Cf. Martin Jay, *Dialectical Imagination: A History of the Frankfurt School and the Institute of Social Research 1923–1950* (Boston, 1973), and *Marxism and Totality: The Adventure of a Concept from Lukács to Habermas* (Berkeley, 1984); Russell Jacoby, *Dialectic of Defeat: Contours of Western Marxism* (Cambridge, 1982).

8.   *Der Mythos des 20. Jahrhunderts* (München, 1933).

9.   *Die Selbstbehauptung der deutschen Universität / Das Rektorat 1933/34: Tatsachen und Gedanken* (Frankfurt, 1983), 9–19; rpt. "Self-Assertion of the German University," *Review of Metaphysics* 38 (1985):470–80.

10. György Lukács, *History and Class Consciousness: Studies in Marxist Dialectics* (Cambridge, MA, 1971).

11. In Max Horkheimer, *Critical Theory: Selected Essays* (New York, 1972).

12. See Hans-Georg Gadamer, *Wahrheit und Methode* (Tübingen, 1960); rpt. *Truth and Method* (New York, 1975).

13. See Lutz Niethammer, *Posthistoire: Ist die Geschichte zu Ende?* (Reinbek, 1989).

14. Clifford Geertz, *Interpretations of Cultures* (New York, 1973); Marshall Sahlins, *Islands of History* (Chicago, 1985); Pierre Bourdieu, *The Logic of Practice* (Cambridge, 1990).

15. This is true of a good deal of post-Marxist social history, of such diverse historians as E. P. Thompson, Herbert Gutman, Carlo Ginzburg, and Hans Medick, who have stressed the role of "agency."

16. See John E. Toews, "Intellectual History after the Linguistic Turn: The Autonomy of Meaning and the Irreducibility of Experience," *American Historical Review* 92 (1987):879–907.

17. Quentin Skinner, *Foundations of Modern Political Thought*, 2 vols (Cambridge, 1978); J. G. A. Pocock, *Politics, Language and Time: Essays on Political Thought and History* (New York, 1971), and *The Machiavellian Moment: Florentine Political Thought and the Atlantic Republican Tradition* (Princeton, 1975).

18. See Gadamer on prejudice (*Vorurteil*) in *Wahrheit und Methode*, 255ff (*Truth and Method*, 238ff).

19. Hayden White, *Metahistory: The Historical Imagination in Nineteenth-Century Europe* (Baltimore, 1973), ix; see also his *Tropics of Discourse: Essays in Cultural Criticism* (Baltimore, 1978) and *The Context of the Form: Narrative Discourse and Historical Representation* (Baltimore, 1987).

20. Donald Kelley, "Mythistory in the Age of Ranke" in *Leopold von Ranke and the Shaping of the Historical Discipline*, eds. Georg G. Iggers and James M. Powell (Syracuse, 1990), 3–20.

21.	Robert Finlay, "The Refashioning of Martin Guerre," and Natalie Z. Davis, "'On the Lame,'" *American Historical Review* 93 (1989):553–71, 572–603, respectively.
22.	Gino Benzoni, "Ranke's Favorite Source: The Venetian *Relazioni*," in *Ranke and the Shaping of the Historical Discipline*, 45–57.
23.	Carl Hempel, "Explanation in Science and History" in *Ideas of History*, ed. Ronald H. Nash (New York, 1969), 2:79–106; Karl Popper, *The Logic of Scientific Discovery* (New York, 1959).
24.	Lucien Febvre, *Philippe II et la Franche Comté: Etude d'histoire politique, religieuse et sociale* (1912; rpt. Paris, 1978).
25.	Lawrence Stone, "The Revival of Narrative: Reflections on a New Old History," *Past and Present* no. 85 (1979):19.
26.	Allan Megill, "Grand Narrative and the Discipline of History," unpublished manuscript.
27.	Georges Lefebvre, *The Great Fear of 1789: Rural Panic in Revolutionary France* (New York, 1973).
28.	Albert Soboul, *The Parisian Sansculottes and the French Revolution 1793–4* (Oxford, 1964).
29.	François Furet, *Interpreting the French Revolution* (Cambridge, 1981).
30.	Maurice Agulhon, *La République au village* (Paris, 1970); Mona Ozouf, *Festivals and the French Revolution* (Cambridge, MA, 1988).
31.	Charles Tilly and Edward Shorter, *Strikes in France 1830–1968* (New York, 1974); Michelle Perrot, *Workers on Strike: France 1871–1890* (New York, 1987).
32.	Robert Darnton, *The Great Cat Massacre and other Episodes in French Cultural History* (New York, 1984).
33.	Lucien Febvre, *The Problem of Unbelief in the 16th Century: The Religion of Rabelais* (Cambridge, MA, 1982).
34.	E. P. Thompson, *The Making of the English Working Class* (New York, 1963); Herbert Gutman, *Work, Culture and Society in Industrializing America: Essays in American Working Class and Social History* (New York, 1975); Carlo Ginzburg, *The Cheese and the Worms: The Cosmos of a 16th-Century Miller* (Baltimore, 1980).
35.	Cf. Hans Medick, "Missionaries in the Row Boat: Ethnological Ways of Knowing as a Challenge to Social History," *Comparative Studies in Society and History* 29 (1987):76–89.
36.	David Sabean, *Power in the Blood: Popular Culture in Village Discourse in Early Modern Germany* (Cambridge, 1984), and *Property, Production, and Family in Neckarhausen, 1700–1870* (Cambridge, 1990). See also Hans Medick's study of the village of Laichingen in Suabia in approximately the same period (forthcoming).
37.	Walt Rostow, *Stages of Economic Growth: A Non-Communist Manifesto* (Cambridge, 1960).

3 Text, Context, and Psychology in Intellectual History

Gerald N. Izenberg

I have two basic purposes in this essay. The first is to argue against a current tendency in intellectual history to devalue or ignore the role of historical context in interpreting the texts with which it often deals, in the name of theories which insist on the self-sufficiency of language or text. The second is to argue for the proposition that biographical-psychological context is often indispensable in intellectual history and always irreducible to other levels of explanatory context.

Anyone arguing the second proposition, however, finds succor on neither side of the contemporary debate about the proper foundations and methods of intellectual history. The most radical proponents of the idea of "textuality," deploying various elements of poststructuralist thought, would do away with all context whatsoever, not least that of the author himself. According to David Harlan, for example, "The belief that language is an autonomous play of unintended transformations rather than a stable set of established references . . . ; the consequent doubts about language's referential and representational capacities; the growing suspicion that narrative may be incapable of conveying fixed, determinate, accessible meaning; and, finally the eclipse of the author as an autonomous, intending subject,"[1] make the enterprise of recovering the original meaning and point of a text not only fruitless but literally without sense. Paraphrasing Frank Kermode on the methodological approach of the art historian Aby Warburg, Harlan writes approvingly, "Texts do not point backward, to the historical or putative intentions of their now-dead authors; they point forward, to the hidden possibilities of the present" (604).

On the other hand, the models of contextualization offered by otherwise implacable opponents of deconstructive "presentists" and narrative "fictionalists" agree with them to this extent at least, that they reject the relevance for understanding texts of the individual as represented in psychology and psychoanalysis. Theoreticians of discourse like John Pocock (in his earlier methodological essays) and Michel Foucault subordinate

40

individual examplars of a discourse to the sets of interlinked terms and assumptions that constitute it, much more interested in its structure across a whole network of texts than in a particular instantiation of that structure. "Authors," writes Pocock, "remain the actors in any story we may have to tell, but the units of the processes we trace are the paradigms of political speech. . . . The historian's first problem . . . is to identify the 'language' or 'vocabulary' with and within which the author operated, and to show how it functioned paradigmatically to prescribe what he might say and how he might say it."[2] Quentin Skinner (and the later Pocock), who does insist on the indispensability of an author's intention for understanding the point of a text, explicitly contrasts intention with a causal category of motive precisely in order to rule out psychological, and sociological, explanations. His notion of intention is meant to identify the illocutionary force of an author's ideas, the meaning an author consciously meant to convey in using certain concepts in a given context of action. So, for example, Skinner explains a British politician's use of a specific political vocabulary in opposing royal policy by identifying it as the expression of a widely accepted set of political principles, and hence as useful in supplying an adequate justification for his otherwise treasonable action; but Skinner explicitly acknowledges that his methodological approach does not vindicate the *sincerity* of the politician's belief in those principles, and does not address the question of what other interests he might have had in opposing royal policy.[3] Finally, Fredric Jameson, who against Pocock and Skinner insists on going beyond the explicit language and conscious intention of a text to those external socio-political conditions which control and limit it, and who in tribute to the importance of Freud's contribution to interpretation makes the idea of an "unconscious" the key to deciphering texts, explicitly rejects the *individual* unconscious: "From the point of view of a political hermeneutic, measured against the requirements of a 'political unconscious,' we must conclude that the [Freudian] conception of wish-fulfillment remains locked in a problematic of the individual subject and the individual psychobiography which is only indirectly useful"[4] – useful, that is, only as an indicator of a deeper social structure which shapes the conflicts of the individual personality.

It might seem otiose for a historian to take time and trouble to argue with the most extreme linguistic and textualist theories. They appear, after all, simply incompatible with the historical enterprise as such, and since that enterprise seems securely protected by the traditional practices of stubbornly old-fashioned historians and by the constraints of the academy's departmentalized institutional politics, the best strategy would seem to be to ignore them. Furthermore, Dominick LaCapra, the intellectual historian who with Hayden White has done the most to make his fellows conscious of contemporary literary theory and its importance for the study of texts, specifically eschews the extreme position adopted by, for example, Harlan. While he has attacked the "documentary" approach in history so sharply that he at times appears to reject contextualism altogether, LaCapra claims to be offering not a substitute for but a necessary supplement to the traditional explanatory practices of historians. The fact that complex texts, through their rhetorical and structural devices, "rework" the historical material they "represent," so that they cannot be reduced to mere instances of their sociopolitical and discursive contexts, does not preclude for LaCapra the necessity of going back to those contexts in order to learn what historical material is being reworked, and hence of applying the virtues of traditional historiography, meticulous research and critical rationality, in investigating the past.[5]

Nevertheless there are some good reasons for a historian to take up and examine the radical linguistic positions. For one thing, LaCapra's actual criticisms of specific works in intellectual history belie the methodological synthesis he purportedly aims for. All efforts these works make to isolate particular themes in the thought and art of a period and relate them to their sociopolitical or cultural milieu are seen by him as reductive synopsis and illegitimate causal attribution. As John Toews shrewdly remarks, "Reading LaCapra's critical commentaries, one begins to wonder if it is possible to avoid the pitfalls of a referential or representational theory at all without ceasing to 'do' history and restricting oneself to thinking about it."[6] To which I would add that this may not be just a matter of LaCapra's contingent critical practice but of something inherent in his theoretical approach, an unintentionally over-rigid distinction between text and context which forces him in practice to a choice that in theory he does not wish to make. A second reason for taking textualist theories seriously is the squeamishness one may feel relying on the argument I suggested above for avoiding argument. For historians to avoid considering certain linguistic theories just because they couldn't continue to work as they have if the theories are true, is hardly a comfortable position to take for a discipline which prides itself on the rationality of its procedures. David Hollinger's attempted rebuttal of Harlan's extreme anticontextualism, while cogently arguing that Harlan's a priori theorizing about the impossibility of context does not tell us what if anything is wrong with existing, well-received studies of ideas in historical context, is weakened by the admission that he has not tackled the theoretical objections to context head-on.[7] Most important of all, however, an examination of certain features of linguistic radicalism reveals fissures in its arguments which both help to explain its own uncompromising ahistoricism and point back to the inevitability of context.

DE MAN AND REFERENTIALITY

Perhaps the most radical version of those theories which deny the referentiality of language, and hence the possibility of contextual explanation of any kind, is the "American" deconstruction of Paul de Man. One of his most notorious texts, "Excuses (*Confessions*)," a discussion of an episode in Rousseau's *Confessions*, can serve as a crux for historians because it deals with autobiography, and hence with the issue of the possibility of truthfulness in the recounting of a historical life.

In Book II of the *Confessions*, Rousseau reports that, while employed as a servant in an aristocratic household, he stole a ribbon from its mistress. When the theft was discovered, he accused a young maidservant, Marion, of having given it to him, and she was dismissed. While acknowledging her innocence and his own culpability in inculpating her, Rousseau attempted to excuse himself in a number of ways. His shame at public exposure was so intense that he had to ward it off even if that meant incurring the guilt of accusing an innocent. Moreover, he had absolutely no desire to be vicious or cruel to Marion; on the contrary, he had stolen the ribbon in the first place to give to her, and so makes what he calls the "'bizarre but . . . true'" claim that it was his friendship for her that was the cause of his accusation.[8] Finally, de Man notes a crucial peculiarity in Rousseau's language which suggests yet a third excuse. Because he had stolen the ribbon for Marion, when he was caught, "'She was present to my mind, I excused myself on the first thing that offered itself. I accused her of having done what I wanted to do and of having given me the ribbon because it was my intention to give it to her.'" One implication of these words is that it was sheer accident, sheer contingency, that Rousseau blamed Marion; her name was simply the first thing that came to mind. As de Man says, "The sentence is phrased in such a way as to allow for a complete disjunction between Rousseau's desires and interests and the selection of this particular name" (288).

Faced with such pleas, Rousseau's reader might be tempted to dismiss the last two as transparently unconvincing rationalizations and to wonder further about the roots of Rousseau's powerful sense of shame. De Man himself offers some psychologically shrewd comments about Rousseau's exhibitionism; he also makes the rather less-persuasive suggestion that, since desire always wishes for reciprocity in love, Rousseau could innocently believe that Marion would indeed have been as willing to steal the

ribbon for him as he for her. It is quickly evident, however, that de Man
offers such psychological analyses only to show that he knows how to play
the psychological game. Fundamentally, however, they are beside the point
for him. What interests de Man is the linguistic implication of Rousseau's
claim that Marion's name was simply the first thing that came to his mind
when he was accused: "any other name, any other word, any other sound
or noise could have done just as well and Marion's entry into the discourse
is a mere effect of chance. She is a free signifier, metonymically related
to the part she is made to play in the subsequent system of exchanges
and substitutions." It follows that "if her nominal presence is a mere
coincidence, then we are entering an entirely different system in which
such terms as desire, shame, guilt, exposure, and repression no longer have
any place" (288–89).

   At this point, de Man's *style indirect libre* paraphrasal of Rousseau's
implicit assumptions slides into unequivocal apology. He introduces a
distinction Rousseau makes elsewhere between lies and fictions, the
latter defined by Rousseau as "useless" facts whose falsity is a matter
of indifference and inconsequential for anyone. Fiction, de Man adds, has
nothing to do with representation but is the absence of any link between
an utterance and a referent. Rousseau's excuse – that he said the first thing
that came to mind – amounted to the claim that his utterance of Marion's
name was a fiction, and, according to de Man, "the fiction becomes the
disruption of the narrative's referential illusion" (292). The "text" of
Rousseau's utterance about Marion is no longer subject to considerations
of moral responsibility or even human agency because it does not refer to
an actual person at all but to a fictive construct.

   De Man realizes that in order to reach this conclusion he has blatantly
reversed the very premise of Rousseau's distinction between lie and fiction.
A fiction, according to Rousseau, is "'whatever, albeit contrary to truth,
fails to concern justice in any way'" and he even insists that "'the absence
of a purposefully harmful intent does not suffice to make a lie innocent;
one must also be assured that the error one inflicts upon one's interlocutor
can in no conceivable way harm him or anyone else'" (292). His mention
of Marion's name when accused of the theft hardly fulfills either criterion.
But de Man attempts to rescue Rousseau against himself by blaming
Rousseau's accusers (read: Rousseau's readers) on Rousseau's behalf for
not understanding what he was doing:

   [T]he fiction, in the *Confessions*, becomes harmful only because it is
   not understood for what it is. . . . If the essential non-signification
   of the statement had been properly interpreted, if Rousseau's accusers

had realized that Marion's name was "le premier objet qui s'offrit," they would have understood his lack of guilt as well as Marion's innocence. . . . Not the fiction itself is to blame for the consequences but its falsely referential reading. As a fiction, the statement is innocuous and the error harmless; it is the misguided reading of the error as theft or slander, the refusal to admit that fiction is fiction, the stubborn resistance to the "fact," obvious by itself, that language is entirely free with regard to referential meaning and can posit whatever its grammar allows it to say, which leads to the transformation of random error into injustice. (292–93)

The last sentence generalizes from the specific example of Rousseau to the basic theory of language it is meant to illustrate. De Man in fact suggests both "soft" and "hard" versions of this theory, though he seems unaware of this and the two are in crucial respects incompatible. The "soft" version allows that language can be referential but insists that it is always ambiguous. One implication of this would run counter to everything de Man has seemed to be saying thus far. While the ambiguity of language means that what is apparently real may be fictive, it also means that what is apparently fictive may refer to reality and fall under moral categories. De Man claims:

> [I]t is always possible to face up to any experience (to excuse any guilt), because the experience always exists simultaneously as fictional discourse and as empirical event and it is never possible to decide which one of the two possibilities is the right one. The indecision makes it possible to excuse the bleakest of crimes because, as a fiction, it escapes from the constraints of guilt and innocence. *On the other hand, it makes it equally possible to accuse fiction-making which, in Hölderlin's words, is "the most innocent of all activities," of being the most cruel.* (293; italics added)

This statement has potentially profound implications for the historicity and moral significance of imaginative literature (and hence for criticism). The possible referentiality of even fiction and poetry would mean that it could be held to be offering morally accountable portrayals and judgments of the world.

The end of the essay, however, proposes a quite different theory. De Man makes the radical claim that not only is the text of Rousseau's story of the ribbon (and by extension the whole of the *Confessions*) not meant to be referential, but that "in order to come into being as a text, the referential function had to be radically suspended." For "without the scandal of [the] random denunciation of Marion" (288), there would have been nothing to excuse. The theft itself could have been completely explained in psychological ways as the product of Rousseau's desire, and that explanation would supposedly have been accepted as sufficient excuse by Rousseau's accusers, who presumably shared and therefore condoned his idea of desire. But the random denunciation of Marion happened, and *it* cannot be explained by psychological reasons. Rather the text is uttered as a fiction, and then Rousseau himself is so appalled by the possibility that his utterance is disconnected and without context that he would rather see it as something about which to be guilty than as something without meaning.

> Far from seeing language as an instrument in the service of a psy-chic energy, the possibility now arises that the entire construction of drives, substitutions, repressions, and representations is the aberrant, metaphorical correlative of the absolute randomness of language, prior to any figuration or meaning. It is no longer certain that language, as excuse, exists because of a prior guilt but just as possible that *since language, as a machine, performs anyway*, we have to produce guilt (and all its train of psychic consequences) in order to make the excuse meaningful. (299; italics added)

It could be argued that de Man's house of cards would have collapsed had he been even more shrewd about Rousseau's psychology than he was. To imagine that the theft was both explicable and expiable as an event powered by love is naive; it omits the likelihood that ambivalence colored Rousseau's apparently unrequited desire for Marion with an anger which expressed itself in his accusing her, and ignores the depth and economy of Rousseau's narcissistic vulnerability which could readily sacrifice others for self-protection.[9] But it is more relevant to consider first the way in which de Man's argument undermines itself and points by its own logic to the need for such psychological explanation. De Man blames Rousseau's accusers for "misreading" his fictional word "Marion" as referential. But in fact the words "Marion gave it to me" could only serve to cover Rousseau's shame if he refused to let his accusers know that they were accidental or fictional. Had he in fact said at the time what he wrote in the *Confessions*, that he uttered those words only because they were the first thing to come to his mind, he would have defeated his purpose. By de Man's own account, Rousseau purposefully *played* on the simultaneous possibilities inherent in language in order to deceive his accusers, or at least make it inevitable in the context that they would draw the "wrong" conclusion. But this means that truth and fiction are precisely matters of intentionality – of the illocutionary force of meanings, or how one intends a reader or listener to take what one has uttered. "Marion" may be a signifier both referring to an actual person and usable for a fictional one, as de Man suggests, but its particular use in a sentence uttered to someone entails the intention to have it taken it one way or the other – or, as in Rousseau's case (at least in de Man's version), to mean one thing while exploiting a context which virtually assures that his audience will take it to mean another. In this case, the inherent ambiguity of language – even if we accept the veracity of Rousseau's claim that Marion was simply the first thing that came to mind – does not lead to the "undecidability" of meaning but to a clearer fixing of his intention.

DERRIDA AND THE (DIS)UNITY OF THE TEXT

Unlike de Man, Derrida does not deny the possibility that texts can unambiguously refer to a biographical-historical reality. To a great extent, of course, Derrida is himself responsible for being misunderstood on this issue, not least because of his misleadingly lapidary and too-frequently quoted formulation that "There is nothing outside of the text." [10] But Derrida's point here is that human experience is available to us only as "textualized," as constructed by language. Derrida is not at all opposed to using biographical material "outside" the actual words of a text to illuminate that text; his well-known reading of Freud's *Beyond the Pleasure Principle*, for example, relies very heavily on biographical information about Freud not supplied in that work itself, and he is quite willing to attribute to Freud psychological motives – indeed, quite "Freudian" ones – in order to explain the inconsistencies, obfuscations, and omissions he discovers in the text. Derrida's conclusions about Freud are ones whose form and logic a conventional psychobiographer could be comfortable with, despite Derrida's claim to differentiate his interpretation from what he calls "empirico-biographical explanation". [11]

Derrida essentially argues that it is impossible to draw a clear line between the "scientific" theories Freud advanced in *Beyond the Pleasure Principle* and the complex of autobiographical motives that went into writing it. Freud, according to Derrida, was personally taken with the famous "fort/da" game that he offered as an argument for the idea of a repetition compulsion or Death Instinct because he saw the game as a simulacrum of his own situation. In the text, Freud describes watching a little boy repeatedly throw a wooden reel on a string into his curtained-off bed with a show of great anxiety as it disappeared, and then recover it with signs of equally great pleasure. The little boy was in fact Freud's own grandson Ernst, the child of his daughter Sophie. For Ernst, in Freud's view, the reel was simultaneously self, mother, and father; Ernst's anxiety over his mother's absences inspired fear for his own identity (hence his duplication of the game with his own image in a mirror), rage at the disappearing mother, and a desire to get rid of the rival father. For grandfather Freud, in Derrida's view, the reel as Ernst's mother – Freud's daughter – represented a struggle over the possession of his own name as the founder and "owner" of psychoanalysis, and the fear that after his death it would belong to someone else, as his favorite daughter already did in marrying and giving up the name Freud.

This brief summary does not do justice to Derrida's procedure in the essay. He is self-conscious about the problem of proof and offers an elaborate and careful series of arguments for asserting Freud's identification – he uses the psychoanalytic term despite (unstated) reservations – with his grandson. As the indispensable foundation of his psychological interpretation, Derrida explicitly points out the inconsistencies and gaps in Freud's reasoning. A criterion of rational argumentation, I have argued elsewhere, is a standard to which a text may legitimately be held if the text itself claims it, and its breakdown is usually sufficient reason for looking beyond the process of argumentation in the text for external reasons to explain the conclusion it reaches.[12] As Derrida notes, the oddity of the fort/da story is that, while Freud supposedly introduces it as a piece of evidence for a principle of behavior "beyond the pleasure principle," it proves no such thing, and Freud himself ultimately acknowledges this (114). If the story had only its avowed purpose, it might well have been left out or written up separately under a different rubric. But its inconclusiveness is only one of a series of equivocations about the episode in the text. Both rational and tonal inconsistencies create a mood of uneasiness that provide the opening for introducing the extra-textual considerations about anxiety of ownership that Derrida sees as the key to the meaning of the text.

Nevertheless, Derrida's claim that he is doing something other than "empirical psychobiography" should be taken seriously. Indeed his procedure in this essay differs strikingly from his usual practice precisely in his adduction of a writer's motives for the inconsistencies of his text. Personal motives are generally irrelevant for Derrida because the point of his deconstructive enterprise is that the contradictions in a text are inevitable, inherent in the nature of language itself. His argument rests on a critique of what he refers calls "logocentrism" in Western thought, the concern of the Western metaphysical tradition from Plato to the present to establish some absolute truth as the ground or foundation of all knowledge and judgment. His procedure has been to examine a series of texts which try to establish the normative truth of certain definitions or practices, such as Plato's effort to establish the priority of speech over writing in human expression, or Rousseau's attempt to determine the essence of "normal" sexuality, and to show how each of these attempts ultimately defeats itself by falling into various rhetorical traps. The key feature of all of these traps is the writer's inevitable inclusion of what he is trying to exclude within the putatively normative definition. One of the most revealing traps is the text's use of figurative language to describe what it is trying to characterize as complete and normative, for example when Plato describes genuine speech, which by contrast to writing is supposed to express immediate truth, as speech "written in the heart." Since the text is purporting to define and delimit the normative practice directly, the use of metaphor, especially of course a metaphor that describes the practice in terms of the very thing it is supposed to exclude, unwittingly announces the failure and impossibility of literal denomination. Ultimately, metaphoricity itself – the figurative nature of language – becomes in Derrida a metaphor for the impossibility of establishing "presence" in language: the unmediated expression of absolute, timeless, and determinate truth. Metaphor shows clearly how one linguistic term can substitute for another in what is potentially an endless play of signification. Since verbal signs signify in virtue of their differences-within-similarity from other verbal signs ("ball" denotes this object rather than that because it is not "bill" or "bull" or "bell"), the whole system of signs is in play in the use of any one signifier, and is at least potentially available for semantic connection with or substitution for that signifier.

Seen as a series of operations uniquely designed for the critique of logocentrism, deconstruction would appear to be a profoundly unhistorical, or uncontextual, enterprise. The treacherous play of language which undermines whatever position a text works to establish as absolute goes on within the closed circuit of the text and should be detectable there. But Derrida's procedure in "Coming into One's Own" clearly shows that this is not necessarily so, or rather that the incoherences and contradictions in the text may be only the beginning of a demonstration of relevant meaning that takes one out of the confines of a supposedly "closed" document. It is indeed one of Derrida's arguments that the rigid opposition "inside/outside" is one of those false absolutes that can be deconstructed to show the inevitable crossover between the two halves of the dichotomy whenever it is deployed in an exclusionary way. In the case of Freud's *Beyond the Pleasure Principle*, Derrida demonstrates how the intrusion of Freud's subjectivity in the observation of his grandson undermines the notion of a "pure" science grounded in the nature of the object itself and reveals the conclusions to be an intextricable mix of the subjective and the objective.

DECONSTRUCTION AND HISTORY

Nevertheless, the inherent tendency of deconstruction, given its concern with logocentrism, is towards an analysis of texts whose basic, indeed sole, purpose is to show how they disrupt their own efforts at univocal expression, at the establishing of one determinate truth or position. It is this bias which leads LaCapra, in adapting deconstructive approaches and techniques, to the sometimes misguided criticisms he makes of contextual interpretations in intellectual history. In a typical example, he attacks the effort of Alan Janik and Stephen Toulmin to relate Wittgenstein's *Tractatus Logico-Philosophicus* to "a precise context: fin-de-siècle Vienna."[13] Their argument that the *Tractatus* was meant primarily as a treatise in ethics rather than logic produces, according to LaCapra, an overly reductive reading which ignores precisely what makes a text a text – its language, style, structure, and so forth (87) – and is, in any case, derived from outside the text rather than from within it (100). Such a reading "serves the interest of a fully unified interpretation" (87) which, in its quest for completeness and unity through "the contextual saturation of the meaning of a text" (99), fails to take into account "a more or less systematic tension or internal contestation between the explicit, direct argument of the *Tractatus* and its own use of language or style" (109).

To begin with, LaCapra is wrong in implying that Janik and Toulmin's interpretation does not appreciate contradictions or "contestations" within the text itself. In fact, the authors build their case precisely on certain blatant inconsistencies both in the text's argument (in his focus on rhetorical, stylistic, and structural features, LaCapra seems to ignore that discursive argument is a defining feature of a philosophical text as a text) as well as on its form and language. The famous utterances in section six of the *Tractatus* which touch on matters of ultimate meaning, death, and ethics are in fact meaningless according to the theory of language of the rest of the book, and ought not to be spoken at all, as the concluding epigram expressly says; their tone, furthermore, is utterly different from anything that has come before, one of exquisitely understated existential passion and anguish. These inconsistencies were indeed sometimes noticed but glossed over by positivist interpreters because of their own philosophical biases. By going outside the text – both to Wittgenstein's direct utterances about the *Tractatus* ("The book's point is an ethical one. . . . My work consists of two parts: the one presented here plus all that I have not written. And *it is precisely this second part that is the important one*")[14] and to the context of fin-de-siècle Vienna's crisis of values, in which it becomes intelligible *why* Wittgenstein might consider the unwritten ethical part the more important one – Janik and Toulmin have cast some light on one mystery of the text.

LaCapra reveals how his own dice are loaded when he imputes to Janik and Toulmin the idea that "fin-de-siècle Vienna is the locus of full intelligibility for reading Wittgenstein's *Tractatus*" (89). Whatever "full intelligibility" might mean, Janik and Toulmin have neither stated nor implied it as their goal. At the time they wrote, they were operating polemically within a context of contemporary views of Wittgenstein, and they were concerned partly to correct, partly to supplement existing interpretations with a reading which addressed the anomaly those views made even more glaring. In crucial respects, as I have argued, their methodological starting point is the same as LaCapra's. But for LaCapra, the exposure of self-contestations in a text is an end in itself because of his normative deconstructionist belief-orientation that texts just *are* attempts at establishing an ultimate ground of truth and unity of structure which are, at the same time, predestined to fail. Revealing the fissures in the work created by conflicts between rhetoric and argument is for LaCapra the whole job of interpretation.[15] Indeed, his notion of inevitable contradiction and failure is constitutive of his definition of a text; a text for LaCapra is "a situated use of language marked by a tense interaction between mutually implicated yet at times contestatory tendencies" (26). He thus finds it necessary to impute to contextualism, whose effort is to explain such contradictions socio-politically or psychologically, the desire to do away with them.[16]

But in interpretation, *tout comprendre n'est pas tout pardonner.* It is a logical error to assume that explaining the conflicting tendencies of a text by something other than the structural features of language explains them out of existence. Derrida's own example in "Coming into One's Own" is a clear case in point, and Janik and Toulmin by no means eliminate Wittgenstein's contradictions through their analysis. Moreover, the deconstructive enterprise, taken out of Derrida's quite specific framework of the Western metaphysical tradition and its presumed logocentrism, begs some rather large questions of interpretation. Not all texts are a priori concerned with establishing the kind of ground or absolute that Derrida is interested in deconstructing. Not all texts are totalizing enterprises which struggle to repress and subdue uncomfortable truths in the name of some

one Truth, and which are therefore adequately explained – that is, demysti-
fied – when its repressions are exposed. This does not mean, however, that
Derrida's analytic techniques are useless outside the special framework of
the critique of logocentrism. Though designed for that purpose, they are not
limited to it and can be deployed separately from it. Separation, however,
opens up new problems of explanation.

A fascinating example of the critical purchase that sensitivity to figurative language can provide for the interpretation even of scientific texts
can be found in Charles Darwin's uneasy discussion of the concept of
natural selection in *The Origin of Species*. He acknowledges that "natural
selection" is a metaphor, one which would seem to have implications
opposed to his own theory, but insists that the metaphor ought not to be
taken seriously:

> In the literal sense of the word, no doubt, natural selection is a false term;
> but who ever objected to chemists speaking of the elective affinities
> of the various elements? . . . It has been said that I speak of natural
> selection as an active power or Deity; but who objects to an author
> speaking of the attraction of gravity as ruling the movements of the
> planets? Every one knows what is meant and is implied by such
> metaphorical expressions; and they are almost necessary for brevity.
> So again it is difficult to avoid personifying the word Nature: but I
> mean by Nature, only the aggregate action and product of many natural
> laws, and by laws, the sequence of events as ascertained by us.[17]

It is almost impossible after Derrida not to read Darwin's vigorous
disclaimer about metaphor as unwittingly ironic, as protesting rather too
much. It is as if he is acknowledging what Derrida has demonstrated,
that metaphor is not innocent, that the "mere" figure of speech is not
simply a *façon de parler* but in fact an argument. And indeed elsewhere
in the *Origin*, Darwin overtly contradicts what he says here about natural
selection as the aggregate action of certain sequences of events. He
attributes a teleology to Nature, a progressive direction to the process
of evolution that is expressly at odds with his insistence that adaptation,
as shown by the survival of lower species, does *not* necessarily involve
progressive development (74): "And as natural selection works solely by
and for the good of each being, all corporeal and mental endowments will
tend to progress towards perfection" (122).

In contrast to the usual textual move as understood by deconstruction,
the effect of the metaphor of natural selection in the *Origin* is ironically
to *restore* the sense of unified meaning destroyed by the work's official

doctrine of the "decentered" randomness of the evolutionary process. For that very reason it leaves us with a puzzle to solve. Without the background assumption that texts necessarily both strive for totalizing unity and simultaneously decenter themselves, Darwin's metaphorical undermining of his own naturalism clearly demands some sort of explanation – unless of course we are willing to rest content with its blatant contradictions. Whether that explanation is to be found in personal, tactical, or socio-ideological considerations, it necessarily takes us out of the confines of the *Origin* narrowly construed to the context of its author's life, beliefs, and Victorian milieu.

Furthermore, even if one accepts in principle Derrida's fundamental theoretical argument about the ultimate indeterminacy of signification – and as we have seen in the case of de Man, for any particular utterance, that notion has to be circumscribed by notions about the illocutionary force of utterances within a community of language users, who operate within certain conventions about their meaning and use – we cannot escape reference to an author's intentions and motives in ascertaining a text's cruxes and ambiguities. Possible alternative meanings for, or associations to, a linguistic term exist only if a linguistic consciousness (or unconscious) has in fact brought those meanings into relationship with one another for itself, and made them available to displace or substitute for one another. This is a point which deconstruction often ignores, but it is implied by Derrida's own ideas about language as a humanly-constructed network. The differences among signs implied by the language system are differences to and for human consciousness.[18] Just as the language user inevitably selects and combines from the potentially infinite repertoire of language, so also he selects from the potentially infinite repertoire of metaphors and displacements which may be associated for him with his linguistic choices. A reader may well have his own associations to a textual utterance, but whether they are also the author's, and not simply the reader's transferential free associations, depends on whether there is any evidence to show that they are within the author's repertoire in general and whether, according to his practice as shown by his writings, they could be germane to this utterance in particular. The punning interpretations of deconstructive reading can be imaginative and clever, but just because the language permits a certain word-play does not mean that the text does. It also follows from this argument that, if there are contradictions or other kinds of self-contestations within a text, the reasons for them will have to be found in the conflicting principles of selection by which the writer created them – that is, in his conflicting reasons and motives.

GOING OUTSIDE THE TEXT

Since those reasons or motives are rarely to be found in the text itself, this means going outside the text as narrowly construed to its wider context. But going outside raises a number of serious questions. One is the question of evidence. Precisely because what is being invoked to explain a problem in the text is not there in a direct sense – if it were, there would be no problem – how can it be shown to be relevant to, or operative in, the text? That question is closely related to another one: what context should be invoked as explanatory? In his critique of Janik and Toulmin, LaCapra faults them for claiming to offer fin-de-siècle Viennese culture as "*the* context" of the *Tractatus* when, in fact, they have described only one among many possible contexts relevant to its issues, and a very partial version of that one to boot (89–95). Harlan draws the more general inference from LaCapra's criticism. If all of the intellectual, artistic, religious and cultural traditions that might have been relevant to a writer's subject, knowledge, form and style are part of his context, "the relevant community of discourse may include all of Western civilization. And more" (595).

This objection, however, rests on a fundamental misconception about the point of invoking context in the first place. We are not usually interested in a text's context simply for its own sake – though if we were, such an investigation would probably escape the strictures of the anti-contextualists because no causal claims would be involved in it. Contextualism would then simply be a harmless, though also unilluminating, description of the milieu in which the text was written. What anti-contextualists in fact object to is that the purpose of contextualization is usually to explain something in or about a text. But to the extent that the purpose of contextualism *is* explanation, it can escape the criticism that everything is causally relevant. This criticism is a version of the more general objection to causal explanation as the attempt to isolate the necessary conditions of an event. It has been argued that defining the cause of something as the set of conditions necessary and sufficient to produce it is an empty formula, because it gives no guidelines as to where to stop: the full necessary conditions for any event, after all, are nothing less than the whole universe. But this objection in turn is based on a fundamental misunderstanding of the purpose and logic of causal explanation. We are generally interested in explaining something because it is unusual or problematic, because it deviates from what we consider to be the "normal" or the desirable. Conditions that are part of the normal state of the object being considered – or part of our normal patterns of expectation about it – do not figure as causes, even though they may be necessary conditions, precisely because they are normal.

Oxygen is a necessary condition for burning, but we do not usually consider the presence of oxygen in the air as the cause of a fire – unless in the "normal" circumstances for that particular event, oxygen should not have been there (as in a laboratory experiment). If a gardener charged with watering flowers fails to do so and the flowers die, we will consider his failure to be the cause of their death, though no one else watered the flowers either.[19] A cause is that which produces something "abnormal" against the background of what are considered normal standing conditions or expectations. But as the examples show, what constitutes "normal conditions" is highly variable, and depends on circumstances and interests. Something that is normal under one set of circumstances may be abnormal in others. Someone with an ulcer may consider "the cause" of his indigestion to be the spicy food that he ate, insofar as he regards his ulcer as part of the normal conditions that regulate his eating; his doctor, on the other hand, will consider the cause to be the ulcer, in relation to his concern for prescribing correct treatment against the background of other possible diagnoses of the pain, while medical researchers will see the cause of the indigestion in the biochemical processes that cause the ulceration. All are right; they are just taking different background conditions for granted as "normal" in relation to the different causal questions they are asking for their specific purposes.[20]

These issues are directly relevant to questions about the possibility and point of contextualism. In understanding a text, we do not want the whole set of conditions for its production; we want only the relevant conditions. But which are relevant? In fact, that question depends on the further question of what we want to explain about a text, what is problematic about it. If we are tempted to "explain" a text at all, it is because there is something about it that *from some point of view or other* is not transparent or self-explanatory to us. The very questions that we ask of the text may then point us in the direction of relevant context. Our two questions above are in fact related to one another. What is missing in the text will point us to what must be supplied from outside the text, which, *pace* Derrida, has left its traces there in its very absence because of the background of expectations we bring to the text. There may simply be gaps in our knowledge of things referred to or terms used in a text that inspire questions about what it means and that drive us to its historical context to understand its references, allusions, or conceptual language. (Part of the point of Pocock's and Skinner's work is that, in considering works written in the past, we ought in principle to assume such gaps, that even the familiarity of a term or concept in a political text may be misleading since it may have meant something different to contemporaries of the text

than it does to us.) There may be, from what we think we know of the times
in which the text was written, anomalous concepts or literary elements that
require clarification. In the case of Freud's *Beyond the Pleasure Principle*,
as in many other discursive texts, it may be the incoherences in their
argumentation, the contradictions between stated or implied purpose and
method and actual procedures, that inspire the need for explanation. And
as we have seen, contradictions are not necessarily peculiar to rational
argumentation. The particular contribution of modern literary criticism to
intellectual history has been to alert us to the fact that it is possible to speak
of structural, narrative, stylistic, and tropological incoherences, and that
tensions in the aesthetic elements of even a discursive text are part of its
meaning and argument.

Only some of these problems point in the direction of psychological
answers. But there is a strong presumption in favor of looking in that
direction precisely when the text contests itself. As we have seen, even
readings that expose ambiguities of meaning made possible by the multi-
valency of language or its figurative character drive us to intentional or
motivational contexts because all meaning is only meaning to a self; in
the end, the particular ambiguities of a text are the result of an author's
linguistic *choices*, though, it must be stressed again, not necessarily of
his conscious intentions. This is true even where the range of choices
is circumscribed by Foucaultian "discourses," or, more loosely, by the
limitations of the historical milieu, which, as Skinner has been at pains
to argue, may rule out as plausible meanings for an utterance those not
generally available to speakers in its time and place. No text writes itself out
of prevailing discourses, however necessary it may be to identify a specific
conceptual paradigm to understand how a certain topic is talked about or
how language is used in the text. The idea of a discourse itself is in some
respects a fiction, an abstraction from a series of individual texts, and while
the reconstructed ensemble of a discourse may be seen as providing *some*
implicit rules for what can be said at a given time, each textual instance
is a subjective selection of elements and emphases from the ensemble as
well as a subjective shaping of them. Moreover, the tendency of interpretive
approaches that stress linguistic paradigms or discourses, even those like
Foucault's that emphasize their partiality and their roots in the social power
of dominant historical groups, is to treat them as coherent systems and to
ignore the internal inconsistencies that point to the internal conflict of the
author's positions.

Awareness of the subjective factor is necessary, however, even where
these inconsistencies are recognized and socio-cultural factors are introduced to explain them. Merely establishing a parallelism, for example,

between the cultural-intellectual concerns of a milieu and a specific text may create a false or at least an inadequate notion of their relationship. LaCapra has a point when he criticizes the central role given by Janik and Toulmin to the Viennese satirist Karl Kraus on the grounds that there is little evidence that Kraus actually influenced Wittgenstein, or when he criticizes them for precipitously rejecting (236) consideration of Wittgenstein's "personal temperament and makeup" because it has no bearing on his concerns in the *Tractatus*. Context is operative only as it is mediated by the author. If trends in the milieu are supposed to explain aspects of the work, its author had to have been aware of them and to have been reacting to them, even if in any particular case of historical explanation, the only evidence we have for such subjective response is circumstantial. Moreover, the existence of a general crisis does not by itself explain a particular individual's susceptibility to it, nor preclude the possibility that particular features of his response to it can only be explained in personal terms.

To argue for the importance of conscious intention and unconscious motivation in the original shaping of a text and the retroactive interpretation of a text, is not to argue against the role of wider historical factors. On the contrary, not only does an author make choices from the arc of possibilities furnished by his environment, but his environment, as Marxists have always argued, contributes to constructing the personality that makes the choices. Nevertheless, it is not an adequate version of the role of socio-historical factors in constructing personality to say, with Sartre or Jameson, that individual personality is at most the necessary mediation between social class and the individual work, that psychoanalysis is the method which enables us to study the process by which the child lives out his class situation within his particular family, and preserves the residues of that family situation in his adult life.[21] This could be true only if Sartre were correct in saying that psychoanalysis has no principles of its own, no theoretical foundations, by which he means that it has no fundamental theory of motivation independent of the kinds of motivations implicit in the theory of historical materialism – the basic needs of producing the means of subsistence and the particular historical motivations accompanying a specific historical set of productive forces and relations of production. This implies, however, that sexual desire, identity issues, and the problem of self-esteem are nothing but the products of a particular historical culture: a highly improbable thesis which is too often confused with the more plausible notion that all of these are psychological features universal to the human being but given particular form – constructed, in the language of contemporary theory – by the social forms, rules, and beliefs of a given culture. It would be as correct to say that social structure mediates the forms that self-esteem can take in a culture as it would be to say that the particular things which confer self-esteem in a culture are mediated by its social structure.

My methodological suggestions make brief examples difficult. I want, nevertheless, to try to illustrate the value and even inescapability of recourse to the biographical and psychological with a glance at some of the problems raised for a modern reader by one of the key documents of early European Romanticism, François-René de Châteaubriand's short story *Atala*, originally published independently in 1801 but intended as part of his great work of Christian apologetics, *The Genius of Christianity*, which appeared a year later.

Like its framing work, *Atala* is meant to argue the virtues of Christianity, particularly over those of the state of nature as represented by Indian culture in North America. In earlier years, Châteaubriand, like many young French radicals towards the end of the eighteenth century, had favorably opposed primitive virtue to the mores of the Old Regime. The oppressiveness and hopeless corruption of the eighteenth-century French monarchy, its aristocratic hierarchical ordering reinforced by the huge inequalities in wealth created by modern commerce, made him a supporter of the French Revolution in its first stage. Before his eyes were two alternative political/moral models. One was classical republicanism, a central strand of oppositionist political theory in the eighteenth century, with its stern ideals of civic virtue, dedication to the common good, universal participation, and the rough economic equality and independence that were their prerequisites. The other was the quasi-mythical image of the state of nature as theorized by Rousseau and as purportedly embodied in the actual society of American Indian tribes. Disillusioned by the bloodshed of the revolution, Châteaubriand had travelled to the fledgling United States in 1791 to observe modern republicanism in action, but even more to find renewed inspiration in the untouched wilderness and the natural emotional and moral life of the American natives.

A first mysterious conversion, triggered by the news of the king's flight to Varennes, brought him back to Europe in the royalist cause as a soldier in the emigré armies and to ultimate flight to England as a royalist refugee. A second abrupt conversion after the deaths of his mother and sister some years later brought him back to the Catholicism he had repudiated as an Enlightenment radical. His works of Christian apologetics were meant partly to atone for the past, partly to offer a new approach to proselyting for Christianity: emotional and aesthetic, rather than rational and dogmatic.

Atala seems like apologia as melodrama. Atala, a young Christianized

Indian woman, rescues Chactas, a pagan Indian youth of another tribe, from the death sentence imposed by her own people. They flee to the forest where, surrounded by idyllic nature, they fall in love. They are about to consummate their passion when a violent storm threatens their lives; they are rescued and sheltered by the missionary Father Aubry in the community, based on Christian love and agrarian communism, he has established with converted Indians in the wilderness. There can be no happy resolution for the lovers in this utopia, however, because Atala has a dark secret. Sickly at birth, she had been consecrated to virginity by her mother in exchange for her life, and as her mother lay dying, she made Atala renew the vow to the Virgin Mary on pain of her mother's eternal damnation. Tempted beyond endurance by her desire for Chactas, Atala poisons herself rather than succumb. Chactas curses the God who chokes off nature, but Father Aubry reproves him sharply for his unruly passion, then tries to console him. The vow of Atala's mother, he argues, was a primitive perversion of the true spirit of Christianity. Christianity does not want to extirpate the passions but to fulfill them. It does not oppose natural sexuality, but it does recognize the inevitable imperfections in human love, the result of human finitude and weakness, and promises in the afterlife the gratification that earthly passion aspires to but can never achieve. Pacified, Chactas promises Atala on her deathbed that he will convert to Christianity.

Even this summary, which gives the story a consistent narrative line, raises a questions for the modern reader. Father Aubry's Catholicism seems quite puzzling, both unhistorical and tonally inconsistent with the Catholicism's traditionally strong ambivalence about sexuality. But my summary itself, while not quite wrong, is crucially misleading. The vow which has apparently caused the tragedy is something of a red herring. Ultimately the tragedy does not turn on a potentially avoidable misunderstanding of the requirements of Christian faith. The brunt of Father Aubry's diatribe is in fact aimed at the godlike pretensions of human love, pretensions which Atala has previously made dramatically explicit when she described the depth of her passion for Chactas. "Sometimes," she confesses to Chactas, "as I fixed my eyes upon you, my desires would go to the wildest and most forbidden extremes. I wanted to be the only living creature on earth with you, or else, feeling some divinity restraining me in my dreadful ecstasies, I longed for the annihilation of divinity, if only, clasped in your arms, I could plunge through endless depths along with the ruins of God and the universe."[22] It is this aspiration to divine self-sufficiency in ecstasy, to be achieved if necessary by annihilating God himself, that Father Aubry confronts and condemns. Yet at the same time, he also validates this aspiration by promising Atala its fulfillment in the afterlife, when in union with Jesus, "the embraces of your heavenly spouse will never end" (67). Humanity becomes divine through religion itself.

But this is not the only hidden paradox in the story. The true barrier between Atala and Chactas turns out to be incest. They are, as they discover, brother and sister, if only nominally, since Chactas was only informally adopted by Atala's biological father. Their kinship seems a disconnected plot element, at best an embodiment of their spiritual affinity, but though latent – it will become fully explicit only in the companion story *René*, published a few years later – brother-sister incest is the key to desire in *Atala*. Union with the sister who is both absolute other and alter ego ("an Eve drawn from myself," René will say in his story) is the metaphor for the love that contains all opposites, selfish sexual desire and selfless affection, self-sufficiency and totality. In maintaining the superiority of religion over natural feeling, Father Aubry is caught in an insoluble contradiction. He condemns native passion as "unnatural" though not culpable in the eyes of God because it is an error of the mind rather than a vice of the heart. Incestuous desire itself, that is to say, *is* natural; the problem is that it is directed at the wrong object, human rather than divine. But this only highlights the contradiction in the desire itself, which aims at personal infinity through self-surrender.

But in the final paradox of *Atala*, the promise of Christianity is brought into question even as it is affirmed. Structurally, the story undermines the hope of an earthly Christian commonwealth by unfolding the tragedy after the depiction of Father Aubry's utopian community. But the narrative also undermines the promise of infinity in the afterlife as well. Despite his oath to Atala, Chactas does not convert to Christianity, at least within the story. He tells it as an old man, long after the events it relates, still not converted, and at the end of his account, he himself wonders at his failure. Only an epilogue by an unidentified narrator indicates that Chactas converted to Christianity just before he was killed in an Indian massacre. The narrator is the only survivor, a lonely wanderer without roots whose sole identity is as a teller of tales.

These paradoxes certainly undermine the overt message of the story. For the historian of ideas, however, exposing them is only the beginning of his task. The paradoxes raise questions which point in specific contextual directions. Why does Châteaubriand define religion, against what appears its every essence, as the fulfillment of the infinite self? Why does he figure desire as incest, a trope that is neither universal or self-evident, and why does he make self-expansion possible only through self-surrender? Why is the female figure in the story, who is the one most explicitly aggressive in the quest for infinity, made to die with only its promise, while the male rejects that promise and survives as a creator, but one whose identity derives only from his connection with his beloved as the narrator of their story?

In other words, as Jean-Paul Sartre said, the work poses questions to the life, the psychological life that includes issues of narcissism, intrafamily relationships, and gender. It is impossible to understand *Atala* without exploring Châteaubriand's developing sense of self through the stages leading up to its writing, his relationship with his sister Lucile, and his developing vocation as a writer. But there is nothing about these issues that intrinsically divorces them from the contextual factors of ideology, social class, political conflict, and historical moment. On the contrary, the very questions I have raised about the text suggest that what, from a purely psychological point of view, might be formulated as a question of narcissism, is also a historical question: what made it possible for Châteaubriand (and we might add, other Romantics) to formulate the question of the self in the way he did at this time? The psychological questions do not preclude historical questions; they are inevitably also historical. But as I have argued above, they are unavoidable. A text as obviously concerned with self and psychological issues as *Atala* only foregrounds what is true about all textual interpretation. While it may not always be the point of interpretation to raise questions about the subjective choices in the text, they are always there in its construction.

Notes

1. D. Harlan, "Intellectual History and the Return of Literature," *American Historical Review* 94.3 (1989):596.
2. J. G. A. Pocock, "Languages and Their Implications," in *Politics, Language, and Time* (New York, 1973), 25.
3. Q. Skinner, "The Principles and Practice of Opposition: The Case of Bolingbroke versus Walpole," in *Historical Perspectives*, ed. N. McKendrick (London, 1974), 127.
4. F. Jameson, "On Interpretation," in *The Political Unconscious* (Ithaca, NY, 1981), 66.
5. D. LaCapra, *History and Criticism* (Ithaca, NY, 1983), 141.
6. J. Toews, "Intellectual History After the Linguistic Turn," *American Historical Review* 92.4 (1987):886.
7. D. A. Hollinger, "The Return of the Prodigal," *American Historical Review* 94.3 (1989):621.
8. Quoted by P. de Man, "Excuses (*Confessions*)," in *Allegories of*

Reading: Figural Language in Rousseau, Nietzsche, Rilke, and Proust (New Haven, 1979), 284.

9. See the discussion of Rousseau's shame in C. Blum, *Rousseau and the Republic of Virtue: The Language of Politics in the French Revolution* (Ithaca, NY, 1986), 74–85 and passim.

10. J. Derrida, *Of Grammatology*, trans. G. C. Spivak (Baltimore, 1976), 158.

11. J. Derrida, "Coming into One's Own," in *Psychoanalysis and the Question of the Text*, ed. G. H. Hartmann (Baltimore, 1978), 140.

12. See my "Psychohistory and Intellectual History", in *History and Theory* 14 (1975):139–55.

13. D. LaCapra, "Reading Examplars: *Wittgenstein's Vienna* and Wittgenstein's *Tractatus*," in *Rethinking Intellectual History: Texts, Contexts, Language* (Ithaca, NY, 1983), 86.

14. Quoted in LaCapra, 100; also in Alan Janik and Stephen Toulmin, *Wittgenstein's Vienna* (New York, 1973), 192.

15. In an effort to defend against precisely such charges, LaCapra reaffirms the documentary or representative function of texts as well as their creative or "worklike aspects" and warns against the danger of "a lemming-like fascination for discursive impasses and an obsessive interest in the aberrant and aleatory – tendencies that threaten to identify all controlling limits [on a text] with totalizing mastery": *History and Criticism*, 141. But despite his abstract disclaimers, his practice reveals the inherent tendency of his theoretical approach to just such a "lemming-like fascination for discursive impasses."

16. This becomes clear again in his critique of Carl E. Schorske's *Fin-de-siècle Vienna: Politics and Culture* (New York, 1979) as an escapist response to the crisis of liberal culture at the turn of the century, which LaCapra terms "the quest for unity through a reductive psychologism superimposed on a reductive socioculturalism": "Is Everyone a Mentality Case? Transference and the 'Culture' Concept," in *History and Criticism*, 84.

17. C. Darwin, *The Origin of Species*, abr. P. Appleman (New York, 1970), 45.

18. Heidegger has argued perhaps the most influential version of this idea for contemporaries in *Being and Time*. See Gerald N. Izenberg, *The Existentialist Critique of Freud: The Crisis of Autonomy* (Princeton, 1976), 90–96. Charles Taylor sees the idea as foundational for understanding the self: *Sources of the Self: The Making of Modern Identity* (Cambridge, MA, 1989), 34 and passim.

19. For the examples as well as the concepts argued here, see H. L. A. Hart and A. M. Honore, *Causation in the Law* (Oxford, 1962), 24–41.

20. Hart and Honore, 34.

21. J-P. Sartre, *Search for a Method* (New York, 1968), 60–61.

22. F-R de Châteaubriand, *Atala/René* (Berkeley, 1952), 61.

4 Whither History? Reflections on the Comparison between Historians and Scientists

Theodore K. Rabb

I

Whither history? Increasingly, those who concern themselves with this question have concluded that it is impossible to come up with an answer. Methods, approaches, and purposes have multiplied so rapidly over the past forty years that anyone who looks at the historical enterprise as a whole is likely to deny that it has any discernable shape or mission. Neither research nor writing appear to be guided by common principles or aims. As a result, both the subject matter itself and the forms of analysis through which it is explored – the very contours of the past as well as the ways used to describe it – evaporate before our eyes. To quote a critic of a much earlier scholar who sought to unify his discipline, Galileo Galilei (and the analogy, as we shall see, is by no means inapt), the efforts "dissolve into so much alchemical smoke."[1]

That observers of the historical scene may reach conclusions similar to those put forward by contemporaries of Galileo is not entirely surprising. The study of nature in the Europe of the 1610s and 1620s was also the product of half a century or more of inconclusive experimentation in theory and technique. Traditional assumptions had been sharply challenged, but the alternatives, each proclaiming its own superiority, merely created confusion. Proponents of new doctrines denounced the Aristotelian, Ptolemaic, and Galenic paradigms that had held sway for centuries, but it was impossible to decide which of their ideas was better, if any. There seemed little chance that renewed certainty, or even confidence about the goals of scientific investigation, could be restored. It was even being suggested (by Francis Bacon and René Descartes among others) that the very substance of the investigations – physical reality – might be something of an illusion. In Bacon's view, "The human understanding is of its own

63

nature prone to suppose the existence of more order and regularity in the world than it finds."[2] And Descartes thought there was a clear distinction between the interpretations we form in our minds and the tangible objects we study. Bacon, moreover, was suggesting that the classic subjects of science – the heavens, optics, motion, and the body – were themselves inadequate, and should be joined by such new topics as heat, earthquakes, and climate.

These issues and arguments sound extraordinarily familiar to the student of recent historiography. Especially since World War II – though the tendency began earlier – dozens of long-standing assumptions have been strenuously disputed. The historian's paradigm-makers, such as Ranke and Marx, have been as directly rejected as were Ptolemy and Galen before them. Advocates of the latest theories of literary criticism have deconstructed reality into no less of an invention of the mind – a possibly insignificant product of discourse, signs, and the signified – than the world envisioned by Descartes. And the array of hitherto neglected themes that has been brought to the fore by demographers, psychohistorians, climatologists, anthropologists, explorers of mentalities, and others can rival the list of 130 new subjects that Bacon proposed.

As we know, the fragmentations and uncertainties of science in the 1610s and 1620s were soon to be resolved. Within a few decades, the methods it used to establish its conclusions were to be the core of a new and assured epistemology. By the end of the century, the universally accepted paradigms associated with Isaac Newton were to restore the faith of European intellectuals in the capacity of the human mind to absorb entirely unprecedented findings and to discover truth even amidst seeming contradictions. But does it seem likely that, in the wake of our own century's reawakened doubts about science and its capacity for certainty, historians will be able to imitate not only the confusions of seventeenth-century scientists but also their ability to regain the confidence and consensus that seemed for a while to have been lost forever?

If recent overviews can be trusted, the answer appears to be a resounding negative. Two in particular, though they survey both the immediate past and the prospects for the future from very different perspectives, seem to agree that the outlook is for continued splintering. To the extent that they can be taken as representative of the spectrum of opinion among historians, it is significant that neither offers much expectation of a restored community of interests or purpose. Nor – and this is even more significant – do they regard this as a particularly encouraging conclusion. It may be instructive, therefore, to see if their assessments could be compatible with a rather different evaluation of the current condition of historical research.

II

The two overviews are by B. G. Mogilnitsky of Tomsk State University in what is now the Russian Republic and André Burguière of the École des Hautes Études in France. Their purposes are quite distinct. Mogilnitsky's concern is to demonstrate the absence of a reliable theoretical framework, and therefore of a progressive body of findings, in western – or, to use his word, in "bourgeois" – historical thought. Burguière's aims seem more limited: to determine whether the methods of the *Annales* school have become obsolete or remain useful guides for scholarly endeavor. Like Mogilnitsky, however, he eventually confronts the implications of the various paradoxes that have left current observers uncertain about historical inquiry as a coherent or even well-defined undertaking.

Mogilnitsky's essay, entitled "Some Tendencies in the Development of Contemporary Bourgeois Historical Thought," focuses on recent work in Germany, England, France, and the United States – with occasional comparative glances at the Soviet Union – in order to discern the "scholarly meaning," "ideological direction," and "laws of development" of the scholarship of the past two decades.[3] Despite his closeness to his subject, and the varieties of the national traditions, he feels able to identify a number of such meanings and directions, and to indicate that the absence of laws is exactly what distinguishes western from theoretical (i.e., Marxist) investigations.

En route to his conclusions, Mogilnitsky describes what he considers representative definitions of the historical enterprise in western work. These range from its status as an almost spiritual means of defense against the looming crises of our age; to its role (much debated) as a source of practical guidance; and on to its potential as a systematic and scientific venture (thanks to quantification and interdisciplinary research). The last of these ambitions, he decides, has been undermined by the competing emphasis on human irrationality, which has left "scientization" as a "superficial" and relativist enterprise, incapable of offering a new model for historiography. It promises neither objectivity nor a synthetic theory of the past, and thus remains "a disaster area." The alternative, the microscopic emphasis on individual cases as a means of displaying history's usefulness (and thus reviving Max Weber's program for the social sciences), is equally futile.

The result, according to Mogilnitsky, is a fragmentation into competing specializations, such as cliometrics and "sociologization," from which western historians have sought a remedy by reviving the emphasis on narrative. They have sought esthetic persuasiveness, an emphasis on words, or a historicist "understanding" – all of which are goals that represent either a denial of objectivity or an escape from generalization into meaningless particulars. The social purpose of history becomes moot, and its practitioners descend into crisis, torn between science and narrative, unable to "modernize" their methods or theories, and forced into "retrograde movement."

The binary pulls of science and narrative also preoccupy Burguière. He opens his essay, entitled "De la Compréhension en Histoire," by asking whether the journal he edits, *Annales*, still has a useful function in an age when "the social sciences are in the midst of a profound crisis, both of identity . . . and of credibility."[4] Two sets of critics, he says, imply that its commitments are obsolete. One group (the equivalent of Mogilnitsky's "sociologizers") believes that *Annales*'s work is over, because its views have entered the mainstream, and the real need now is to bring political and institutional history, which the journal has ignored, to the forefront of attention. The other group consists (as in Mogilnitsky's account) of proponents of narrative, who reject the emphasis on social science and quantification with which *Annales* has "disfigured" the "intelligibility" of history. They prefer the faithfulness to life, the ability to create "understanding," that is offered by narrative.

Burguière's response to these critiques is, first of all, to suggest that they are not new. Bloch and Febvre, the founders of *Annales*, would themselves have argued that sources do not speak for themselves – whether presented in statistical tables or in narrative, they have to be manipulated – and that there is no history except of the present. Nor is this subjectivity contradicted by the adoption of scientific methods, which merely expand the armory of the historian as that "chercheur" tries to reconstruct the past. And even the advocates of narrative are hardly raising a fresh issue. It was precisely to get away from the "alchemy" and "magic" of older, more instinctive interpretations that *Annales* created its "Copernican" revolution of a focus on groups rather than individuals, structures rather than events, economy and society rather than politics. The new attack on this "Copernican" shift in the historian's priorities is therefore no more than a revival of old longings. Fearful of the analytic and theoretical demands of the tough *Annalistes*, these critics hope nostalgically that they can restore a lost age of narrative insight and understanding.

Burguière admits that the dichotomy has in fact pervaded recent historiography. As a result, such specialists as historical demographers and historians of science – the two examples he cites – create their own distinct worlds, unattached to larger visions. He admits that this fragmentation lends credence to the accusation that our splintered discipline is losing its "epistemological identity" and is in danger of disappearing completely.

And yet, he argues, both basic approaches, the social scientific and the narrative, have roots in the early days of *Annales*. For Bloch and Febvre, *mentalités* were as important as structures, and he sees their influence in the work of Michel Foucault as well as Ernest Labrousse. Yet differences certainly remain, exemplified for Burguière by the contrast between the books of Philippe Ariès and Michel Vovelle on attitudes toward death. What he finds surprising is that, whereas Ariès (like Foucault) seems almost ahistorical, creating "understandings" that are esthetic rather than analytic, he seems more persuasive than the systematic Vovelle, with his carefully argued structures of intellectual and social causation. Burguière suggests that it is the predictability of Vovelle that lessens his impact, and the unexpectedness of Ariès' picture that touches us. But what Burguière wants is both. Although quantification may not have delivered on its promise of a Cartesian mathematicization and unification of the historical enterprise, despite its dominance during the "thirty glorious" years of prosperity following World War II, it still is needed as a grounding and as an arbiter for the provocative and fertile, but uncertain, speculations of the intuitive historian. Only in combination are these two modes – both of which, in his view, keep alive the *Annales* tradition – able to convey the intensity as well as the nature of the changes that make up the subject of history.

Burguière may seem more optimistic than Mogilnitsky. He certainly believes that, under the umbrella of *Annales*, western historians (primarily the French) still have a purpose and direction that transcends their divisions. Of what this purpose consists, however, he does not say, though he does imply that it includes making important discoveries, such as the "demographic transition" that now helps to define modernity. Whether that kind of advance, limited and specific as it is, would satisfy Mogilnitsky's demand for general and theoretical understandings is extremely doubtful. Indeed, the Russian's much more gloomy appraisal, with its emphasis on fragmentation and disintegration, and its refusal to provide the easy reassurance offered by the Frenchman, seems truer to the mood of the 1980s. If one ignores the political agenda that lies behind his appraisal – which is not difficult, since it does not really affect the conclusions – one has to recognize that he captures much of the unease and Donne-like crumbling "to his atomies" that pervades the profession. Mogilnitsky simply seems more convincing than Burguière – or at least more in tune with the times – when he addresses the consequences of the bifurcation of historical research.

What is suggestive is that, regardless of their different aims, both see the competition between "social science" and "narrative," between analysis and intuition, as the essential division among historians. On the assumption that this conclusion, which unites not only the two disparate (and almost polar) assessments considered here, but much of the literature of the past decade, is both correct and widely held, an attempt will be made in what follows to resolve the dilemmas that it seems to cause. Even if the split is not merely binary, but a fragmentation into many parts, there are reasons – or so it will be argued – not to abandon the sense of purpose, cohesiveness, and confidence that, until recently, seemed characteristic of the historical enterprise.

III

It will cause little surprise if a historian is inclined to suggest that, in order to go forward, we should first go back. But that is how I think we can most effectively proceed. In particular, I believe we should return to that seventeenth-century scientific revolution which, as was indicated above, offers such interesting analogies for our predicament. Burguière makes a number of references to science – it is the source for his comparison of *Annales* to Copernicus; the writing of its history provides him with instances both of fragmentation and of achievement in research; and (in company with Mogilnitsky and most commentators) he sees it as the model for the quantitative and other "social scientific" impulses of recent work. But in these usages, science is a metaphor, an example, or merely a subject that historians study. What I would like to propose is that we think, not of science, but of *scientists*, and consider whether they once behaved, as a collectivity and at a time when their concerns mirrored ours, in ways that are analogous to our own. To the extent that we can make this a direct analogy, and not merely a metaphor or a cautionary tale – though it is important to emphasize that this is a heuristic comparison, not an attempt to blur genuine differences – we may be able to reach more optimistic conclusions about the internal divisions that preoccupy us.

The principal reason for approaching the issues in this fashion is that the scientist is so often the yardstick against whom the historian is measured – and usually found wanting. At the 1989 Mellon Fellows' Conference, for example, a session on the sciences and humanities focused primarily on the methods of the various disciplines. Although there were spirited claims of equivalence, the standard of comparison was consistently the scientist, whose supposed objectivity, influence, and sense of community, not to mention clear-cut methods, were a model for the humanist.[5] As is frequently the case, however, the touchstone is the modern scientific establishment, and the image it projects. The picture changes dramatically if we look more closely at its precursor in the sixteenth and seventeenth centuries.

For the natural philosophers of the generations between the arrival of Copernicus in Padua and the departure of Newton from Cambridge resemble no intellectual group so much as the historians of the different schools and persuasions described by Mogilnitsky and Burguière. Anyone studying the physical world must have felt that none of the assumptions of the past was safe. Indeed, it took a hardy soul to assert with confidence that, amidst the many alternatives of the day, one was clearly right. In Kepler's famous letter to Galileo, for example, the advocacy of Copernicanism rested as much (if not more) on faith and hope as on evidence:

> "You advise us . . . not to expose ourselves or heedlessly to oppose the violent mob of scholars. . . . Would it not be much better to pull the wagon to our goal by our joint efforts, . . . and gradually, with powerful voices, to shout down the common herd? . . . Be of good cheer, Galileo, and come out publicly. If I judge correctly, there are only a few of the distinguished mathematicians of Europe who would part company with us, so great is the power of truth."[6]

Kepler's call to arms echoes all too vividly the claims which, in recent decades, have been trumpeted forth to announce the many new heralds of historical truth, from psychohistory to quantification.

Nor was Kepler wrong to feel embattled. After all, Galileo had just admitted to being reluctant to come out publicly in favor of Copernicanism. It was a period awash with new theories, and this fragmentation, which bedeviled almost every area of natural philosophy, ensured that pioneers and conservatives alike could anticipate disagreement – and even professional difficulties with patrons or academic institutions – if they espoused unpopular views.

No field was immune. The astronomers of 1590, for example, could follow Ptolemy, Copernicus, or Brahe. That the disputes were still very much alive in the 1620s was abundantly clear from Galileo's many quarrels. And some views were simply ignored: thus, although Kepler's Rudolfine Tables provided important support for Copernicus, even the Copernicans overlooked his planetary laws, which served the same cause, for over half a century. In physics, there were hard choices between Aristotle and Archimedes, not to mention the variety of emphases preferred by Gilbert, Galileo, Descartes, Pascal, or Boyle. And the latter's approach to chemistry only slowly replaced the competing vision of the alchemist, while in medicine and anatomy the practitioners included Galenists, Paracelsians, iatrochemists, and followers of Vesalius or Harvey. As if that were not Babel enough, astrologers, hermeticists, kabbalists, and other magicians were also offering their own theories about the natural world. No wonder Descartes started on his journey with immense caution: "like a man who walks alone in the darkness, I resolved to go so slowly and circumspectly that if I did not get ahead very rapidly I was at least safe from falling."[7]

As we look back on this era of trial, innovation, and revolution, we do not judge the enterprise of the natural philosophers to have been so uncertain, so divided, so filled with competing systems and techniques that it lost all coherence. We accept the centrifugal forces, but we nevertheless find reasons to regard those who studied nature in this period – discord and peculiarities notwithstanding – as a cohort basically engaged in a shared enterprise. They themselves may have lamented the doubts, the factions, and the insecurities, but we perceive an overall narrative line, a common project, that links all the disparities within a single overall venture: the determination to understand the natural world.

What is especially revealing, as this story unfolds, is a continuity that enables us to see modern investigations in a new light. For the result of natural philosophy accumulating, in its many branches, both ideas and knowledge, was that it became what we now call science – with sharper means of judging precision and validity, it is true, but otherwise bearing many resemblances to its past. Although this new – that is, newly defined – undertaking may seem more distinct, it has been characterized by no fewer conflicts, certainly no fewer separate disciplines, and no more obvious unity of purpose or philosophy, than its ancestor of the 1610s and 1620s.[8] For these investigations have only rarely been well-equipped – despite the claims of their advocates – to deliver universal and unassailable certainties. If, therefore, we think of science as a model for the cohesion that history lacks, we need to reconsider (in light of the lessons we can learn from its seventeenth-century developments) how the comparison should be made, and what the appropriate implications are.

Can one deny that the splits and antagonisms of the age of Bacon, Kepler, Galileo, and Descartes bear a striking resemblance to the divisions among historians in the late-twentieth century? Are there not similar epistemological doubts, similar internal fissures, a similar concern that, with old structures crumbling, nothing is taking their place? The enterprise certainly seems to be as bereft of a clear mission, or even of an agreed subject matter or methodology, as the science of the 1610s and 1620s. Nor do the two undertakings differ in the causes of their fragmentation, brought about in both cases by the varied and exclusionary standards of judgement they tolerated, by the competing definitions of the nature and aims of research they embraced, and by the lack of unified purpose they condoned. Both, moreover, had corrosive effects on the values of the world they inherited.[9] For there is no mistaking their assault on the most cherished beliefs of their respective cultures: the scientific revolution undermined ancient theological and cosmological doctrines, while the modern historical revolution has challenged a long-standing and profoundly felt consensus about Western superiority, magisterial subject matter, and progress.

To the extent that this comparison seems persuasive on the negative side of the coin, however, it is equally applicable on the positive side. As soon as one grants that twentieth-century historians and seventeenth-century natural philosophers share similar problems when they try to specify what is universally acceptable, either in form or in content, one can suggest that they also share a cohesiveness that persists despite their internal differences. I have written elsewhere about the elements of that coherence, which imposes common standards of judgement that transcend the apparent divisions of historical research.[10] In what follows here, I shall take that argument one step further, and suggest how the model of the scientist can help convince us that there is indeed a shape to the study of the past, even amidst the centrifugal forces and binary splits described by Mogilnitsky and Burguière.

IV

The immediate objection will doubtless be that a Newton is unimaginable in this field. It is only because of the synthetic achievements of Galileo and Descartes – so this argument might run – and then the decisive contribution of Newton, that we can find, retrospectively, a pattern in the kaleidoscope of earlier natural philosophy. Without the unifying laws and methods these geniuses provided, the entire effort would continue to look like aimless and inconclusive meanderings. Since no such expectation seems plausible for historians, what remains is chaos and disparity, without any prospect of harmony or integration.

Against that Whiggish view, in which only *finis coronat opus*, one must posit the historicist belief that every period is equal in the sight of God. What that suggests is that the study of nature in Kepler's lifetime was not inherently less valid or less governed by common assumptions than it was in Newton's. If we have learned anything from Thomas Kuhn's insights into the paradigmatic foundations of scientific research, it is that each system carries its own justification.[11] Aristotle's thesis that every body is naturally at rest may not easily solve as many problems as the principle of inertia, but it served western civilization perfectly well for nearly two thousand years. It was no less effective or coherent – in its time – than the theory that replaced it. And that conclusion may also be applied to the various competing scientific paradigms and interpretations of the early seventeenth century.

Just as historical research in the 1990s appears to be split among dozens of topics and techniques, so the natural philosophers, magicians, and engineers of the 1610s followed a multitude of quite distinct paths. It is true that convergence was just around the corner: the great figures would find ways of combining the different approaches and materials, and creating entirely new unities of method and content. But that is not to imply that the work of the earlier period was any less animated by a sense of purpose and, ultimately, common enterprise. Argument and dispute were, in the end, means of discovery, and everyone was hoping to unlock the secrets of nature. Nor did the splits vanish in response to a Galileo, a Descartes, or a Newton. There was a growing Baconian, experimental tradition that had little to do with the preoccupations of the mathematically inclined disciplines of ancient subjects like astronomy and dynamics.[12] And the divide extended through subject matter as well as approach, not to mention a wide array of sub-disciplines.

If this condition sounds familiar, that may be because it can also describe – with little change – the historical research of the last third of the twentieth century. The main difference is one that will be challenged here. For, despite the similarities, the practice of history does not enjoy a privilege – an essential source of confidence and cohesion – that has been extended, from Newton onward, to the investigation of nature. Regardless of its internal divisions, we have managed ever since to see the entire enterprise as a unity, and in the last century and a half to refer to all of its elements as science: diverse, often rent apart, and often uncertain, but always joined, even if only tenuously, by a single rubric and a common set of techniques and purposes (cf. footnote 8, above). What has happened to historians is that they have entered this culture of diversity; they have contrasted it with the canonical unity they believe to have prevailed in an earlier era; and they have found the new situation so unfamiliar that they have concluded, like Donne, that all coherence is gone. But in the end Donne was wrong, and so are they. For the pessimism that is implicit in assessments like Mogilnitsky's and Burguière's rests on misunderstandings, not only of the historical discipline in earlier times, but also of the real lessons of science.

Before we conclude too easily that the splendid unity of a bygone age has been irrevocably lost, we should recall how few were the commonalties – of approach, let alone subject matter – in the work of our predecessors. Are there any two historians today who are more dissimilar than, say, Herodotus and Thucydides, or, to come to the time of the giants who are our immediate models, than Ranke, Michelet, and Burckhardt? The nostalgia for the community of purpose that supposedly ruled the profession in earlier days, when the coterie was so much smaller, is misplaced. If we look back some eighty years, for example, where would we find the unifying themes that connected such distinguished contemporaries as Thomas Frederick Tout, Karl Lamprecht, and Frederick Jackson Turner, not to mention Charles Beard? In other words, the multiplicity has always been with us; what is more, the spectrum has often been just as wide as it is in the 1990s. Since in retrospect our forefathers seem to have been joined in a distinct and cohesive profession, despite their diversity, why cannot the same indulgence be extended to our own chameleon generation?

It is not as if there has been some decisive break. Like the scientist who, for all the Kuhnian implications of equivalence among paradigms, does build on earlier discoveries – in Newton's famous image, as a pygmy on the shoulders of giants – so does the historian pursue a cumulative enterprise. That may not always be obvious when each new type of research is heralded as unprecedented, and when old topics undergo wholesale revision. Yet it is clear nevertheless. Fresh ways of looking at long-standing problems may appear, and original questions may arise, but the continuities remain inescapable. One of the liveliest areas of historical revisionism in recent years, for example – the reconsideration of early Stuart politics and the origins of the Puritan Revolution – has often caused the staunchest critics of previous research, the loudest detractors of Whiggish tendencies, to demand emphases that are reminiscent of a great nineteenth-century Whig scholar, Samuel R. Gardiner. Similarly, the proponents of an apparently novel, "general crisis" interpretation of seventeenth-century Europe, though buttressed by theoretical elaborations of the meaning of "crisis," and by totally new methods of research like historical demography, have still relied heavily on the groundwork completed long ago by historians from Gustav Droysen to Eli Heckscher.[13]

Like the scientist who may never have read Newton, or considers his views obsolete, the historian cannot help leaning on the work of predecessors. Just as Galileo used Aristotle, so today's historical climatologist relies on previous generations of economic historians. And the influence remains even if it is not consciously absorbed. Although a graduate student seminar, for instance – and my consideration of these issues benefitted greatly from such a seminar during the spring of 1990[14] – tends to seek the latest word on current trends, its members are usually aware of the findings of the monuments in the field, whether or not they read them. To an older generation, it may be sobering that an innovative book that, for us, still seems hot off the press, like Keith Thomas's *Religion and the Decline of Magic*, strikes the young as a classic not inherently different from a work that is fifty, rather than twenty, years old, like Robert Merton's "Science, Technology, and Society in Seventeenth Century England."[15] A student who does not actually read them, however, still gets to know what their major achievements have been.

In other words, nothing important is ever lost. Old ideas are combined with the new; significant contributions leave an indelible mark; ancient questions continue to shape our research. And that is why it makes little sense, innovation and acts of scholarly patricide notwithstanding, to deny that history is a cumulative discipline – "progressive," to use Mogilnitsky's word. It shares crucial and abiding points of reference, and not only in bibliography. For the story does not end when we say we are all aware, if only dimly, of a Mommsen or a Weber, and that we build, like Newton, on the shoulders of our predecessors. We also have in common certain standards of judgement, and certain fundamental assumptions about the value and values of history.

Although these are, again, matters I have treated elsewhere with reference to the coherence of historical research,[16] they also bear on the issue of cumulation. For it is striking that, whereas to the nineteenth and early twentieth centuries – to a Tocqueville or a "new historian" like James Harvey Robinson – the French Revolution was the measure of human behavior, in the second half of the twentieth century (as Keith Baker made clear to me during an illuminating conversation) it has been replaced by the Holocaust. Whereas once the extreme – the yardstick against which more normal phenomena could be compared – was summoned up by reference to 1789 or 1793, now it is evoked by mention of Hitler or Auschwitz.[17] The Terror has become tame; and even the other side of the French Revolution, its idealism, has been superseded as a touchstone by more modern radicalisms. Stated more simply: we move on together. Our common points of reference include not only previous scholarship but also the landmarks we use to test our conclusions, the criteria by which we assess our normative statements. Moreover, as these gauges of professional discourse grow and change, they do so across the entire discipline.

Historical research is thus cumulative both in its retention and development of past achievements and in its adaptation to new standards of value and judgement. In this respect, moreover, history can actually be regarded as a model for science, which in the late-twentieth century, especially in its medical, nuclear, and ecological investigations, has developed moral concerns which hitherto have been implicit rather than explicit.[18]

V

The conclusion seems clear. If historians, like chemists, can study tiny aspects of their subject, and do so in a multitude of different ways, why should they not be considered – as chemists are – participants in a basically coherent and distinct enterprise? The analogy with science is, like any heuristic device, not exact, but the comparison is sufficiently plausible to suggest that the inferences that have been drawn from the diversity of recent historical research are unnecessarily pessimistic.

It is true that the binary divisions identified by Mogilnitsky and Burguière could be multiplied. As in Descartes' generation, there are profound epistemological doubts that trouble the theorists of the discipline. There are open conflicts between proponents of narrative and proponents of analysis – between the "anecdotalists" and the "number-crunchers," to cite the disparagements they apply to one another. The former are accused of being purely subjective, which they (like Collingwood) deny, but even the quantifiers struggle with the perennial question of objectivity. Is history rhetoric or is it logic? Humanity or Social Science? And so it goes, with even the materials and topics considered worthy of study sometimes becoming as controversial as the methods that are brought to bear on them. One side claims that the microstudy, however pursued (demography, *mentalités*, etc.), is mere antiquarianism; the response is that the macrostudy, frequently interdisciplinary, ceases to be history when it begins to lean heavily on sociology, anthropology, or even the history of art. Yet this kind of fragmentation and debate does not justify the conclusion that history lacks the common purpose that can distinguish it from other disciplines.

For the disagreement is over means, not ends. We all seek to understand the past, and we have time-honored questions, evidence, and forms of explanation and persuasion that advance our cause. If anything, the disputes should be heartening: signs of vitality and engagement, not disintegration.

Indeed, they offer the best support for the view – which I would endorse – that the past half-century has been a golden age for the historical profession. And our analogy is helpful on this score, too, since it is difficult not to conclude that the first third of the seventeenth century – the era of conflict and uncertainty – was just as fruitful a time for science as the last third. Its many discoveries notwithstanding, the age of Newton, Boyle, Huyghens, and Leibnitz was marked by an air of respectability and consolidation that makes it in some ways less vibrant than the bubbling excitements of the period of Gilbert, Kepler, Bacon, Galileo, Harvey, and Descartes. And it is suggestive that astronomical research lost steam after Newton, whereas it gathered steam during and after the life of Kepler. Might it not be more interesting for historians to operate (as they do) in Kepler's world, rather than Newton's – that is, with uncertainties all around them, but with boundless opportunities as well?

Instead of deploring the divisions, or worrying about incoherence, the discipline should see its current state as a challenge. Its chief feature is not aimlessness but energy. Our task is to maintain the momentum, not to change direction. To our opening question, therefore – whither history? – the most appropriate response should be: more of the same. The hope for unity, or for comprehensive, overarching syntheses is essentially beside the point – after all, if we agree, how can we learn from one another? Instead of chasing the chimera of harmony, and deluding ourselves that consolidation is possible (or even desirable), historians would do better to concentrate on a far more urgent mission. For their most grievous genuine problem is that few outside the confines of the profession are aware of the excitement of historical investigation in recent decades, or of its consequences.

A quick tour through any general bookstore reveals that, to the world at large, history remains its familiar, traditional self: a chronicle of famous lives and notorious wars. To educate the reading public into recognizing (and appreciating) that in recent decades historians have revolutionized our understanding of the past; that their work is pervaded by a liveliness, a boldness, a variety, and a pioneering spirit that recall the glory days of the scientific revolution; and that they are indeed in the midst of a golden age – that would be a worthy common goal, a suitable shared purpose, for history's practitioners. Their most pressing task is to mount a crusade, not to harmonize the diversity of scholarship or to reconcile its competitive visions, but rather to convey to a wider audience the sense of vitality and promise that is characteristic of historical research in the 1990s.

Notes

1. Comment by Monsignor Querengo of March 5, 1616, quoted in Giorgio de Santillana, *The Crime of Galileo* (Chicago, 1955), 124.
2. Francis Bacon, *The New Organon*, ed. F. H. Anderson (New York, 1960), 50: Book One, Aphorism XLV.
3. Mogilnitsky's essay originally was published in *Voprosy istorii* no. 2 (1987) and, in a translation by Sidney Monas, appears in *Western and Russian Historiography*, ed. Henry Kozicki, intro. Sidney Monas (London, New York, 1992), 45–70.
4. André Burguière, "De la Compréhension en Histoire," *Annales* 45 (1990):123–35. The translations are mine.
5. *Proceedings of the 1989 Mellon Fellows' Conference on Teaching*, ed. Bonnie S. McElhinny (Princeton, 1990), 170–91.
6. Quoted in Santillana, *Galileo*, 14–15.
7. René Descartes, *Discourse on Method*, trans. Laurence J. Lafleur (New York, 1960), 14. For the comments about the nature of the sciences in modern times (as well as the seventeenth century) which follow, support can be found in Stephen Toulmin, *Cosmopolis: The Hidden Agenda of Modernity* (New York, 1990).
8. Indeed, it still seems far more appropriate to speak of the enterprise as sciences rather than science, and to see its links to the wider culture (especially the reverence is inspires) as timebound, the product of particular circumstances in the seventeenth century and thereafter, until our own more skeptical era.
9. An insight I owe to Joseph M. Levine.
10. See Theodore K. Rabb, "Coherence, Synthesis, and Quality in History," *Journal of Interdisciplinary History* 12 (1981):315–32.
11. Thomas S. Kuhn, *The Structure of Scientific Revolutions* (Chicago, 1962).
12. Thomas S. Kuhn, "Mathematical vs. Experimental Traditions in the Development of Physical Science," *Journal of Interdisciplinary History* 7 (1976):1–31.
13. Surveys of these two recent scholarly controversies can be found in Theodore K. Rabb and Derek Hirst, "Revisionism Revised: Two Perspectives on Early Stuart Parliamentary History," *Past & Present*, No. 92 (1981):55–99; and Geoffrey Parker and Lesley M. Smith, eds, *The General Crisis of the Seventeenth Century* (London, 1978).
14. The members of the graduate seminar in question, for whose helpful comments I am most grateful, were Alastair Bellany, Hilary Bernstein, Brad Gregory, April Shelford, and Benjamin Weiss.
15. Thomas's book was published in London in 1972; Merton's study appeared in *Osiris* in 1938.
16. In my "Coherence, Synthesis, and Quality in History."
17. For a brief while, World War I may have served as a benchmark, but it was soon overwhelmed by World War II. Before the French

Revolution, the Thirty Years' War was the *locus classicus* of extreme behavior. The deep unease caused by those who, in recent years, have tried to suggest that the Holocaust can be understood as a product of standard historical developments, such as the struggle between the Right and the Left in the twentieth century, is a manifestation of the profession's shared assumptions. For it is precisely because the Holocaust is seen to lie *outside* the realm of normal behavior or analysis that efforts to account for its history by normal means of explanation seem so inappropriate.

18.   The point about science's moral concerns is made forcefully in Toulmin, *Cosmopolis*.

5 The Sociological Historiography of Charles Tilly

Leon J. Goldstein

I

A dialectical tension pervades B. G. Mogilnitsky's essay, "Some Tendencies in the Development of Contemporary Bourgeois Historical Thought," [1] in that he seems to be saying two different kinds of things about bourgeois historiography at odds with each other. I do not believe that statements seemingly at odds are immediately self-canceling. On the contrary, statements that express an inherent tension sometimes serve us better than those that do not conflict.[2] Thus, social structures are both stable and changing at the same time; the Old Testament covenant of God and Israel is both an agreement between two parties and a gift from one party to the other; and societies are both individual and non-individual. What we need are concepts that are able to encapsulate the inherent tension in each such pairing.[3] But, on the other hand, not every tension need be admissible. And, I must confess, I have my doubts about the one pervasive in Mogilnitsky's essay, namely, that bourgeois historiography is both the causal result of certain social factors and is, at the same time, an ideological instrument of bourgeois class-interests and the imperialism of the western states.

On the one hand, bourgeois scholarship is caught in the grip of social forces which shape the course of its growth and character. But, in Mogilnitsky's view, bourgeois scholarship is not itself capable of the degree of self-reflection that would be necessary for it to discover for itself what its nature is. To accomplish such a thing, it would be necessary for it to possess the character of science, and that is precisely what bourgeois scholarship cannot possess. Yet, on the other hand, time after time Mogilnitsky seems to be telling us that bourgeois historiography has a job to do. Its job, to be sure, is not to reveal to us the historical truth about the human past. It is, rather, to further the cause of capitalism and western imperialism. It is hard to know how a mere epiphenomenon of social and economic forces can undertake a task with a specifically determinate goal.

79

I suppose that, from the vantage point of Mogilnitsky, the nefarious schemings of bourgeois historiography is no real cause for concern. Why be fearful of a foe who cannot do anything right? Time after time, he tells us about this or that bourgeois pretension. In particular, there is no science about the scholarship he impugns. It is always pretension. Bourgeois historiography has a pretension to work scientifically or to introduce scientific materials. It is prone to crisis. It has placed its unity and autonomy at risk. It is, clearly, in a very bad way.

But it occurs to me that perhaps I am not reading Mogilnitsky in the way he means to be read. We have, after all, learned from Leo Strauss[4] and his disciples that we must sometimes distinguish between what a writer appears to be saying – indeed, wants to appear to be saying – and what he is really saying to those who know how to read. When Spinoza tells us that God creates out of the necessity of his being,[5] he presumably hopes that the dolts of the world – among whom he expected that the censors were to be included – would be assured by the idea of a god who creates, and not notice that, whatever that means, it is withdrawn by the idea of the necessity of his nature. Presumably, those who know how to read will grasp the point easily.

While reading Mogilnitsky's essay, it seemed to me that it could be read as a caricature of Marxism, when, in due course, the point of Straussian reading occurred to me. Where, after all, do we find such pretension among historians to be working in scientific ways – indeed, in the only scientific way it is given to an historian to work – but in the Marxist camp? Is it possible that really to understand what Mogilnitsky is doing is to recognize it as a piece of self-criticism? Perhaps. We will simply have to wait until some Straussian subjects the paper to the sort of exegesis that Strauss himself provided for Xenophon's *Hiero*[6] – and his disciple, Vaughan, for Vico.[7] But there need no cause for fear or alarm. Even if Mogilnitsky's secret is out, we live in a time of *glasnost* and *perestroika* and nothing untoward can happen.

II

Mogilnitsky's paper seems to focus on two points: science and historiography. Perhaps it is only one point: scientific historiography. In any event, it seems to have a great deal to say about bourgeois historiography, and it is incredible how large a number of western historians are cited in a paper of modest size. But even cursory attention to what the paper actually contains makes it clear that it says nothing about bourgeois historiography.

There are many quotations from historians, but it is historians talking about history, not actually doing it. Carl Becker spent decades of his life producing works of historical scholarship, yet, for whatever reason or reasons, he became skeptical with respect to the possibility of historical knowledge.[8] Surely, an account of Becker's historiography, the principles which inform it, the methods which produce it, cannot be based on some skeptical assertions. Rather, one must attend to the details of the work itself. We find no such attending in Mogilnitsky's essay. What we find instead are all manner of quotations about history; these give expression to their authors' reflections about history and its character, but that is not the same as actually producing works of history. It is common enough that writers – even really good ones – are not always dependable in presenting accounts of what they do. In any event, historiography is what historians write as historians, not what they say they do or what they say about history. In order to do what he wants to do, Mogilnitsky should have presented detailed accounts of actual works of history. Of course, to deal with all the historians he cites in his paper would require a tome of massive proportions, yet if he wants to condemn western historiography, he has to do it in terms of what it actually is. And that he fails to do.

What about science? And scientific historiography? The Marxists have no doubt that they know what it is, and Mogilnitsky has no doubt that the bourgeois historians he cites do not. This may be unfair, but Mogilnitsky leaves me with the impression that he takes science and scientific method to be rather a settled thing. In those ancient days when I was a student, we seemed to have had a similar attitude. Science is, to be sure, an ongoing and changing enterprise, but what science is – its generic nature, as it were – seemed reasonably stable. Do you want to know what it is like? Simply read the right authors: Carnap, Feigl, Hempel, Popper. Given what science is, if we want history to be scientific we need only figure out how to apply the canons of science to history.[9] When archeology began to become self-conscious about its identity – wanting to eschew, as it happens, its connection with history and insist that it is a social science – it discovered the philosophy of science of logical empiricism, particularly in the shape it received in the writings of C. G. Hempel.[10]

The archeology case may reflect a bit of cultural lag, since by the time the "new archeology" came on the scene our general certainty as to what science was was undergoing remarkable change. Did we really think that a scientific historiography required the application to history of the philosophy of science of logical empiricism, particularly its conception of explanation by subsumption under laws? Don't give it a moment's thought, we were told by Michael Scriven, because that model of explanation is not ever to be found in the practice of natural science which is alleged to be its source.[11] And then Paul Feyerabend tried to show that there are no specific methods or ways of thinking that were characteristic of science. Anything that seemed to work, that would push the project forward toward discernable progress, could be used and would be used in any endeavor which purported to be scientific.[12] Furthermore, there was no specifically determinate project or program which was science. Rather, the very nature of the enterprise was subject to radical shifts in the course of time, as conceptions of nature and the way in which nature ought to be studied underwent change. There was no one science possessed of an essentially identical character, but in the course of the history of systematic human study of the world in which we live, different ideals of natural order,[13] reflecting different conceptions of the way things are and ought to be studied, led to the emergence of a succession of not fully compatible paradigms[14] or research programmes[15] within which different kinds of science would be practiced. I'm sure that it comes as no surprise to people like Mogilnitsky that the philosophy of science of logical empiricism is no longer the methodology it was around mid-century, but there is a lesson for all schools in the manner of its passing. And that is that there is no way to settle for all time what science is.

III

I suspect that it is easier to say what history – the discipline – is, than what science is. Some insist that history is a form of literature and others that it is a means whereby we may correct the mistakes which inform our social bias. There are those who think that properly-done history is the means whereby we may predict the future, while others are satisfied to believe that it is a way of uplifting the human spirit. The list could be enlarged. What these views have in common is that, by and large, they focus on the uses to which history is to be put rather than on what history, the discipline, is.[16]

Surely, the purpose of history is to make known to us the character of the human past. We may, of course, use that knowledge in whatever way we deem pertinent to our interests – as reformers, revolutionists, or just individuals concerned about the human spirit. There is, thus, no ambiguity about the status of history. Some who think that history ought to be science – whatever that is – become ambiguous about the status of history *vis-à-vis* sociology and other social sciences. It may be that sometimes history provides facts that social science may put to use,[17] and it is hard to doubt that the social and behavioral sciences contribute to historians' ideas of the humanly possible.[18] But far from suffering from any ambiguity with respect to its status or identity, history is the only discipline that has the task of making known to us the character of the human past.

Charles Tilly has identified himself as "a sociologist who often works with historical materials,"[19] but one must recognize that he is also an historian. He may use techniques that are not typically used by historians, but who is to say that future historians may not broaden their repertory of methods precisely owing to his successes. It is, of course, the case that Tilly does not produce narratives, and there are those who take it that history is a special form of story telling; history, W. B. Gallie tells us, is a species of the genus story.[20] On that view, Tilly is not to be counted as an historian.[21] Gallie – and Hayden White, Louis Mink, F. R. Ankersmit,[22] and others – take it that history is a mode of discourse, whereas for me it is a way of knowing, which is the only way that makes any sense to speak of historical truth and falsity, historical objectivity, factuality, and reference. The *manner* in which a historian presents his conclusions cannot be essential to the nature of the discipline.

The use of sociological thinking, insight, and theories does not affect the character of the work as historical, if the purpose of it is to realize typical historical goals, namely accounts of what the human past was like. The emergence of the social and behavioral science affect our sense of what is and is not possible in the sphere of human activity.[23] Science in history is simply the using of the best conceptual tools available to make known to us what happened during some span of the human past. It would, thus, seem to me that, notwithstanding the longstanding tendency to oppose the analytic and the narrative in historical writing as science vs art, to the extent that, in producing her finely-crafted narratives, Cecil Blanche Woodham-Smith made use of the best available methods for acquiring the knowledge she presents, there is no reason to deny that her work is scientific.[24] She makes no appeal to specifically formulated theories and uses none of the mathematicizing techniques that characterize the work of the cliometricians, yet there is method and system to what she does with the evidence before she produces her narratives.

IV

But surely this is not how we have come to think about science in history. Ever since Hempel published his classic paper "The Function of General Laws in History," the advocacy of science in history has been in the hands of those who defend the covering-law point of view: the view that explanation in history – as in everything else – must be by deduction from one or more relevant general laws and antecedent or boundary conditions. There is, however, no reason to identify science with explanation,[25] and even if one inclines to be more open as to what counts as scientific than allowed by the philosophy of science of logical empiricism, it should be possible to see the point of the nomological-deductive theorists as to the nature of explanation. What can you mean, they seem to be asking, if you say that this *A* explains that *B*, yet it need not be the case that *B*s are always explained by *A*s? I have myself been inclined to be sympathetic toward that view.[26] Whatever one may wish to say about the nomological-deductive point of view, one thing is clear: it has application only to a retrospective justification of what has already been accomplished. The historian – to limit ourselves to that – has produced an account of something, and the account seems reasonable.

How does one justify it? One way would be to produce the sort of general theory according to what the historian has done in his particular case is rendered intelligible. But this tells nothing about how the historian's account was produced. It comes into play only after that has been completed, and I suppose that may make it seem like the correct way to go to those who believe that philosophy can only be concerned about the context of justification, never about the context of discovery. But the obvious consequence of this attitude is that we simply overlook entirely the actual character of historical knowing, paying no attention at all to what the historian actually does as he tries to determine what actually happened – meaning what it is reasonable to believe happened – in a human past we can never witness. Surely, there is method to that. Surely, there is theory – or common sense informed by theory – in such determination, particularly inasmuch as it is not, contrary to what many people think, simply copied out of surviving documents. I should want to say that, at its best, the work is scientific, but surely not accomplished by deduction from general laws.[27]

Before turning to the task of discussing what is scientific in the sociological historiography of Charles Tilly, I should like to strengthen the position that I have been trying to take here by attending to what Arthur Stinchcombe does in his account of the use of theoretical methods in the practice of social history.[28] The problem of his book is to explore the way in which the practice of social history is informed by theoretical commitments which historians bring to their work. The heart of it is the middle two of its four chapters. In each of them, the work of two writers is compared. Chapter 2 deals with Trotsky's *History of the Russian Revolution* and Tocqueville's *The Old Regime and the French Revolution*, works of history by any reasonable criteria.[29] Chapter 3 is concerned with contributions to history by two writers who are actually sociologists, Neil Smelser and Reinhard Bendix,[30] but, to the extent that they contribute to our knowledge of what the human past was like, they perform as historians.

What Stinchcombe supports is the notion that there is science in the effort to come to know what the human past was like. It is true that he often speaks of explanation and, thus, creates the impression that the focus of his attention is in the use of theory to explain past events, however they come to be known. Thus it would appear that Stinchcombe's book is an attempt to justify the covering-law point of view, albeit with a knowledge and sophistication with respect to sociology and social-science theory that philosophical defenders of the covering-law position never have. This is not, in fact, the case,[31] but the interesting thing about the book is the way it points to the role of social-scientific theoretical models in the acquisition of historical knowledge.

With writers like Trotsky and Tocqueville, one would suspect that their broad visions concerning the character and direction of the sociopolitical world – what Stinchcombe calls their "epochal" theories – would determine how they characterize the historical material with which they deal, but he claims that this isn't the case. Of course, their epochal visions are to be found in their histories, but the way in which they handle the detail of the course of events is, he argues, independent of them. Rather, embedded in their description are more limited theories which bear on the specific sorts of thing they discuss. And, in Stinchcombe's view, the two writers are actually in broad agreement with respect to the character of the material and the strategies appropriate to the study of the material.[32] The point is as follows. The two historians produce narrative accounts of the material of their respective studies, but the character of the presentation and the authors' respective senses of what the possibilities and actualities are, are informed in essential ways by the theories they take to be true and relevant. In that way, then, science – not understood as deduction from general laws, but, rather, as the use of the best available conceptual tools for the production of the historical account – is seen to be a characteristic of their work.

Stinchcombe explicitly identifies Smelser and Bendix as sociologists, but the focus of discussion is on how they handled what are certainly historical issues. Of course, as trained sociologists their theoretical material is not merely implicit. Rather, they are aware of what sociological notions figure in what they do, and one may suppose that their appreciation of the sociological side of historical research is more sophisticated than is more usually the case. But that has nothing to do with the principle at issue. Sociological instruments may be more finely honed in their hands, and they may be more explicitly aware than other historians of what current sociological thinking accepts as genuine possibility. Smelser's study is concerned with the behavior of workers during the course of the industrial revolution. Over time, one discovers certain kinds of change in that behavior. What actually is happening? Stinchcombe says that "the most original argument of the book is that 'collective behavior' of cotton workers in the first part of the nineteenth century was caused by the necessity to reorganize family roles, brought on by the growth of factory labor separate from the family, and ended when that reorganization had been successfully carried through" (83). That factory behavior and concerns for the family – particularly, as it happens, the children – are elements of the same course of development need not be all that obvious, and for Smelser to put them together the way he does is presumably owing to the way in which theory – his scientific instruments – leads him to construe them. There is no sociological-deductive derivation of the course described by Smelser, nor of any of the sub-events which make it up, but there is a method, a science, to the way in which his historical account is produced.

V

Sociological historiography is different than historical sociology. I have not found in Tilly's writings any historical sociology, though it does seem to me that he makes important contributions to sociological historiography. Let me say briefly what I take the difference in these ideas to be. The job of history is to provide accounts of the human past, to tell us how things were and why. For that reason, historians' work seems directed at particular historical entities or events, the French Revolution and not revolutions as such, Caesar crossing the Rubicon and not the general problem of upstarts challenging established authority. An historian may use whatever deepens his understanding of his problem and clarifies for him the limit of human possibility, but, *qua* historian, his attention is not on these things: he merely uses them for some other purpose. Sociologists, on the other hand, are oriented toward general theory. They may, to be sure, make use of historical data that, in their opinions, contribute to the testing of the theories they work on, but it is the theory, not the historical fact, that is at the center of their attention. Thus, Lewis Henry Morgan was not interested, as such, in the reforms that Cleistehenes introduced in ancient Attica, but, rather, dealt with those reforms only as illustrating the theory he had worked out on the evolution of culture.[33] And certain facts of the religious history of Norway were of interest to John Flint only as they bore on theories in the sociology of religion, and, in order to use them in a way he deemed appropriate, he felt it necessary to redescribe the accounts of historians in the language of sociology.[34] This was not because sociologists are happy only when they have us all drowning in the jargon of their discipline, but because, unless he could present the material in terms of the variables of the relevant theories, there would be no way to use that material in the way that he wanted.

I do not want to exaggerate the distinction, though I think it fundamental. That an historian uses theories from the social sciences in ways that are productive for his own purposes, must surely be understood as providing some additional reason for taking the theories seriously: additional confirmation, as it were. And to the extent that some piece of historical constitution proves useful to a sociologist in testing or in otherwise enhancing his theoretical work, one may suppose that the historical work is given some additional support. Thus, there is a mutuality here, not rigid boundaries which cannot be crossed over. Yet it is clearly possible to distinguish between historical sociology, which is a theoretical approach to the social by means of historical data, and sociological historiography, which is the attempt to realize goals of the discipline of history by utilizing the resources and methods of sociology.

The work of Charles Tilly is, clearly, of the latter sort. If it is to prove possible to offer an account of the character and direction of western – bourgeois, if you like – historiography, we are required not, *pace* Mogilnitsky, to cite general remarks historians may make about history, but, rather, to attend to examples of the actual practice of history by large numbers of historians. And it seems appropriate to offer an example here. Since so much is made of "science" – by Mogilnitsky and others – it is not unreasonable to examine the historiography of one whose work is clearly informed by the methods of social science.

The Vendeé was Tilly's first major work.[35] After the 1789 French Revolution, the counterrevolution called the Vendeé took place in the 1790s in the western part of the country rather than in some other parts. It would seem that, by the application of the theories of sociology, Charles Tilly has offered an explanation for it, almost as if he is on the road to applying sociological covering laws to suitably chosen boundary conditions in order to deduce by means of the techniques of logic an event called "the Vendeé." All I can say is that this is not how the book reads to me.

Even if such an explanation could be carried out, what would be deduced? One doesn't simply deduce the Vendeé, a global event[36] called by that name. What would be deduced is an historical description of the Vendeé, and given what that is, it is clear that such a description

would require a very large number of statements in terms of which
to be expressed. Indeed, it would require a book-length collection of
statements, which is one reason to be doubtful about the realizability of the
explanation-by-covering-law project. Tilly's book seems not a response to
the question, How shall we explain the Vendeé? but, rather, to the question
– What is the Vendeé? I should suppose that the accounts we find in
different works of history are not different explanations or interpretations
of the global event which is the Vendeé, but, rather, different accounts or
descriptions of what the Vendeé consists of.[37] Tilly's book has a great deal
to tell us about what the Vendeé was like, who participated, who opposed,
and so on. What is untypical of historical writing is that, to a major degree,
his account is teased out of the evidence by means of the application of
sociological theory and technique.

In Tilly, we are not confronting a counter-revolutionary outburst as
something complete in itself. Rather, the outburst is part and parcel of a
socio-economic and religious complex which is expressed in the outburst.
The Vendeé is the totality of it, and in order to have a sense of what it is,
we need to know more than that in 1793 there was an armed uprising in
the west of France against the Revolution; we need to have a sense of the
whole complex of factors which is the Vendeé. The spirit of this research
is contained in the following passage from Tilly's book:

> It is all too easy to stumble into the assumption that the Vendeé
> counter-revolution was simply the natural response to the Revolution
> of a backward region. This convenient formula explains nothing. It
> fails because it begs three crucial questions: What do we mean by
> "backward"? What is the "natural" political behavior of backward
> regions? Was the Vendeé significantly more backward than sections
> of France which did not rebel? An examination of urbanization in
> western France provides some of the elements of answers to these
> questions. (16)

In order, then, to know what precisely the Vendeé was, we need to focus not
merely on a "response," but, rather, on the total character of the sections of
France which rose in revolt. Tilly begins by attempting to determine what
urbanization is, and that concept is to be applied to the various sections
of France. Urbanization is, of course, a notion that is bequeathed to us
by sociology, and so we find that sociological methods are used here.
By thinking sociologically about the data uncovered from the historical
remains, Tilly is able to get some idea of the differential urbanization in
the sections of France in the late-eighteenth century.

Likewise relevant to the outbreak of the counter-revolution are differences with respect to classes in the various parts of the country, and what we find Tilly doing in Chapter 4 is going through the preserved documentation in order to derive from it relevant information. But this can only be done if he brings to his reading of the documentation the theoretical methods – again, derived from sociology – that enable him to discover the class structure and relations in the communities he studies. That information is there only if one knows how to read it or, more likely, constitute it out of the documentation. Consider the following analogy: I look through a microscope at a culture but see only a glob, but a biologist would discern a bacillus of a determinate strain because a conceptual apparatus enables him or her to see it. But the identification of the bacillus is not an explanation of anything. It is, rather, part of a description of what is given, that may, perhaps, be in need of explanation. That is what Tilly does in *The Vendeé*. He is engaged in the historian's task of constituting or constructing some part of the historical past, and, since what he is dealing with are phenomena of the social realm, the conceptual tools of sociology are relevant and useful to the realization of his purpose.

Succeeding chapters of *The Vendeé* deal with the religious aspect (Ch. 6), economics (Chs. 7 and 10), power (Ch. 8), each carried out through the application of sociological thinking. We get description – not narrative with heroes and plots – that simply could not be produced without scientific method.

A dozen years later, Tilly contributed to and edited a multi-authored book, *The Formation of National States in Western Europe*, which attempted to identify the factors that contributed to the rise of the national state. The different contributors focused on different elements: Samuel E. Finer deals with the role of the military, Gabriel Ardant with financial policy, David H. Bayley with the police, and so on. In addition to a general introduction and a concluding essay, Tilly contributed an essay dealing with food supply and public order.

The Vendeé breaks out in 1793 and goes on for a few years. The time perspective of this second book is much longer. The process of national-state formation takes centuries. It begins, obviously, before any states emerge, and while some states – Spain, France, England – emerge relatively early, others – Italy and Germany – do not become fully formed until the nineteenth century. But I do not want to suggest that the analytical work which informs Tilly's constitution of the Vendeé is limited only to the small number of years of the counter-revolution. Given Tilly's view that a proper account of the counter-revolution requires a presentation of the character of the social world in the different parts of France at the time of the outbreak, he is required to produce tables and charts which show that character over a period of time prior to the outbreak. The outbreak seems to be not simply a radical deviation from what existed until 1793, but, rather, an expression of that social, political, economic, and religious reality in reaction to the events of the Revolution. But for all that, the project of the first book is more narrowly circumscribed so far as its temporal spread is concerned than that of the second book.

It is not possible to exaggerate the importance of food and not difficult to understand that the capacity to control the food supply is a source of power. Thus, it is not unreasonable to take seriously that, part of the effort to establish national states and the centralization of political power involves the attempt to control the food supply. Not only is such control itself a source of power, but the growth of the central state created new demands for food where they didn't exist before – or existed to lesser extent – because it was necessary to feed growing armed forces and to channel food to national capitals where increasing numbers of people who were no longer involved in food production were concentrated to serve the growing state. This defines the problem that Tilly explores in his contribution to the book on national-state formation.

The growing need for food could be fine – especially for farmers – if means exist to increase its supply. That isn't always easy, and, to the contrary, from time to time, for whatever causes or reasons, food is found to be in short supply. Government may have the power to take what it wants, but ordinary people do not find the need of the state a sufficient reason to suffer hunger passively. And so we have the phenomenon of the hunger riot. If one thinks of history as simply a sequence of happenings, one might note that, in this place at that time, the masses gave violent bent to their need for food, but that is not the sort of thing we find in Tilly's essay. Instead, we get a sociologically-constituted account of the nature – Tilly calls it here a "physiognomy" (385) – of food riots. And this is followed by a construal of the "political significance of food" (392 ff) which deals with the way in which food and the controversies over it contributed to the rise of the national state. All in all, Tilly's essay is not a narrative account. It is, rather, an attempt to deal with an aspect of a long-term historical course by means of applying to the surviving manuscripts and documents conceptions of human social possibility and plausibility as those have been worked out within one of the systematic disciplines concerned with such things.

The last of the three works of Tilly that I consider here is *The Contentious French*.[38] This, too, is a work of long temporal spread, namely, four-hundred years, and its focus is upon the character of popular struggle or contention in France during the course of that period of time. Tilly's claim is that the elements of contention in France are taken from other aspects of French culture and display considerable persistence (140 ff). The kinds of thing which give rise to contention change over the course of generations as different problems and different interests come to the center of attention, but contention itself is something specifically determinate that has both a history and a tendency to be stable in its expression. Tilly – here and elsewhere – uses the methods of sociology to constitute or reconstruct a swath of the historical past.

VI

I use Tilly's material in order to point to certain conclusions. The first, to go back to the beginning, is that there is no way we can have a sense of the historiography of the west – or the east – simply by noting what historians say about history. There are no such general remarks in Tilly. Besides, no such quotations could begin to give the reader a sense of the rich character and multiple texture of the work that Tilly has produced as an historian.

The second has to do with what history as scientific can mean. In "Toward a Logic of Historical Constitution," I ask, "What makes an historical reconstruction acceptable?" (19), and discuss what conceptions historians bring with them to the task of characterizing the human past. In earlier times, before the rise of the modern social and behavioral sciences, the historian operated in terms of the sophisticated common sense of educated members of his society, but, increasingly, that common sense is now informed by the findings of the social and behavioral sciences, even if the historian is not particularly trained in any of them. In that paper, I noted that these define the limits of human possibility, what can or cannot be accepted (42–45), what may or may not be presumed to be possible given the evidence that exists.

In some cases, however, we see historiography move beyond the sophisticated common sense of historians toward the direct application of social science to the historian's task. What is that task? There is an old, somewhat wooden conception of the relation of history and social science which sees that relation as entirely external to the practice of either one. History provides facts about the human past. Social science produces theories about human possibility and how social systems work. The historian's facts may be useful for the testing of the social scientists' theories. The social scientists' theories may be useful in explaining the historian's facts. Certainly, many of us think, if there is to be room for social science in history it can only be in the area of explanation, a term, I fear which is rather promiscuously overused in writings on history (in which respect it resembles "interpretation"). The historian's task is to recreate the human past, and what we are seeing increasingly in our time is the use of social science in the realization of that task. In their famous *Time on the Cross*,[39] it does not seem to me that Fogel and Engerman use the cliometrician's perspective in order to explain pre-established facts. Rather, they use it in order to establish facts not hitherto known, which could not be known until the evidence was subjected to their kind of questioning.[40] That is the sort of thing we find in Tilly's work. The methods and insights of sociology are used to give us new ideas as to what the historical past was like.

Notes

1. Mogilnitsky's essay originally was published in *Voprosy istorii* no. 2 (1987) and, in a translation by Sidney Monas, appears in *Western and Russian Historiography*, ed. Henry Kozicki, intro. Sidney Monas (London, New York, 1992), 45–70.

2. See Leon J. Goldstein, "Reflections on Conceptual Openness and Conceptual Tension," in *Freedom and Rationality: Essays in Honor of John Watkins*, eds. Fred D'Agostino and Ian Jarvie (Dordrecht–Boston–London, 1989), 87–110.

3. The problems presented by Rousseau's "General Will" are entirely owing to the fact that, starting with a individualist methodology, Rousseau sought to articulate his insight into the fact that there is a non-individual sociocultural context within which the individual functions.

4. See, e.g., Leo Strauss, *Persecution and the Art of Writing* (Glencoe, IL, 1952).

5. Baruch Spinoza, Ethics, Prop. XVII, Corollaries 1 and 2; cf. Prop. XXXII and Prop. XXXIII note 2. I wish to thank Dr. Amihud Gilead for furnishing these references to me.

6. Leo Strauss, *On Tyranny*, rev. edn (Ithaca, 1968).

7. Frederick Vaughan, *The Political Philosophy of Gianbattista Vico* (The Hague, 1972).

8. See Leon J. Goldstein, "Historical Realism: The Ground of Carl Becker's Skepticism," *Philosophy of the Social Sciences* 2 (1972):121–31.

9. See Hempel's now-classic paper, "The Function of General Laws in History," *Journal of Philosophy* 39.1 (1942):35–48.

10. See P. J. Watson, S. J. Leblanc, and C. L. Redman, *Explanation in Archaeology: An Explicitly Scientific Approach* (New York, 1971); and M. Alison Wylie's doctoral dissertation, *Positivism and the New Archaeology*, State University of New York at Binghamton, 1981.

11. Michael Scriven, "Truisms as the Grounds for Historical Explanations," in Patrick Gardiner, ed., *Theories of History* (Glencoe, IL, 1959), 443–75.

12. Paul K. Feyerabend, *Against Method* (London–Atlantic Highlands, NY, 1975).

13. Stephen K. Toulmin, *Foresight and Understanding* (New York, 1963).

14. Thomas S. Kuhn, *The Structure of Scientific Revolutions* (Chicago, 1962).

15. Imre Lakatos, "History of Science and Its Rational Reconstruction," in *Method and Appraisal in the Physical Sciences*, ed. Colin Howson (Cambridge-London-New York-Melbourne, 1976), 1–39; see also his "Falsification and the Methodology of Scientific Research Programmes," in *Criticism and the Growth of Knowledge*, ed. I. Lakatos and A. Musgrave (Cambridge, 1970).

16. Before historians write up their narratives – the only form of historical expression the history-as-literature theorists take to be the legitimate expressions of historical knowledge – they must engage in all manner of historical research and historical thought which, to my way of thinking, is what the discipline of history actually is. Thus, on the narrational view, the discipline of history is undertaken for the purpose of writing narratives.

17. Cf. what Guy E. Swanson does with the historical facts of the Reformation in his *Religion and Regime* (Ann Arbor, 1967).

18. See Leon J. Goldstein, "Toward a Logic of Historical Constitution," in *Epistemology, Methodology and the Social Sciences*, ed. R. S. Cohen and M. W. Wartofsky, *Boston Studies in the Philosophy of Science*, vol. 71 (Dordrecht-Boston-London, 1983), 19–52.

19. *The Formation of National States in Western Europe*, ed. Charles Tilly (Princeton, 1975), 83.

20. W. B. Gallie, *Philosophy and the Historical Understudy* (London, 1964), 66.

21. I have had my say on that issue years ago. See Leon J. Goldstein *Historical Knowing* (Austin, TX–London, 1976), Ch. 5.

22. Hayden V. White, *Metahistory: The Historical Imagination in Nineteenth-Century Europe* (Baltimore, 1973); Louis O. Mink, *Historical Understanding*, ed. B. Foy *et al.* (Ithaca, NY–London, 1987); F. R. Ankersmit, *Narrative Logic* (The Hague–Boston–London, 1983).

23. See my "Toward a Logic of Historical Constitution."

24. As in, *The Great Hunger: Ireland 1845–1849* (New York, 1962), or *The Reason Why* (New York, 1953).

25. Nor, for that matter, with prediction. Those who think of explanation in the nomological-deductive way, identify the logical form of explanation and prediction, and there is a tendency – exaggerated in my opinion – to think of prediction as the goal, or main goal, of science.

26. See Leon J. Goldstein, "Theory in History," *Philosophy of Science* 34.1

(1967):23–40; also in *Boston Studies in the Philosophy of Science*, vol. 4, ed. R. S. Cohen and M. W. Wartofsky (Dordrecht, 1969), 277–302.

27. See my "Toward a Logic of Historical Constitution," 24–28.

28. Arthur L. Stinchcombe, *Theoretical Methods in Social History* (New York, 1978).

29. Leon Trotsky, *History of the Russian Revolution*, trans. Max Eastman (New York, 1932); Alexis de Tocqueville, *The Old Regime and the French Revolution*, trans. S. Gilbert (Garden City, NY, 1955). To be sure, such elements of Trotsky's history which are in defense of his own role would not be genuine history.

30. Neil J. Smelser, *Social Change in the Industrial Revolution* (Chicago, 1959); Reinhard Bendix, *Work and Authority in Industry* (New York, 1956).

31. See my review of Stinchcombe's book in *Journal of Interdisciplinary History* 10.3 (1980):517–19.

32. E.g., see Stinchcombe (49) for the way the two historians treat what he calls "Authority and Dual Power."

33. Lewis Henry Morgan, *Ancient Society* (New York, 1877).

34. John Flint, "The Secularization of Norwegian Society," *Comparative Studies in Society and History* 6.3 (1964):325–44.

35. *The Vendée* (Cambridge, London, 1964).

36. See Henri-Irénée Marrou, *The Meaning of History*, trans. R. J. Olsen (Baltimore-Dublin, 1966), 314.

37. See Leon J. Goldstein, "A Note on Historical Interpretation," *Philosophy of Science*, 43.3 (1975):312–19, where I try to argue in a similar way about what are alleged to be different "interpretations" of Bacon's Rebellion. There I show that, far from being different interpretations of the same event, the different account of Bacon's Rebellion are not compossible in the same historical world inasmuch as each of the historians dealt with describes the rebellion in different ways, such that some of what it is alleged to consist in, according to one historian, is logically incompatible with what is alleged to have happened according to another historian.

38. *The Contentious French* (Cambridge–London, 1986).

39. Robert W. Fogel and Stanley L. Engerman, *Time on the Cross*, 2 vols (Boston-Toronto, 1974).

40. See my discussion of Lee Benson's revision of the idea of Jackson's democracy (in his *The Concept of Jacksonian Democracy* [New York, 1984]) in my *Historical Knowing*, 82–91.

6 Dialectical Rationality in History: A Paradigmatic Approach to Karl Marx's *The Eighteenth Brumaire of Louis Bonaparte*

Michael A. Kissell

There are two principal approaches to the investigation of the nature and methods of historical knowledge: deduction within the frames of philosophical systems, and analytical reflection based on real history. The general tendency in the history of socio-philosophical thought is the shift from the first approach to the second. In the post-World War II period, analytical method was practiced in a two-fold way, as in the manner of the early and the later philosophy of Wittgenstein. His first (early) version of analysis presupposed the construction of model language in the light of which every actual statement must be corrected or thrown out if such a correction is impossible. From this point of view, the language of history is hopelessly damaged, and so history becomes a form of pseudo-knowledge. The second type of analysis – taking as its subject ordinary language in the real world – is much more liberal because it assumes "different linguistic games": not just one language inherent in the empirical natural order. Thus arose the analytical philosophy of history which investigates the morphology of historical writings, different levels of historical knowledge, and the connection with other forms of creative spiritual activity.

The rise of the so-called "historical school" in the philosophy of science enriched the achievements of the analytical approach, combining with the latter the procedures of historical and sociological thinking. As a result, the paradigmatic method of Thomas Kuhn rejects verificational and "functional" criteria of scientific truth-value and, instead, proposes a criterion that is not ideal, or theoretical, but real or actual. Not an idea, the fact to be discovered by ordinary means of historical inquiry is of a special kind as regards the works which are considered by a given community of scientists to be of the highest scientific value at a given time. *Almagest* by Ptolemy, Aristotle's *Physics*, the *Principia Mathematics philosophiae naturalis* by Isaac Newton, Maxwell's *Treatise on Electricity and Magnetism* – all can be used as paradigms for scientific knowledge (in the field of natural science) in different epochs of European history. In order to know the criteria of scientific value at a given time, we must analyze the books treated as paradigms by contemporaries.

I propose to consider Karl Marx's *The Eighteenth Brumaire of Louis Bonaparte* as one such paradigm. It is generally considered to be an outstanding product of historical thought, not only by Marxists but by opponents as well. To begin with, Marx demonstrates here an old truth: a good historian must have talent. No methodology can save an historian without certain natural and consciously developed qualities of mind: without skills of historical penetration, and without the art of historical writing.

Let us begin with the art of writing. That history is narrative is an evident truth. The historiographical tradition has many great writers belonging to the history of literature in general. Herodotus, Tacitus, Michelet, von Ranke, Carlyle, Macaulay, N. I. Kostomarov, and V. O. Kliuchevsky – all are not only representatives of the science of history but fine writers or, as they say in Russia, "prose makers." *The Eighteenth Brumaire* has great literary merits. It is not a dry exposition of chronological events, but a complex work containing protocol statements of facts, a sociological scheme of explanation, dramatically vivid pictures of political collisions, and valuations of different kinds, especially moral and aesthetical. Of course, we find also the "employment" which Hayden White, deems the primary function of historians.[1] In Marx's work the coup d'etat of Louis Napoleon is the "plot" which converts the rich and chaotic world of facts to a meaningful historical narration. The aim of an historian is to organize facts in such a way as to show the organic and "natural" connection between beginning and end. This organicism has long been considered an attribute of successful aesthetic creation. Yet this similarity between a work of art and a work of history is not tantamount to identity (as White seems to think).

The essence of the matter is that the historical picture of events is considered to be a true picture and not an imaginary one. Truth-seeking in history is not an illusory and misleading procedure, even though the inevitable presence of the aesthetic element complicates the problem and makes the analysis of historical knowledge even more difficult than in the case of natural science. In the work, we analyze aesthetic features that appear from the very beginning. Marx states that world-historical personalities emerge twice as large in the context of tragedy than in the context of buffoonery.[2] These are aesthetic categories.

But in analyzing the work of Marx, we easily understand that the aesthetic valuations are not primary but secondary. They appear as the emotional charge resulting from scientific analysis of events. They are not *a priori* conditions defining the content of narration from the very beginning. Rather, they are determined by the content and therefore have a subsidiary function in the whole. In the same manner, Marx introduces moral qualifications, which do not violate an historian's impartiality and objectivity but act in just the opposite sense.

Aesthetic and moral qualifications are not superfluous, because without them history ceases to be humanitarian knowledge, i.e., knowledge about man in all his manifestations. What is needed for an historian to be objective is not an absence of moral and aesthetic judgments but the presence of a clear self-consciousness in using them truthfully, especially when different sets of values clash. Marx was a revolutionary but, in analyzing the revolution of 1848 in France, he concluded that a socialist transformation of society was not the immediate task of the workers' movement of that time. Rather, this would take place in a relatively remote future. The value of truth overcame (in this case) the revolutionary sympathies of Marx. The contradiction between the requirements of scientific objectivity and the historian's personal attitudes – brought about by nationality, geography, and culture – is the source of many distortions in historical thinking. But when the contradiction is resolved in favour of scientific truth, we have a model work deserving to be a pattern for generations of subsequent historians.

An historical work demonstrates its organic nature by the causal links that develop throughout the narration, unifying events by means of rational arrangement in such a form as to explain the result, given the initial conditions. The result is the victory of Louis Napoleon proclaiming himself to be a life-president. The explanation of this result is not a procedure as in natural science. It does not subsume a given event under a general covering law, say that of the class struggle, which would be only natural in the case of Marx. But he was too good an historian to do so (as his own dogmatically minded followers did many times after his death).

The victory of Louis Bonaparte was not an ordinary but, rather, a unique event which almost nobody foresaw after the monarchy of Louis Philippe was overthrown by the February revolution of 1848. The reputation of "a nephew of the great uncle" at the start of events was very low. He was considered to be somewhat a comical figure with a record of dubious adventures behind him. Marx with great skill shows the way through which this insignificant person (very canny and smart indeed) moved step-by-step from one success to another and finally ascended the throne. By this explanation we begin to understand that this "miracle" is no miracle indeed but the natural result of special circumstances created by the struggle of social forces and the purposive actions of a mediocrity who could use these circumstances to his advantage. This explanation in no way can be represented by "iron" laws from which deductions may be drawn. The success of Louis Bonaparte was not inevitable from the beginning. But, on the other hand, it was not accidental, as many light-minded observers concluded. To proclaim an event "accidental" means to escape from explanation and to deem it irrational.

But "not inevitable" also does not mean irrational or unexplainable. The event has causes and the aim of an historian is to discover them. This aim is the *differentia specifica* of history, because science seeks immutable regularities and treats particular events only as examples or manifestations of laws. In history, every genuine explanation is singular; i.e., causes discovered are not applicable to other cases without modifications which cannot be found without historical inquiries specific to those cases.

Thus in history we have explanations, but of a strange kind: explanations not forever, so to speak, but for a given case only. Even so, the task is very difficult. To achieve his aim, an historian must take into consideration all the chain of previous events and build the logical sequence of facts to demonstrate the linkage of cause and effect. This implies a great power of analysis but coupled also with quite another capacity: that of a "living" imagination. The historian must resolve contradictory qualities: those of a scientist and of a writer at once. That is why genuine historians are so rare. These capacities must not only be present but maintain a certain equilibrium: the writer must not suppress the scientist nor vice versa.

Marx was one such genuine historian. Let us examine the causal line constructed by Marx on the base of empirical facts. Marx defines the general course of events since the revolutionary February of 1848 as the "descending line of the revolution, incessant shift of power from the left parties to the right ones. At first the extreme left-proletarian's party was crushed, then petty bourgeois representatives and bourgeois republicans at last. And all the time the war slogan was one and the same: Property, religion, order" (8:127).

In the name of the holy trial, the adventurer Louis Napoleon ascended to the throne of the French kings and restored the Empire which was so similar to that of Napoleon I, as he himself was similar to his great uncle. This is the comical aspect of the event. But there is also the tragic one. Social struggle brought with itself the constant use of violence or the threat of it, and the army gradually became the chief instrument of the internal policy of the republican state. People habitually saw the army playing the role of the highest arbiter in social conflicts and were not surprised when, suddenly, out of these military interventions the rule of one person arose. But this end was not predetermined from the beginning. Events could have taken another (if not opposite) direction. There were unrealized possibilities of resistance, and of preventive war by political means against approaching dictatorship. The failure to use them was not predetermined either. Marx has shown what mistakes – what wrong appreciations of a situation, what lack of self-consciousness on the part of the leaders – had led to the final success of a comic personage who would bring France to a great catastrophe afterwards. The catastrophe itself happened in 1870. Marx's book was published in 1852 but the reader of the book has no doubts about imperial ambitions, successful through violence and blood within the country that, to perpetuate itself, needed violence within and outside.

Louis as successor of Napoleon the Great must be great too and such greatness is reached by one way only – through wars. Thus, the subjective side of events must not be abstracted from the real historical process. To do so would be, as A. N. Whitehead used to say in quite another context, the "fallacy of misplaced concreteness." But the turn to concreteness (in the philosophical sense) is one of the chief attitudes of the dialectical approach developed by Hegel and then by Marx himself. Certain followers of Marx have forgotten this rule of dialectics and thus improperly simplified Marxist historical conceptions to a considerable degree. Real history is an inseparable unity of the objective and the subjective. Or to put it another way, history is human. This is the truth which is the fundamental presupposition of all subsequent reflections in the field. The dominance of pure "objective laws" – always the same despite differing cultural horizons, value systems, and individual motivations – is nature "misplaced" for history. The best Marxists never shared this simplified version of historical materialism in which the dialectics of the process with its opposing poles of subjective and objective, evaporated completely.

In Marx's analysis, "objective laws" are not mysterious "trans-historical" forces. Rather, they operate exclusively through purposive human activity: the struggle of interests and of political parties. The law of class struggle would remain true if Louis Napoleon had been defeated by his enemies. Hence, from general law we cannot deduce real events. Law gives only the abstract possibilities of achieving certain results, results which can be incompatible with respect to one another. Only the real actions of individuals, groups, and, in the last resort, classes, decide which possibility will become real. But the victory of one possibility means the death of all the others. Hence, the illusion of the inevitability of the actual result that occurred.

This is the historical fatalism which took many different forms in the past, from open faith in Providence to the contemporary faith in the irreversible laws discovered by science. This point of view is attractive to people, especially to those who seek firm convictions with minimal intellectual efforts. Such a view provides security and certainty in the future, which is a valuable attitude for practical aims. But not only theoretically and from a practical point of view, the attitude is rather dangerous because it diminishes the significance of the conscious choice within the alternatives created by a given situation. Moreover, it is blind to the errors committed in the struggle. Fatalism is capable of converting errors into truth to justify the past in all its details. Then the problem of unrealized possibilities disappears altogether and the role, say, of top officials in choosing the right line of actions appears to be quite negligible.

The ascent of Louis Napoleon to power is not only the result of his own capacities to act purposively without moral restraint, but also the result of a series of blunders on the part of his enemies. Marx is inexhaustible in depicting in satirical colors the leaders of different bourgeois parties, with their exaggeration of their significance in history and their complete misunderstanding of the coming reality. Clear self-consciousness and the capacity for deep penetration into the interrelation of social forces (an interrelation which is ever changing) are necessary for a real political leader, as is the capacity to forecast the actions of other parties, along with the by-products of his own actions.

Marx recognized the role of subjectivity, of realistic self-consciousness, and saw at the same time the other side of the question: the social determinism of behavior. The political leaders of republican parties belonged to the bourgeoisie intimidated by the revolutionary uprising of workers in June 1848. Thus, they were afraid of the masses more than they were of the adventurer with his troops of semi-criminal and simply criminal people. Louis Napoleon understood the fact very well, built his tactics according to it, and won his case. But every time that resistance to his plans became very strong, the comedian was ready to fall on his knees; one blow more and the pretender to a throne would have returned to his private life of unsuccessful adventurer. In Marx's own words: "Instead of being intimidated by the perspective of the new mass movements . . . the party of order [i.e., the chief political party of republican bourgeoisie] might open the place for class struggle, although to an insignificant degree and as a consequence of holding the executive authority in the state of dependence" (8:182).

To hold power it is necessary to have courage and be capable of risk-taking. The lack of these qualities in his opponents gave the advantage to Louis Napoleon, who was a coward but a canny, energetic, and wholly immoral man. Thus, military violence opened his way to a throne. But not only are crude material forces the factors of historical changes; pure spiritual formations play their role too. Louis Napoleon's election as president of France was determined by the voices of the French peasants who voted for him, by virtue of being overwhelmed by the "Napoleonic legend." Listen to Marx himself once more: "Historical tradition generated the mystical faith of the French peasants that the man who had a name of Napoleon returned them all their losses. . . . Idée fixe of a nephew was realized in actual existence because it coincided with the idée fixe of the largest class of French society" (8:208–9).

The faith in Napoleonides was an illusion, but this illusion was among the chief causes of the rise of the second Empire in France. And this illusion was destroyed only by an artillery cannonade at Sedan in 1870. Here we can see the necessity, in historical research, of taking into consideration all the important facts and not only those covered by known sociological laws. That is why history is creative in its nature and not simply imitative "scissors-and-paste" procedure, as R. G. Collingwood used to say.

We must make a selection of the most significant factors in a situation, disentangle them one from another, and show them operating in the production of an event. This was done by Marx in his investigation of Louis Napoleon's coup d'etat. But this particular inquiry raises a wider range of problems. One of them is worth noting here, the role of the state in contemporary society. Here Marx stands in line with Tocqueville who was, probably, the first to note the overcentralization of state power in France as a result of the Revolution of 1789. Marx discovered just the same effect in the subsequent history of France. The state grows in power from age to age, gradually transforming itself into immense executive structures that control society. The twentieth century demonstrates on a large scale both the great dangers inherent in this structure, as well as the possibility, of course, of benevolent interference in the affairs of civil society.

Thus, we cannot agree with the opinion – especially defended by Wilhelm Windelband and Heinrich Rickert – about the inevitable "ideographic" method in history. History has *res gestae* as its own legitimate domain, but it does not give an oath not to cross the established frontiers between different branches of social knowledge. Real history, as exemplified in the great works of the tradition, is much more complex than all existing historical methodologies. This is my deep conviction based on the paradigmatic study of certain monuments of historiography.

An historian most of all wishes to do the work well and not to remain within the limits of a methodology however splendid it would appear to be. Such is the case in the field of science. Hence the importance of a paradigmatic method that permits us to come nearer to the best practice of historical writing. Defenders of different methodologies have their own ideal model of history, not of that history which is, but that history which must be. Of course, partially they depend on facts but facts speculatively generalized.

Thus, one-sidedness may be observed in neo-Kantian methodology or neo-Hegelian, or positivistic ones. With regard to Marxism, we can say that creative work in the field took place only in the very beginning. In Marx, we can see, sociological explanations are introduced into the tissue of a narration. Intermingled as they are with the historical method, the peculiarities of narration become even more conspicuous. Sociology appears only as a subsidiary "moment" of the whole procedure of historical method.

Reconstruction of a past in its living quasi-reality leads to a dominance of description, which has quite another function if compared with science. In science, description precedes explanation, separated from the latter and preparing the new material only. After the explanation had been made, description becomes superfluous and provides only separate instances as illustrations of a general law.

In history, there is quite another state of affairs. Here, description in the sense of science is only a chronicle, a primary collection of facts remembered without logical arrangement and critical appreciation. So-called "facts" are in reality only "testimonies of the sources" and not facts in a genuine sense. Thus, description is not impartial but a final result of the whole study when all necessary facts are obtained, causes discovered, and accents put.

In the structure of a historical narration the peculiar nature of an object is reflected as a dialectical interpenetration of description, explanation, and valuation, with description leading and fundamental and the other two subsidiary and additional. Explanation and valuation, being included in description, bring with them the character of causality in the pure chronology of events and the living meaning inherent in man as a free historical agent. Historical explanation can be separated from description only in an abstractive process for the sake of establishing the artificial similarity between history and science. In science, descriptivity is considered to be the attribute of childhood, which it is necessary to pass through in the process of scientific growth (the "descriptive sciences" are traditionally subsumed under the name of "natural history").

In history, description is the attribute of history's full growth and, even more, of clear self-consciousness of its own essence. But there is description and description. What I mean is description of a special kind, where the crude "facticity" of events is transformed into a rational sequence which is self-explanatory and consciously value-burdened. Valuations are not incompatible with the objectivity of genuine knowledge if they do not contradict the emotional charge inherent in verified facts. Thus, Marx's definition of Louis Napoleon as "a serious comedian considering his own comedy to be world history" (8:168) is based upon his analysis of the pretender's behavior. The valuation is not an *a priori* emotional prejudice of the historian but the necessary element of the historical description itself. Of course, valuations of an historian are the source of innumerable mistakes and unconscious distortions of meaning. But these distortions can be corrected, and were corrected by subsequent generations of historians: the scientific community that exists and maintains the value of objective truth. In this relation, history is indiscernible from science.

The dialectical structure of historical thought lies at the foundation of this unity of description. But I do not mean the external process of subsuming facts under the ready-made dialectical scheme in the manner of Hegel. The dialectical art of Marx in his historical inquiry consists in the reconstruction of this fragment of the historical process as the organic interrelation of its elements, especially the subjective and the objective. Generalizing this procedure, we can state that dialectics is not the search for pre-existent structure, but needs creative rediscovery of itself by means of genuine inquiry: rediscovering in the facts themselves the governing law or the "essence" of the events described. In Leibnitzian terms, dialectics is the unity of *vérités de fait* and *vérités de raison*. This is the function of dialectical rationality in historical thought.

Notes

1. Hayden White, *Metahistory: The Historical Imagination in Nineteenth-Century Europe* (Baltimore, 1973), 7–8.
2. Karl Marx, Friedrich Engels, *Polnoe sobranie sochinenii (Works)*, 2nd edn (Moscow, 1957), 8:119. Subsequent references given in parentheses in my text.

Part Two
Sources, Resources, and Explanations

7 "A Fetishism of Documents"? The Salience of Source-based History

Arthur Marwick

A year or so ago, solid piles of Norman Davies's splendid history of Poland, *God's Playground*,[1] suddenly invaded the central London bookshops: demand was rising, too, for histories of other East European countries. As ethnic violence erupted in parts of Soviet Asia most of us had scarcely heard of, we repaired desperately to the "Russian history" shelves of our college and public libraries. Quite possibly some obscure young man, grittily pursuing his Ph.D., with a dissertation on "Population Movements and Social Change in Old Tajikistan," found himself famous overnight. Long before the freeing of Nelson Mandela we knew that we had to supplement and revise our reading in the older, white-oriented histories with the work of the recent generation of black African historians. Wherever the glorious events, wherever the crises, wherever the killings, the circumstances giving rise to them lie in the past: inevitably, in trying to comprehend them, we turn to the historians and their histories. Even when we take time off, clambering over the stones of Ephesus or sidling along the shaded side of the narrow streets of San Gimignano, we earnestly consult the guide book. Whence comes the distilled, or, more likely, distorted, information for the opening "background" chapter? Why, from, at whatever remove, the history of the professional historians. We need reflect only for moments to realize: first, that we not only *crave* knowledge of the past, we *need* such knowledge (to the question, "what is the use of history?" the only answer required is, "try to imagine what it would be like living in a society in which no one knew any history at all"); and, second, what an astonishing amount of historical knowledge exists on a staggering range of periods, countries, and topics.[2]

To understand the nature of historical study and scholarship (this is the first point in my argument), it is necessary first to understand the purposes and achievements of the discipline of history. Though these, as my opening paragraph was intended to show, are straightforward to the extent of banality (and thus, of course, highly suspect in a world of over-refined intellectuality), their establishment faces a wilderness of obfuscation, mystification, and pseudo-problematics. By "the discipline of history," I mean what goes on in our history departments, or at least what I hope goes on in them: that is to say, "the systematic study of the human past." The first problem raised against this definition is the philosophical one that the human past, being past, simply does not exist, so that, the allegation goes, there is no subject matter "out there" to be systematically studied. Yet most of us have little difficulty in believing in our own personal past: we are where we are now (I confine myself for the moment to a manageable short view) through choices made by our parents, through courses of study we pursued, through job applications we filed, through marital choices of our own; if we look back at old birth certificates, letters, postcards, home movies, there is no great problem in connecting up the past which we remember, and mis-remember, to these sources, and in perceiving that a serious, systematic study of these sources could yield quite a rounded account of our past, full of surprises no doubt, but one which, if we were prepared to be dispassionate about it, we would recognize as "true." One can extend the same reasoning to parents, to grandparents, and, taking a long view, to our more distant forebears. Clearly generation succeeds generation, and clearly each generation leaves sources of exactly the sort which, from our own direct experience, we can confirm as evidence of the "reality" of the past. But personal and family experience is only the start. Everywhere in our cities we can see old buildings being demolished, new ones being erected; from time to time we encounter a building which draws attention to itself through some distinction or peculiarity of style: a church, a disused warehouse, now perhaps serving as offices for architects or accountants, or a row of houses, carefully preserved, or perhaps falling into decay. Perhaps we feel sad at the demolition, perhaps we tell ourselves that buildings constructed to meet the needs of earlier times have no place in our modern city; as we contemplate the church, the warehouse, the row of houses, we will, even the most ignorant among us, be aware that they were built in an age other than our own. These are not the past, but they are surely as tangible evidence that the past really did exist, as the scientist receives of the chemical composition of a distant planet. It would – I now move far beyond our own direct apprehensions – take a very determined obfuscator indeed to deny that the imprisonment and freeing of Nelson Mandela, the ethnic problems of the Soviet Union, the communal conflicts in Ireland, the Near East, and in so many parts of the world, had their origins in past movements of population, past persecutions, past injustices. If the injustices are real, then so must have been the past in which they were perpetrated.

"What a naive fellow," they'll be saying in the ivory towers of linguistic materialism: "doesn't he know that not only is there no past, there is no society, only language, only competing discourses." (This new clerisy may, to their own satisfaction at least, have abolished "the subject"; have they also abolished the succession of generation by generation of which I have just spoken, and with it their own genesis?). Actually, I do point out to my own students that much of what they think they know directly, they know only through language: even those who lived through the World War II (the Open University teaches mature students, some of them very mature) experienced only a minuscule part of it, all of the rest coming through radio broadcasts, newsreels, conversation, hearsay, perhaps newspapers. But to recognize the significance of language is not to agree that there is only language; or rather, to deny the claims of the linguistic materialists is not to neglect the importance of language (at the very core of the activities of the traditional historian, after all, is the scrutiny and evaluation of the language in which the sources are written). Not for the last time in this essay, I am stressing that the world of scholarship is not a world of either-or: one can recognize the considerable contributions of Marx to historical study without being a Marxist; one can criticize the fundamentals of Marxism without being in the pay of the CIA; more pertinent to this inquiry, one can recognize that all human activities are socially (or "culturally") *influenced* without accepting that they are socially, (or "culturally") *constructed*, as one can welcome the insights of linguistic and cultural theory without genuflecting to the absurd absolutes to which their adherents push them. To go further here would be to become embroiled in a dialogue of the deaf. In the end, it comes back to the fundamental issue of purpose and achievement. If one believes it is important (and therefore, of course, *possible*) to study the origins of nationality problems in the Soviet Union, the political, social, cultural, and religious circumstances of the building of San Gimignano, or the origins of the World War I, then the miniatures produced by the discourse theorists, intellectually exciting though some of them are, will seem rather trivial, throwing no light on major historical problems, finding only what their authors put there in the first place: that is, competing structures of dominance "imbricated" in different discourses.[3] The retort, of course, is that the "history" of which I speak does not produce systematic analysis of major issues, but is itself simply "discourse," "ideology," or "rhetoric," certainly no more germane to its ostensible purpose than the perceptive fiction of a novelist. Some who make this kind of assertion would apply the same treatment to the natural sciences: science, too, is simply a dominant discourse, a function of ideology.[4] Without wasting time setting out the relationships between science, applied science, and technology, I shall simply state that a fundamental premise of this essay is that the existence of science as a systematic activity yielding objective achievements is demonstrated by the manner in which linguistic materialists, cultural theorists, etc., travel to Tuscany, or Turkey, or whatever by jumbo jet rather than donkey, employ word processors rather than quills, and, more than likely, have strong views about the foodstuffs consumed by themselves and their families. Others, however, claim for their approaches the status of natural science: theirs is the true rigor, theirs the conceptual integrity, theirs the power to expose the utterly unscientific nature of the history of the historians.[5] As this essay progresses, much of it will necessarily have to engage with that assertion.

Behind the notion of the history of the historians as merely ideology or discourse, there lies, for all but the most bleakly ahistorical of the clerisy (those clinging to the imperatives of the earliest structuralism or fixated on the daemonic pronouncements of Louis Althusser;), a sense of "history" as a process of shifting power relationships linking past, to present, to future. What post-modernism is, and who the "post-modernists" are, can be left to the different cults to fight out among themselves; but, given the frenzied determination of "cultural materialists" and "new historicists" to appear *à la mode*, it is instructive to remember that the notion of history having meaning is essentially a pre-modern one, and that it reached its fullest elaboration and most characteristic modes of expression (*language!*) in the nineteenth century. There have been various versions of this curiously dated conception of history, but the only one needing attention is Marxism, whose various elaborations, one soon discovers, form the basis of those "isms" which, quite correctly, see source-based history as their greatest enemy, and so devote much energy to attacking its claims. The standard ploy of the whole assembly of linguistic and cultural theorists is to disavow the economic determinism of "vulgar Marxism," as if jettisoning one unsubstantiated speculation automatically conferred credibility on a series of other unsubstantiated (and, indeed, exploded) speculations: about class formation, class consciousness, class conflict, patterns of dominance, the dialectic (a figment with as venerable a history as that of the Holy Ghost, but no more securely based in empirical evidence). Although many cultural theorists write as if ideology (in the "critical" or "Marxist" sense – the word, of course, has a perfectly valid, neutral usage as signifying "cluster of ideas, values, and beliefs")[6] has a given existence independent of Marxist doctrine about how emergent classes establish and maintain their dominance; it has, in fact, no meaning outside these (dubious) doctrines. Thus instead of there being any onus on historians to refute the allegations that their histories are merely ideology, the onus should be on the cultural theorists to demonstrate that ideology (as they understand it) exists in the first place. (Historians, of course, know that much "history" *is* self-serving or nationalistic propaganda; it is exactly because of the scholarly, systematic, work of generations of historians that it *is* possible to distinguish between authentic accounts of the past and fabrications, as Marc Ferro has done in *The Use and Abuse of History*.[7] Historians also know – indeed, that is the essence of their training – that we are all products, even captives, of the age and society in which we live: but in modestly recognizing the limits upon their own historical vision, historians are also in rather a strong position to recognize the limitations on the vision of Hegel, Marx, Weber, Althusser, Foucault, and all the johnies-come-lately of linguistic materialism or new historicism.)

The prophecies of Marxism, notoriously, have not come to pass, and even events in what was already past when Marx wrote – "the English Revolution," the French Revolution, the Revolutions of 1848 – do not, we now know, come anywhere near to conforming to Marxist models.[8] Indeed, it is the failure of Marxism as a convincing mode of intellectual analysis which led to the invention of ever more desperate expedients: "hegemony" (as developed by Gramsci), "Americanization" (the force alleged to have seduced the European working class from its historic destiny), and discourses in conflict (more recondite, and therefore more difficult to analyze critically, than mere classes in conflict). At every stage, the obstacle to Marxist speculation has been systematic source-based history. Hence, then, the denigration of sources and of source criticism in E. H. Carr's *What Is History?* (which has furnished me with the first part of my title). And hence the increasing flight into fantasy and away from anything which could possibly be tested against sources of the latter-day upholders of the revelation that everything is dominance and nothing what it seems.

But before I deal with Carr, and his more sophisticated successors, I must expose the manner in which so many professional historians, discontented (as I have already hinted) with the apparent banality of their tasks, have provided sustenance for the implacable enemies of their discipline. Traditionally, the fault lay with snobbish and overly self-confident Europeans (particularly the English); in our own day it has been greatly aggravated by bumptious and overly insecure Americans, desperate to assert the distinctiveness and originality of the approach followed by themselves and their particular school. While Oxford gentlemen presented history as an esoteric intellectual game, American professionals compile meticulous surveys of the separate sub-histories, feverishly assessing their current standing in some great Super League: Intellectual History "dethroned";

both the "New" Cultural History and the "New" Political History riding high; with, no doubt, both "Old" Political History and "Old" Cultural History up for sale – has no one ever reflected that "New," perennially in use by the manufacturers of toothpastes and mouthwashes, is just about the most boringly, unoriginal, and unpersuasive a label it is possible to apply to an intellectual movement?[9] *The Past Before Us: Contemporary Historical Writing in the United States* provides masses of information on *what* historians were doing in the previous decade (together with their anxieties over specialties in decline and hysterical triumphalism over "new" ones on the way up) but very little on *why* or *how* they were doing it. Now, it is unfair to criticize on this score: historians among themselves know well enough how they go about their own business and how, as Canary and Kozicki have remarked, the "cook-book" can be of only limited interest within the profession;[10] likewise, constant self-justification quickly becomes tiresome. My point is simply that the cultural theorists, zealous in their misunderstanding of what it is historians do, do not have much guidance to hand, given that they are invariably too lazy to read the monographs which form the best exemplification of what historians actually do. Worse, when historians do make pronouncements on their subject, in Inaugural Lectures or the like, they often, presumably because it isn't always easy to find something novel or arresting to say, go in for the rather silly and unrepresentative *tour de force*.

My fundamental argument is that the purpose of historical study is to increase knowledge of the human past, knowledge meeting both social needs and human cravings. But that does not mean that I wish to assert some sterile concept of "utility" against the manifest intellectual complexities and subtleties of the subject, not the least of which are questions of history's relationship to literature, art history, philosophy, science, etc.[11] It happens that I work for the University which, perhaps more than any other in the world, has successfully pioneered fully integrated, interdisciplinary courses.[12] I chair both the Open University's "Arts Foundation Course," which brings together History, Literature, Music, Art History, and Philosophy, and the course "War, Peace and Social Change: Europe 1900–1955," which includes poems and extracts from novels, a video-cassette composed of excerpts from fiction films, an audio-cassette featuring passages from Stravinsky, Shostakovitch, Elgar, etc., and another one which discusses a pack of twelve reproductions of paintings.[13] As key members of the intellectual community, historians should engage in writing and discussion appropriate to that community. My worry is that, in a very proper anxiety to disabuse the layman of the idea that history is simply a given body of uncontested knowledge, historians speaking about their subject go too far in giving the impression that history is not a body of knowledge at all, that it is not concerned with anything as humble as finding things out (scientists are proud of their discoveries – why should not historians be too?).

When I was young I was taught that the supreme debunker of naive misconceptions about the monolithic nature of historical knowledge was the Anglophile Dutchman, Pieter Geyl. I cannot but believe that in their own naive and unreflecting pronouncements, Geyl and his like did great harm to the understanding among outsiders of the real nature of history. Geyl began his *Debates with Historians* with a reference to one of Britain's best-loved, if least literate, authors of detective fiction:

> Agatha Christie, in one of her books, *The Moving Finger*, introduces a girl fresh from school and lets her run on about what she thinks of it. "Such a lot of things seem to me such rot. History, for instance. Why, it's quite different out of different books!" To which the sensible elderly confidant replies: "That is its real interest." [14]

The manner in which interpretations change with time and political allegiance is a serious matter with which historians have to reckon, but it should not be confused with the real tasks of historical enquiry: unhappily, writing books about other books is always easier than doing the research and solitary thinking necessary to produce a book of one's own. I don't doubt that Geyl knew that well enough. Certainly his famous *Napoleon: For and Against* was clearly thrown together with the minimum of anything resembling serious research, or even deep thought. Here are two passages from the introductory chapter, "Argument Without End":

> My aim in this book is to set forth and compare a number of repre-sentations of Napoleon as given by leading French historians. Striking differences will emerge, but this is hardly surprising. History can reach no unchallengeable conclusions on so many-sided a character, on a life so dominated, so profoundly affected, by the circumstances of the time. For that I bear history no grudge. To expect from history those final conclusions which may perhaps be obtained in other disciplines is in my opinion to misunderstand its nature . . .
>
> . . . the scientific method is certainly not to blame. The scientific method seems above all to establish facts; there is a great deal about which we can reach agreement by its use. But as soon as there is a question of explanation, of interpretation, of appreciation, though the special method of the historian remains valuable, the personal element can no longer be ruled out, that point of view which is determined by the

circumstances of his time and by his own precautions. Every historical narrative is dependent upon explanation, interpretation, appreciation. In other words, we cannot see the past in a single communicable picture except from a point of view, which implies a choice, a personal perspective. It is impossible that two historians, especially two historians living in different periods, should see any historical personality in the same light.[15]

Serious source-based, history is certainly "argument without end." Historians, like scientists, build upon the discoveries of their predecessors, bring new evidence, new techniques, and new approaches to bear in refining, correcting, and, sometimes, rejecting existing interpretations. But what Geyl suggests is that each argument (one apparently as good as another) is totally replaced by a new argument; thus, unwittingly, he makes the case that history is merely discourse. The implied sequence of discrete stages – (1) sources provide "facts"; (2) "facts," combined with the "personal perspective" of the historian, yield interpretation and explanation – is a false one; of course, historians do present differing interpretations and explanations, but they do not do so in a manner detached from the sources, which at all times they must cite in showing how they have developed their train of reasoning. The concentration on a single political figure is outdated and misleading. Historians are seldom concerned solely with biographical topics: with Napoleon, as with any other single individual, there will remain aspects of his psyche which can never be penetrated, but, with respect to his actions and their impact, the evidence exists, and has been used to present interpretations which in essentials do not radically differ from each other. The disabling weakness of Geyl's book is that it does not, in fact, study serious, source-based, monographic work on Napoleon, but offers no more than a series of extremely short and schematic chapters based on the writings of political propagandists whom no one would ever mistake for historians, or on the brief treatments provided in textbooks of general European history. *Napoleon: For and Against* retains some credibility as what might loosely be described as a history of changes in broad popular conceptions about Napoleon; as a study of scholarly practice, it is a non-starter.

Rather more substantial, though no less mischievous in their effects, were the writings on history, in particular *The Idea of History*,[16] of R. G. Collingwood (1889–1943). As I have written elsewhere on this philosopher and archaeologist[17] (he was no more a trained historian than was E. H. Carr, Carr being a classicist, diplomat, and journalist, who had little experience of handling the sorts of sources most historians use), I shall confine myself to quoting the curtly dismissive words of Sir Geoffrey Elton in the hope that they will make clear that Collingwood's eccentric ideas – a gift, of course, for discourse theorists – have no status among such working historians as have devoted serious thought to the nature of their own activities. Elton writes of Collingwood's "unreal and unrealistic notion that the historian understands history by reenacting it in his mind . . . "18

In making the case that Cultural History is now *the* style for the fashion-conscious historian, Social History definitely *vieux jeu*, Lynn Hunt several times invokes E. H. Carr's *What is History*? Just as one suspects that those within the profession who cheerfully praise *Napoleon: For and Against* or *The Idea of History* have not themselves looked at these books since they were students, one often also feels that those who commend *What is History*? can't possibly remember the ludicrous positions it adopts. Since Carr lived in an era when it was still possible for intellectuals, with perhaps only a half-portion of self-delusion, to perceive the Soviet Union as the civilization of the future, it is perhaps unfair to dwell on his Hegelian faith in "great men" such as Cromwell and Lenin, who "actualize" their age, his apparent support for "drugs consciously used to influence human behavior, and surgical operations designed to alter human character," and most definite support both for education concerned "with the shaping of society in a particular mold" and for that exploitation of the environment which has subsequently proved so catastrophic in Russia and East Europe.19 It is Carr's conception of what constitutes objectivity in history which is truly pernicious. Actually, the first of the two points he makes is an excellent and important one (and indeed one which undermines his second, major, and utterly absurd one). He observes that the objective historian, first of all,

> has a capacity to rise above the limited vision of his own situation in society and in history – a capacity which . . . is partly dependent on his capacity to recognize the extent of his involvement in that situation, to recognize, that is to say, the impossibility of total objectivity. (123)

It is the serious professional historian, with his or her detailed understanding of the way in which belief structures change from age to age, and whose entire training illustrates awareness of how human beings are always prisoners of their own social and intellectual environment, who is best equipped "to rise above the limited vision of his own situation in society and in history": it was, after all, the professionals – Pollard, McIlwain, and their successors – who exposed how medieval parliaments had been envisaged by the first historians (Stubbs, Tout, etc.) who sought out and preserved the sources (a considerable achievement in itself) through the eyes of Victorian constitutionalism, and Namier who revealed how the politics of the reign of George III had been misconceived as belonging to the same Victorian thought-structures. The connections between our understanding of the present and the understanding of the past, can never be completely severed, and we can never, as Carr recognizes, achieve complete objectivity. But the essential concern of history is with the substantiable truth which painstakingly, and often opaquely, emerges from the sources, not with endless, and ultimately sterile, discussion of what the "new" historians said, what the "Consensus" historians, and what, again, the "New Left" historians. Re-focus on aims and achievements and the point is made: of course, there will always be variations in the accounts historians produce of the building of San Gimignano or the politics of Tajikistan, but it is the (hard won) substantiable knowledge which serves society, not any high-flown critique of the cultural and the ideological origins of the various disagreements the historians will undoubtedly have had along the road of producing this knowledge (always provisional, never definitive, I fully recognize, but usually better than no knowledge at all, or sheer myth).

The second, and major, point said by Carr to characterize the objective historian would be hilarious were it not that the very same sentiment lies at the heart of the much-vaunted theories of today, in whose name are perpetuated the distortions and misrepresentations of the systematic study of historical sources. The objective historian, Carr says,

> has the capacity to project his vision into the future in such a way as to give him a more profound and more lasting insight into the past than can be attained by those historians whose outlook is entirely bounded by their own immediate situation . . . some historians write history which is more durable, and has more ultimate and objective character than others; and these are the historians who have what I may call a long-term vision over the past and over the future. The historian of the past can make an approach towards objectivity only as he approaches towards the understanding of the future. (123)

This, of course, is a classic instance of the historian *not* rising "above the limited vision of his own situation in society": this "long-term vision over the past and over the future" was no more and no less than the woolly Marxism espoused by so many of Carr's generation and class. If we excuse Carr his simple faith in the Soviet Union, and his grotesque passion for social engineering, as belonging to his day and generation, we are equally bound to dismiss his claims to "understanding the future" as being similarly the product of a particular time and outlook.

It was, of course, through his arrogant belief in his own superior objectivity that Carr contemptuously dismissed what he termed a "fetishism of documents" (16):

> The documents were the Ark of the Covenant in the temple of facts. The reverent historian approached them with bowed head and spoke of them in awed tones. If you find it in the documents, it is so. (16)

That nineteenth-century historians, like many badly trained writers with Ph.Ds. today, too often simply transcribed, or paraphrased, their documents is not to be denied (Carr did a fair amount of this in his own Soviet histories); but Carr showed no understanding of what for a modern scholar "finding it in the documents" entails in skilled intellectual analysis. Nor did Carr, whose own work was almost exclusively confined to official documents, have any conception of the powers of intellect and imagination required in the hunt for relevant documents: an absolutely critical element in the success of *The Making of the English Working Class* by E. P. Thompson, (a Marxist, but then it is no part of my purpose to deny that some of the ablest historians have been Marxists) was the way in which previously scarcely thought-of sources were deployed to throw light on the working-class experience.

Carr posed a famous question, following it with an extremely silly answer. "But what when we get down to it, do these documents – the decrees, the treaties, the rent-rolls, the blue books, the official correspondence, the private letters and diaries – tell us?" The answer:

> No document can tell us more than what the author of the document thought – what he thought had happened, what he thought ought to happen or would happen, or perhaps only what he wanted others to think he thought or even only what he himself thought he thought. (16)

Let us consider the documents specified by Carr. A decree records a definite decision by a ruler or government. Whether the decree was actually implemented would be a matter for further investigation, and, like all sources, the decree would have to be set within a context of other relevant documents, but a decree certainly tells us far more than what its author (supposing one single author can be completely and persuasively identified – a large supposition) thought. Consider the Edict of Nantes, *signed* by Henry V of France on 30 April 1598 (but not necessarily the pristine expression of the unassisted regal thought processes), and (roughly) giving Protestants and Catholics parity of status. What Henry, whose earlier "conversion" from Protestantism to Catholicism had brought him considerable political advantages, really "thought," or even "thought he thought" about religion has been a matter of considerable debate and speculation. Henry at the time was embroiled in war with Spain and, at the same time, threatened with civil war by his former Protestant supporters (the "Huguenots"). The Edict reflects the dangers of Henry's situation, the claims advanced by the Protestants, the advice given by his advisers, and the balance between whatever predilections he may have had himself and political calculation, in what he almost certainly intended as a temporary expedient. A many-layered document indeed, yielding riches far beyond Carr's footling foolery, to, that is, the trained historian: master also of the Edicts of Mantes and Poitiers, utterly familiar with the peculiar nature of the claim to public worship made by the Protestants, with the technicalities of *bailliages*, *sénéchaussées*, *parlements* and their special chambers, etc. Treaties record what has been agreed between two or more powers; again, a treaty may not be fully carried out,but it will certainly indicate the balance of power and aspirations between the principals, the best bargain each can obtain. As it happened, just two days after the Edict of Nantes, Henry (or, more accurately, the advisers who were concentrating on this issue) concluded the treaty of Vervins with Spain. Is it, then, perhaps what Philip II of Spain "thought he thought" that we learn? To any one not intoxicated with his own rhetoric, as Carr was, it is obvious that these two documents of record will tell the historian with the necessary skills a great deal about the nature and assumptions of both politics and religion and their interrelationships at the end of the sixteenth century. Quite obviously, they are indispensable to the study of both. And without all the other sources turned up by the systematic and imaginative work of historians, we wouldn't have a *clue* (for once, the everyday cliché is completely appropriate) as to, say, who or what the Huguenots were, or even about the basic sequence of events.

Or, for a moment, reflect on the treaty of Versailles, the ideals it enshrined (political equality for women among them), the follies it propagated – Carr's feeble trivialization is but a passing of wind. Decrees, treaties, as also official correspondence, and (in published form) private letters and diaries were what Carr himself, in the historical studies he came to relatively late in life, was most used to. Even an official letter usually amounts to rather more than the personal thought of one person, though, of course, as ever, the professional historian will check it against, and collate it with, the other relevant sources (a fundamental procedure which Carr ignores). Carr was unfamiliar with the sorts of letters and diaries used by social historians to piece together, say, structures of belief and patterns of family life. Again his comments reveal only his own ignorance, but – and this is the point of taking a sledge hammer to what may seem like a peanut – that same ignorance pervades the work of the cultural theorists who denigrate source-based history, without having any understanding of how historians actually use their sources. If we come back to rent-rolls, we are again in the domain of the document of record: since it is certainly not in the interests of a landowner to enter the rents due to him incorrectly, this kind of document is a valuable source of statistical information, offering clear evidence for social and economic relationships into which the element of thought stressed by Carr scarcely enters. "Blue Books" are the reports of the commissions and committees of investigation which figured prominently in nineteenth-century British politics: a report on the conditions of women and children in the mining industry might well be inflected by the opinions of the investigators (as indeed we know *from the studies made by historians of related documents*) but quite patently has a significance for historians far beyond what Carr allows. With all of these documents, historians find much of value in the assumptions which lie behind what is written, as well as in the overt thought being expressed. Carr, it may be noted, says nothing of archaeology, place names, the landscape, physical artifacts, visual sources, film, and all the other non-traditional sources which historians use: but, then, it's rather difficult to indulge in the joke that the field plan of a medieval village shows only what someone "thought he thought."

This discussion of Carr's contempt for and misunderstanding of "documents" (the very word reeks of Carr's nineteenth-century mental set), brings out that my earlier definition of history, the history whose achievements I identified at the beginning of the essay, was incomplete. We cannot directly apprehend the past as, say, we can apprehend the circulation of the blood in the human body, or the river system of Tibet; we can only apprehend the past through what it has left, sources in all their manifold variety. Thus history is "a body of knowledge about the human past *based on the systematic study of sources.*" The standard objection at this point from those who know a little about history, but very little about the actual practices of historians, is that, since the past is in effect infinite, sources cannot truly be the "base," or the true starting-point of historical study; on the contrary, the true "base" or starting-point must be some initial theory or organizing principle. Often there is a confusion here between "sources" and "facts." Clearly, the facts of the human past are infinite, multitudes of them utterly trivial, and others likely to remain forever unknowable. But, in any case, historians do not set out to know everything: they address specific, limited, clearly defined questions or topics. History, it is too often forgotten, is a cumulative subject: we advance where our predecessors have previously prepared some of the ground, stimulated by the questions they have left unanswered, or, sometimes, by their manifest errors. Or the stimulus may come from the discovery or opening of a new archive (not in itself "infinite," and to be exploited in conjunction with work already done by others in other archives), or from the development of new approaches and techniques (the possibilities of computerization, for instance, which, indeed, reduce even further any potentially random elements in allegedly "infinite" researches). In many areas of historical study, the problem is rather of too few sources than too many. Sources are not an undifferentiated morass; fragmentary and frequently difficult to interpret they undoubtedly are, but still they can be categorized into different types, each presenting different technical problems, each contributing greatly to some types of research, and not at all to others.

Of course, the individual historian will have a *strategy* in embarking on any piece of research; but, contrary to the speculations of the theoreticians, this does not imply an a priori theory or ideology; it simply entails (though it is never that simple) a mastery of the existing secondary sources, an identification of the questions which require answering (though, as often as not, as research progresses, a whole set of new questions will be thrown up), and at least a provisional inventory of the types of sources to be examined (one set of sources, as all historians know, will often throw up problems which then require the study of another set – this is open, not predetermined, but it is not haphazard). In short, the denigration of source-based history on grounds of the infinity of the past, and, therefore, of the sources left by the past, is itself based on the failure to see that individual historians, aided by the work of others, address manageable sectors of the past, and on the confusion of strategy, derived from the nature of the topic and existing knowledge about it, with *theory* or *ideology*.

Declaring all sources to be "ideology" or "discourse" sounds cleverer than saying what is actually more precise and to the point, that every source comes into being for a particular purpose (two I have already discussed, for instance, having had the purpose of resolving certain problems facing Henry IV). No historian has ever imagined that a document is transparent, a straightforward statement of some truth. Finding out the precise purposes of a particular document may be a lengthy process: once known, the historian will begin to be able to discount the biases, the subterfuges, the untruths which all documents contain. At the same time, he or she will squeeze out the unwitting testimony of the document: presumptions, attitudes, value-systems, beliefs, the things that the authors of the document and its recipients took for granted and which, therefore, are no part of the purpose of the document, but which may be invaluable to the historian who has the knowledge and skill to prise them out and to make use of them. It is knowledge and method, above all, which are needed, not theory. To bring out these points I am going to do what writers who theorize about what history isn't, or what it ought to be, never do, categorize the main types of historical source. How sources are grouped, or categorized, by historians can be seen in the bibliographies to substantial works of scholarly research, though (as already suggested) few works encompass the entire range of possibilities, which can be organized under thirteen (in themselves capacious) headings:[20]

1. *Documents of record.* As we have seen from the examples of the edict and treaties already mentioned, these, taken in conjunction with other sources, offer an enormous variety of insights and perceptions, but they do also record something that actually happened; they record a "fact" or "event," the very edict or treaty itself – in that specific and limited sense, they cannot be "ideology" (they are "fact" not "opinion") – though, of course, as historians know better than anyone, minutes, reports of meetings, and so on, recording what a body as a whole *agreed* its decisions to be, can be incomplete and slanted. They may, as with, say, parish registers or rent-rolls, record hard factual information – the "facts" will be subject to human error in the original entries, though scarcely to ideology, and will require specialist skills to extract.

Documents of record have a range and variety that the mockers of "a fetishism of documents" have never dreamed of. E. P. Thompson, and other historians of the working class have made great use of police records; in reconstructing the life of Montaillou, Le Roy Ladurie used the records of the Inquisition; one of the most illuminating sets of sources for sexual behavior in *ancien régime* France are the *déclarations de grossesse*, statements required by law from unwed mothers. These, it need scarcely be said, are *records*, subject to the accuracy and honesty of the scribes, of what the women *said*, not necessarily of what actually happened. No one but the historian can comprehend the fascinating variousness of sources, and what can be done with them; no one better than the historian knows their dreadful fallibility.

2. *Surveys and reports.* These will always have a point of view, as with Carr's Blue Books, but then it is one of the historian's first tasks to be sure that he or she has fully grasped what that point of view is; the task is not to pin down an ideology (rather easy when there seem to be so few on offer, of which, of course, much the most popular is "bourgeois") or identify a

type of discourse, but to penetrate far more deeply in order to isolate such bits of hard evidence as the source does contain.

3. *Chronicles and histories.* Historians, who for a couple of hundred years or more have been used to the mishmash of superstition and myth, mixed with the occasional recording of fact or attempt at assessment, to be found in monastic and chivalric chronicles and town histories, are entitled to feel some weary resentment at latter-day preachers on the problems of "deconstructing" texts; medieval historians try as far as they can to avoid undue dependence on such sources (yet how glad we are to have them for such places as Tajikistan or Vilnius); a few authentic chronicles, difficult though they will be to interpret, are worth any amount of specious theory.

4. *Family and personal sources.* Diaries and memoirs intended for publication will obviously be assessed differently from letters written solely with the purpose of, say, begging for a job, or informing a husband of how the household is faring in his absence; all diaries will have to be treated as the products of rather untypical human beings: but when purpose, social background, personal peculiarities, immediate context, literary conventions – as relevant – are taken into account, how much information there often is for those skilled enough to perceive it!

5. *Polemical, hortatory, and prescriptive documents.* Pamphlets, treatises, sermons, political manifestos are among the most used of historical sources: the naive may think that these are simply conflicting discourses, Catholic against Protestant, Tory against socialist. In fact, apparently competing discourses often reveal common assumptions, which may be their prime interest for historians – both seventeenth-century sermons and twentieth-century manifestos reveal shared assumptions about the nature of social structure. Conduct books, advising or prescribing on etiquette and behavior – often for women! – are much used by historians these days, fully aware that they have to pin down who wrote them, who read them, and how far, if at all, they corresponded with actual behavior.

6. *Studies of customs and folklore and other academic works; textbooks, works of sociology, etc.* Some important recent books have made considerable use of contemporary studies of folklore and customs – folklorists have their prejudices and blindspots like everyone else, but, on the whole, their driving force tends to be a dedication to their subject, so that again the historian, employing the appropriate wariness and cross-checks, can learn much. Neither the writings of Max Weber, nor of Talcott Parsons, tell us how class actually is or was; but they give insights into perceptions of class in, respectively, the late-nineteenth century and the mid-twentieth century. Works of contemporary cultural theorists don't tell us much about either culture or history, but they will tell future historians much

about the strange ideas put forward towards the end of the twentieth century.

7. *Guides, handbooks, directories, and other works of reference*. I am deliberately making a distinction between these and the conduct books and other sources included under heading 5: guides to social customs, etiquette, and fashion, as perhaps also guides to the contemporary social scene, may straddle the divide – the historian will have to work out whether the intention is to prescribe a desired behavior, or whether it is simply to report on actual behavior (often something of both), but codifications of the law, guides on parliamentary procedure, directories and handbooks, and educational manuals will (rather like a guide to home computing today) have to be accurate, or they will be of no value to their potential customers. Guides to "Ladies of the Town" are an interesting sub-category: of course they inscribe prevailing values, a slightly more complex matter than those whose unvarying response to the practices of the past is outrage, would have us believe.

8. *Media of communication and artifacts of popular culture*. With newspapers, cartoons, etchings, and other illustrative material, posters and advertisements, films, radio tapes, television tapes (none, of course, mentioned by Carr), we move into fields where the cultural theorists also like to trample: no harm done, and perhaps something for historians to learn, provided always the fundamental purposes and achievements of history are kept firmly in mind – not to illustrate predetermined generalizations about competing discourses, or dominant ideologies, but to illuminate the past. These sources are very rich for attitudes, assumptions, mentalities, and values.[21]

9. *Archaeology, industrial archaeology, history-on-the-ground, and physical artefacts*. It has to be recognized that these are sources not directly used by the majority of working historians; yet most would consider it at least an ancillary part of their job to be knowledgeable about the built environment of whatever period or society they are studying and to be familiar with surviving physical relics. The area most affected by archaeological discoveries, obviously, is that traditionally termed "ancient" or "classical" history. A major point is confirmed: discovery or application of new sources alters interpretations – in other words, history *depends* on sources. We have to focus again on the relatively limited territory (though to the worker, vast enough!) on which individual, or groups of, historians concentrate. A choice example comes to hand as I write this: excavations at Edinburgh Castle suggest that human settlement in Scotland's capital (which also happens to be my home city) dates back to about 1,000 B.C.; there also being evidence that the place was an important center in the

Roman period; previously there had been few sources to demonstrate that Edinburgh pre-dated medieval times.[22]

How cities originate and develop is surely one of the most significant branches of historical study, and one which offers fascinating microcosms of the interrelationships between society, politics, the arts, economics, and technology. It happens that at the very same time that the excavations were proceeding at Edinburgh Castle, the centenary was being celebrated of the Forth (railway) Bridge a few miles to the northwest. The very building of that bridge is an important and fascinating historical subject. The major document, of course, is the bridge itself. But a complete history of the Forth Bridge requires documents from practically every type of source identified in this list. And that is really what I want to drive home here: single documents, of whatever type, are in themselves uncommunicative, imperfect, freighted with prejudice, difficult to read. But the history of the historians is not the reproduction of two or three texts, but a distillation from as large a number as it takes to produce convincing answers to specific questions, each individual source being subjected to both vigorous internal criticism and tested against the evidence suggested by the other sources. The argument can be further sustained from contemplation of one of the most evocative settings in the City of London; standing at a particular point near the Museum of London in the Barbican, one can take in: (1) a high-rise block of modern flats, part of the Barbican development itself; (2) in front, to the right, the square tower of the medieval church, St Giles, Cripplegate; and (3) low down to the left, an impressive section of the wall, originally built round London by the Romans. At one very fundamental level (not to be scoffed at), this little scene gives the spectator a very potent impression of three different eras in London's history. But, alas, these three magnificent pieces of history-on-the-ground cannot be taken at face value. From a wealth of other sources (including engravings and photographs, as well as written documents) historians know that while St Giles Cripplegate actually survived the Great Fire of London, it had in fact been burnt down over a century before, in 1545, that it was punitively "restored" by the Victorians, and that it was practically destroyed in the blitz of December 1940 – much of what we see today is a restoration completed in the 1960s; we know also that the wall was in continuous existence till the seventeenth century, constantly reconstructed and rebuilt, and has been subject to deliberate conservation since then: we see the Roman contours, but mainly seventeenth-century materials. As it happens, historians don't actually know when St Giles was originally built: without corroboration from other sources they are disinclined to believe John Stow, whose *A Survey of London* of 1598, which (like all the "histories" in category 3, it is both delight and delusion) claims that it was founded in 1090. As well as demonstrating what is known (all knowledge, inevitably, being in some sense provisional), the scrupulous citation of sources also reveals candidly what is not known: sources are salient both positively and negatively.

10. *Literary and artistic sources*. Many of those who are in the van of condemning the fetishism of documents would maintain that "art" and "literature" are meaningless terms; but then they would also maintain that all of the other sources studied by the historian are – like novels, plays, paintings, etc. – merely forms of discourse. The historian who wishes *to produce results* (as distinct from elaborately trapping out predetermined conclusions) does best to stick to categories based partly on the physical nature of the source, but mainly on its fundamental contemporary purpose. Paintings are not painted to serve the same purpose as acts of parliament, nor novels drafted to bring wars to a close. Indeed, a criticism which could legitimately be made of an earlier generation of historians who generalized about age of marriage from the plays of Shakespeare, and about Victorian living conditions from the novels of Dickens, is that they forgot that plays and novels are *deliberately* works of the imagination. There are important bodies of critical theory which the historian would be extremely foolish to ignore. Every historian, for instance, should be aware of the conventions within which an artist of any particular period or style operates in representing reality, the *schemata* he employs, as Gombrich puts it.[23] But historians will also adhere to their own proven methods: not reading the text in isolation, but studying all the other sources which indicate the origins of the work of literature or art, the intentions of the artist or writer, the conditions under which it was produced, the way it was marketed, and how it was received. If information is to be taken from the text it will, in the usual way, be checked against other relevant sources. In the study of values, attitudes, and assumptions, artistic and literary sources can be invaluable to historians, who, however, neither forget that they are fiction, nor exempt them from the critical caution applied to every other source.

11. *Processed sources*. This inelegant title, redolent of down-market foodstuffs, points to some of the most up-market activities indulged in by historians today: paleontology, serology, aerial photography, the study of place names, and, of course, the application of advanced computer technology to statistical material. To take the last first, the actual raw data will have to be collected from the various other categories of sources listed here: in origins, it is indisputably primary source material, but it only becomes usable through being processed through a computer. Aerial photographs are not in themselves sources left by the past; rather the taking of an aerial photograph is a *process* through which the contours of a medieval

village, say, or of old field plans, not apparent to someone standing on the ground, become clear. To be absolutely accurate, one should probably say that the actual configurations of the landscape, invisible though they may be to the unaided human eye, form the true primary source. Likewise, the true primary sources for the study of place names are surviving towns, villages, and geographical features and their names, together with all the other categories of sources from which place names may be extracted (old maps, chronicles, etc.). The study of place names is a process or technique for making use of the data assembled from many sources. As is well known, English towns ending in *by* and *thorpe* have been used to plot the extent of Viking settlement. But place-name evidence is no more free-standing or infallible than any other. The date we first *hear* of a place name may not be the same as the date at which it first *came into existence*. P. H. Sawyer made considerable use of this discrepancy in arguing that the basic pattern of English settlement had already established itself by the seventh century, and not, as usually thought, only in the eleventh century. Paleontology is the study of pollen cores from peat bog and lake sediments, giving knowledge of vegetational (and therefore cultivational) change. Serology uses the distribution of different blood groups in societies of today, to indicate settlement patterns of say (in Africa) different tribal groups or (in early England) of different nationalities (Anglo-Saxons, Norsemen, etc.). In both of these cases, process and basic source are inextricably intertwined. Historians, I hope it is now clear, exploit every possibility, go to every last resort in the naked pursuit of hard information – how very different is that pursuit from the facile manipulation of so-called "ideologies" and discourses.

12. *"Oral history" and oral traditions.* I put "oral history" in quotation marks because this phrase, though now absorbed into the language shared by historians and the general public, can be misleading. What is usually meant is "oral testimony" (that is to say, "oral sources"), the recording, whether on tape, or in shorthand, or by any other means, of personal recollections (though sometimes what is meant is a fully written-up history based almost exclusively on such sources). For some areas of historical study, including much recent Third World history, such source material is absolutely invaluable. Naturally, it takes great skill, and a mastery of whatever other knowledge is available, to make effective use of what is inherently (given the fallibility of human memory) a highly problematic source. Oral traditions (which take us back far beyond living memory) are especially valuable for societies where the written word is little used. Folk songs and folk sayings can give insights into the attitudes and mentalities of ordinary people in the past. It is in this category of source that we really

do encounter the "stories" which the linguistic materialists tell us are the only sources out of which we construct our lives. It is, on the contrary, fundamental to systematic historical study that realistic distinctions are made between "stories" properly so-called and the many very different kinds of evidence I have itemized here.

13. *Observed behavior, surviving customs, technical processes, etc.* Regrettably, there is still a considerable market in the United States for handguns individually crafted as they were in the late-eighteenth and early-nineteenth centuries before the mass production of fully interchangeable parts: for economic and military historians alike the study of a contemporary craftsmen at work in the old manner provides a peculiar, but unique, kind of source.[24] When Marc Bloch was alive, it was still perfectly reasonable for him to believe that, in studying the French peasants of his day, he would learn about their past. In our day the focus of such approaches has had to switch to the Third World, where medieval historians can still reasonably hope that the study of practices current there will throw light on behavior in the Europe of earlier times. I don't wish to exaggerate the importance of sources and techniques not widely used in mainstream history; I am simply concerned to drive home the point that those who wish to mock the historian's concern with sources should be careful first to be clear that they really do understand what these sources comprise, and should certainly not remain under the illusion that E. H. Carr had anything like the last word on the subject.

In setting out, and explicating, my taxonomy of sources, I have indicated some of the key activities involved in constructing the body of knowledge known as history. I have ignored the whole series of further processes (of which the most critical is the devising of a coherent intellectual structure) through which the end product, article or book, comes to be written. What I am stressing here is that, without the systematic study of the sources, none of these processes can come into play, and that the very discovery and study of the sources, far from being a routine, mindless activity, involves skilled and taxing work. The problem is that, aided, as I have suggested, by the utterances of certain professional historians desirous of endowing their subject with (phoney) glamour, the fashionable theorists of our time deny this account, reducing history, at best, to a multitude of stories, not different in character from novels, or, at worst, to an activity without relevance to contemporary society. Historical documentaries on British television continue to be of a high standard, yet one can detect in them, and in high-quality television criticism, the desire to keep up with intellectual fashion by "admitting," or declaring, that history is *no more than* culture-bound interpretation, based on a deployment of sources which is in itself deeply suspect. Historians cannot, therefore, simply ignore the cultural theorists, the linguistic materialists, the new historicists, particularly since, on the one hand, many of these theorists themselves make use of a highly naive form of history, and, on the other, as items 5, 8, 10, and 12 on my taxonomy of sources indicate, historians must themselves be involved in the realms of the arts, tradition, popular culture, etc., and must carry their own standards into these realms. My arguments against the theorists are that they pay no heed to, or dismiss, what it is that historians are actually trying to do (substituting instead aims which are neither possible for, nor proper to, historical study), and that, accordingly, they do not ever study what it is historians actually do (a time-consuming occupation), contenting themselves, at most, with studies of what others have said historians do, or more usually, of what historians *ought* to do. In fact, a discipline with such an outstanding record of achievement hardly needs the advice and criticism of outsiders (my battle cry!) whose own achievements, by comparison, are both rather modest and somewhat tiresomely repetitive.

It is time to look at some of these comments and criticisms. *Explanation in Social History* by Christopher Lloyd is the very paradigm of the sort of book which concludes, as it starts out, that history is, or should be, a unified, "sociological" discipline based, not on the study of sources, but on Marxist theory, as developed by Habermas, Foucault, etc. There is no examination of what historians actually do, only of what has been written about what they do. The case for source-based history is disposed of, to the author's satisfaction at least, though a brief critical discussion of the writings of Maurice Mandelbaum.[25] Gregor MacLennan, in *Marxism and the Methodologies of History*, insists that those who claim that there is a systematic body of historical knowledge based on the systematic study of sources are as ideologically motivated as any Marxist postulating that any proper body of knowledge must be based on Marxist theory, but, instead of examining any of the source-based articles and books which practising historians write, he confines himself to a quick run through various Inaugural Addresses which, as I have already said, are often more orientated towards rhetorical effect than towards the more boring "cook-book" task of explaining how historians actually go about their business.[26]

At first sight one might well feel that rather more attention should be given to the collection of essays edited by Attridge, Bennington, and Young, *Post-structuralism and the Question of History*, yet, on investigation, it turns out that the editors in their "Introduction: Posing the Question" place great weight on a brief essay by Mark Cousins purporting to analyze

"The practice of historical investigation."[27] The principle Cousins seeks to contest, they note, is "that the rise of modern historical scholarship involves a non-theoretical but a decisive technical distinction between primary and secondary sources" (130–31). The only reference given here is Part V of Collingwood's *The Idea of History*, which dates back to 1946 – and, as I have said, Collingwood is something of a soft hostage for history's enemies; no other historian *at all* is cited. Cousins's brilliant scheme for discrediting source-based history is to draw an entirely spurious parallel between the practices of history and the practices of the law. This method does not rebut, let alone refute, the value of the systematic study of sources; it does not even begin to engage with it. Instead the entire concentration is on the (alleged) nature of historical explanation. Cousins has noticed that historians do not usually attribute major historical developments to individual persons (though Cousins himself does not actually go into examples, it is perfectly true that historians speak of demographic factors, ideological trends, structural pressures, and so on). Agents in history, he says with a certain understatement, are "not necessarily persons"; it is, he says, the same in law:

> For it is the law which enables us to consider non-humans as agents. . . . Whether it be a limited company, a branch of the executive or a private citizen it can be a legal subject, can be legally reasoned about, can be said to act and to cause events. (134)

This piece of ludicrous fantasy, which contrives to equate limited companies and branches of the executive with the demographic factors or structural pressures of the historian, I should point out, is absolutely devoid of anything which could be construed as scholarly apparatus.

Cousins, along with Attridge, Bennington, and Young, would presumably see the law as a culture-bound, but not entirely negligible, human activity and would give history the same sort of conditional tolerance. But Barry Hindess and Paul Q. Hirst have absolutely no tolerance at all for what they see as an utterly irrelevant and valueless activity, the history of the historians. They identify their *Pre-capitalist Modes of Production* as "a work of Marxist theory,"[28] and draw a distinction between science on the one side and history (and the social sciences) on the other: their claim is that their approach, based on the "explicit theoretical construction of their concepts" is "scientific," in contrast with the "empirical" approach of history. This empiricism "ensures" (Hindess and Hirst are nothing if not dogmatic) that historical "'facts' are ideological constructs" and historical "'theories' are, at best, sophisticated theoretical ideology" (2–3). There is nothing in this string of bold assertions that a mere empiricist would recognize as argument, let alone evidence: the assertion, indeed, amounts to no more than "what I do is theory, what you do is ideology." In my *The Nature of History* I have claimed that the argument that history is a social necessity is sustained by the fact that from the very earliest times most societies have supported a form of "history" (have preserved records, mounted historical pageants, employed chroniclers – I *do* give examples: 2, 14–15). Hindess and Hirst apparently know better (though, as is their way, they offer no substantiation of their statement): "The absence in many literate societies of the writing of history and of history as an object of knowledge should indicate that history is not a given, that it is an object constituted within knowledge" (308). History, they go on to say is "useless," because, they repeat, it cannot escape from empiricism and is therefore ideological (310–11). Lacking any means for substantiating their assertions, the authors resort to repetition: "The study of history is not only scientifically but also politically valueless" (312). I deliberately began this essay by giving clear examples of the "uses" of history, and a major purpose of the remainder of it is to argue that history is useful only in so far as it is empirical (i.e., based on sources). That it does not on the whole serve the cause of Marxism is certainly true, but that the natural sciences have "political value" in this sense would seem to be an extraordinarily dubious notion. At least Hindess and Hirst are not bashful about declaring the sources of their thought (my concern, indeed, over less monochrome exercises in anti-historical cultural theory is that they fail to see that their notions of conflict and of ideology are actually based on two or three highly debatable Marxist *assumptions*): "All Marxist theory, however abstract it may be, however general its field of application, exists to make possible the analysis of the current situation" (312). Just in case this should be forgotten, the statement is repeated ten pages later. We now see clearly why the theorists love to invoke Collingwood, whose "insistence on history being written from the standpoint of the present," Hirst claims elsewhere, "explodes the myth of historical 'evidence'."[29]

History, I have said, is indeed important to the present, but it is only truly useful to the present if it is written in as "objective" a way as possible: that "objectivity" is to be achieved through the systematic study of sources which, of course, is scorned by Hindess, Hirst, and their like. There are many approaches to history, depending upon the particular problems being addressed (social history, quantitative history, feminist history, etc.): characteristically, Hindess and Hirst employ only grand, utterly outdated labels, "idealist" history, and "positivist" history: "positivism" has simply degenerated into a valueless term of abuse, and, in their actual writings, historians, of course, consider both "ideal" and "material" factors – the notion that one must automatically have primacy over the other finds no validation in the works of professional historians and is simply another relic of nineteenth-century philosophy. "Save for mindless antiquarianism or utter skepticism, "declare our two "scientists," "there can be no history without a philosophy of history" (312). Well, I've referred to the provision by historians of substantiable information on major contemporary trouble spots, on the places we like to visit, on urban development, on the building of a major technological wonder, and economic and social investment like the Forth Bridge: whether such matters are "mindless antiquarianism" is, I suppose, a matter of opinion; whether one could begin to study conflict in Northern Ireland, or in the Lebanon, without a fair dose of "skepticism" would seem less a matter of opinion, unless the opinion be that of a religious bigot. "We reject," Hindess and Hirst grandly conclude, "the notion of history as a coherent and worthwhile object of study" (321). What Hirst wants, as he explains elsewhere, is "a 'strategic' historiography informed by current concerns"; this he contrasts with what he refers to as "an endless poking in the potentially infinite archive of the 'past'." Historians, I have already said, do have their "strategies," but strategies which arise from their identification, within the developing body of historical knowledge, of topics which require exploration; they select particular archives, which they study systematically, neither endlessly poking, nor being daft enough to take on an infinity of archives. Perhaps that rebuttal is scarcely needed when one considers that Hirst's next sentence reads: "History without this strategic dimension can be a diversion for the Left."[30] The equation of left-wing propaganda with science would seem utterly laughable were it not that so much of the rejection of sources as the basis for historical study arises from the disappointment of the Left that history so studied does not always turn up answers favorable to their cause.

Nevertheless, one of the most powerful defences of source-based history was mounted by that notable man of the Left, E. P. Thompson.[31] Thompson is a major target for Hindess and Hirst, and for Anthony Easthope, who approvingly refers to their work. Easthope raises the question: "How can anyone, situated as they must be within discourse, come to have a knowledge of reality since that knowledge can only be constructed in and through discourse?"[32] This, it will be readily perceived, is both a high-falutin' re-phrasing of the old (and valid) recognition that the historian is situated within his own culture, and a pseudo-question in that nowhere in the literature of discourse theory is there any *validation* of the *assertions* *"must be"* and *"can only be."* However, in the assertion made, and, of course, swallowed without further thought, the contention is that: "Whereas the Althusserian stylistic situates itself in its material existence as writing, Thompson's language wishes to be a *voice speaking*" (97). Yes, Thompson wishes to be a "voice" presenting an account of significant aspects of the past, explaining clearly how he knows what he thinks he knows (i.e., referring to the sources) Easthope, actually, is a *"voice speaking"* as well, and a rather emotional one at that, as when he refers to Hirst's criticism of Thompson: 'Playing off against Thompson's native English, Hirst's review is written in a style with a new edge, its theoretical rigor sharpened into tones of sardonic anger and contempt that recall the stylistic of Marx" (99, 59). Here we go again: "your sardonic anger and contempt is a *voice speaking* (an insult evidently, though what on earth voices are supposed to do if not speak, beats me), our sardonic anger and contempt recalls the Redeemer Himself." Unfortunately, there is no space here to explore the way the cant phrase "theoretical rigor" is splashed around in this form of discourse (I use the word in its "ordinary," "neutral" sense), as if it expressed some ineffable virtue instead of connoting, as it does, inexpressible narrowness of vision (the echo of *rigor mortis*, I always think, is most serendipitous).

Easthope, in common with other contemporary cultural theorists and linguistic materialists, is always at pains to disavow the crude economic determinism of "vulgar Marxism," as if this somehow made it all right to maintain most of the other unproved assertions of Marxism: Although in every epoch "the ruling ideas are nothing more than the ideal expression of the dominant material relationships" (Marx and Engels 1970, p. 64), they are nothing less than them either, an "ideal" and therefore to some extent autonomous expression:

each new class which puts itself in the place of one ruling before it, is compelled, merely in order to carry through its aim, to represent its interests as the common interest of all the members of society, that is, expressed in ideal form: it has to give its ideas the form of universality, and represent them as the only rational, universally valid ones (*ibid.*, pp. 65–66).[33]

What enormous edifices have been based on this handful of lines from the great "scientific" theoreticians. Empirical studies, of course, have for many years now shown them to be complete nonsense. Long before the nineteenth century, aristocrats in Britain, many of them of "bourgeois" origins, had espoused what Marxism perceives of as "bourgeois ideology"; "bourgeois" figures, throughout the nineteenth century, continued to be happy at being governed by the aristocracy, while the most successful elements sought, not to put themselves in the place of the aristocracy, but to join it. Class, as it is revealed to be by empiricist studies, continues to be an important element in modern societies. It is the theoreticians who create muddle and confusion, because of the gap between what their theory says ought to be, and what actually is. Within a few lines on one page of a recent study, Alan Sinfield speaks of "the leisured upper-middle class," "the middle class," and "the middle and upper classes," subsequently swinging dizzily between "upper-class," "middle-class," "dominant class," "leisure class," and "leisure elite," all, apparently, the same wicked bunch. The fact is, hampered by the vague and embarrassing category "bourgeoisie," and not having made any empirical (source-based) study of the British class structure, he simply doesn't know what he is talking about.[34] Class is important, but if we are to foster knowledge rather than propaganda, considerably more precision in the use of terms is required, and such precision, of course, can only come from an assiduous study of the relevant sources.

Concepts, generalizations (that is well-trodden ground), and indeed theories (but not one over-arching macro-theory) are integral to historical study. But all must emerge from the evidence, be constantly tested against the evidence. Marxism postulates the notion of "class consciousness," so that in book after book, any sign of a sense of class identity, any sign of protest over wages or conditions, is immediately written up as evidence of class consciousness (which, by the theory, automatically entails class conflict). I have suggested that what the evidence more often shows is what could properly be termed "class awareness," a phenomenon that cannot automatically be conflated with class consciousness in the Marxist sense.[35] I believe that the muddle into which the theoreticians get themselves is well-illustrated by this passage from a famous book by the eminent British sociologist Anthony Giddens:

> An initial distinction can be drawn between "class awareness" and "class consciousness." We may say that, in so far as class is a structurated phenomenon, there will tend to exist a common awareness and acceptance of similar attitudes and beliefs, linked to a common style of life, among the members of the class. "Class awareness," as I use the term here, does *not* involve a recognition that these attitudes and beliefs signify a particular class affiliation, or the recognition that there exist other classes, characterized by different attitudes, beliefs, and styles of life: "class consciousness," by contrast, as I shall use the notion, does imply both of these. The difference between class awareness and class consciousness is a fundamental one, because class

awareness may take the form of a *denial of the existence or reality of classes*.[36]

In other words, "class awareness" in the Giddens usage means "not being aware of class." Giddens is forced into performing this trick because of his *a priori* assumption that class consciousness is a real and proper condition for the working class: just to show awareness that one is working class, or that other classes exist, is sufficient to be written up by Giddens as class consciousness with all the other (in my view quite unwarranted) assumptions that term includes. Class awareness in the sense in which I use it is simply not allowed for, because that would make an enormous hole in the whole interrelated schema of Marxist assumptions. Giddens's notion of class awareness is so insubstantial that it is very hard to think of what evidence one could use to demonstrate its existence. My line of argument has been that the evidence which Marxists cite to demonstrate the existence of class consciousness does no more than demonstrate the existence of class awareness: but of course the implication of Giddens's formulation would mean that any evidence that I used to demonstrate class awareness would automatically be taken as demonstrating class consciousness – which, of course, is the beauty of the formulation from Giddens's point of view!

Again, there is no space to multiply examples. I have already maintained that the critics of source-based history do not understand what historians really do, and misrepresent the aims of history; I am now adding the contention that, for all their affectation of superiority, their own ventures into history are confused and confusing.

Hindess and Hirst manage within a few pages to dismiss the utility of empirical evidence, then make an appeal to empirical evidence ("the absence in many literate societies of . . . history as an object of knowledge") while at the same time not actually giving any evidence for this apparently empirical statement (the evidence actually is very much to the contrary). In supporting a conception of ideology, which is in fact based on a handful of (discredited) Marxist assumptions, John B. Thompson follows the same procedure:

> There is little evidence to suggest that certain values or beliefs are shared by all (or even most) members of industrial societies. On the contrary it seems more likely that our societies, in so far as they are "stable" social orders, are stabilized by virtue of the diversity of values and beliefs and the proliferation of divisions between individuals and groups. The stability of our societies may depend, not so much upon a consensus concerning particular values or norms, but upon a lack of consensus

at the very point where oppositional attitudes could be translated into political action.[37]

In fact there is a great deal of evidence which, at the very least, does *suggest* that certain values are shared throughout society. It is to deal with this awkward fact that the theory of ideology was invented in the first place, and indeed the deeper implication of what Thompson is saying is that it is because of ideology that the point of translation into political action never actually materializes. But what I particularly want to draw attention to here is the slither through an apparent general appeal to empirical evidence without for a moment stopping to consider what that empirical evidence really is.

The claims to being "scientific" are mildly risible, till they become hilarious when "scientific" is conflated with "serving the interests of the Left." I prefer the views of a genuine scientist, Fellow of the Royal Society and internationally acclaimed biologist, Lewis Wolpert:

> My own feeling is that what I do really differs very little in essence from the work of a historian; a search for explanation and connections, the process of validation or verification, the falsification of ideas. What makes the study of history different is less the approach than the subject matter.[38]

In considering the question of "subject matter," I return to my opening remarks. The nature of history is to be defined by its aims and achievements which, in different ways, have considerable significance for the present. Historians have been highly successful in providing explanations and connections, in validating their accounts, and in exposing myths; these achievements are based on the systematic study of sources. The theoreticians have at once too grand, and too limited, a view of history. The historian can no more (and should not try to) provide an over-arching account of historical "meaning," nor of the relationship between past, present, and future, than the scientist can provide an over-arching explanation of the physical universe[39] Historians, like scientists, attack coherent, manageable areas within what is truly an immense subject. Yet the variety of topics explored by the historian far outstrips the curiously restricted notion that the subject matter of history is limited to shifting structures of power, and the way in which classes, or discourses, conflict with, overthrow, or accommodate to, each other. These who want to know about Tajikistan, or San Gimigano, or the Forth Bridge, or who are trying to get to grips with the problems of world poverty or world peace, will not be helped by some speculative theory about the unfolding of history or the inescapability of their situation within discourse, but will want to feel that the explanations, interpretations, and information they are provided with are based on a serious study of the evidence; and it will do them no harm at all if they are also made aware that all sources are fallible, that all study of them must be carried out in accordance with the strictest principles, and that there are always things which we do not know with any certainty.

History's critics need to appreciate that there *is* a crucial distinction between *primary* sources (which include the stories and narratives the postmodernists love to go on about, as well as the whole vast range of materials with whose imperfections historians have to grapple), and *secondary* sources, the history which historians produce through the systematic, disciplined, study of the primary sources. Despite postmodernist fancy, the scholarly history of the historian is in a very different category from the novels, stories, plays, or poems of the creative writer. We expect such texts to exploit the ambiguities and resonances of language. In history, on the contrary, conclusions should be lucidly expressed, evidence painstakingly cited, and conjecture unambiguously separated from securely established fact.[40]

Notes

1. Norman Davies, *God's Playground: A History of Poland*, 2 vols (Oxford: Clarendon Press, 1981).
2. These points are expanded more fully in Arthur Marwick, *The Nature of History*, 3rd edn (London: Macmillan, 1989), 1–27.
3. I am particularly grateful to two distinguished British discourse theorists, Professors John Barrell and Marcia Pointon, for accepting my invitation to deliver papers to the 1988 Social History Society Conference which I coordinated: these papers appear in *The Arts, Literature and Society*, ed. Arthur Marwick (London: Routledge, 1990). John B. Thompson, in *Studies in the Theory of Ideology* (Cambridge: Cambridge University Press, 1984), comments that "the various forms of discourse analysis have yielded results which are disappointing in many ways" (8).
4. The classic account is Peter L. Berger and Thomas Luckman, *The Social Construction of Reality: A Treatise in Sociology of Knowledge* (New York, 1966); for postmodernist views of science as (like history!) "just another set of narratives," see David Harvey, *The Condition of Postmodernity: An Enquiry into the Origins of Cultural Change* (Oxford: Blackwell, 1989), 9.
5. See Paul Q. Hirst, *Marxism and the Writing of History* (London:

Routledge, 1985), and other works discussed later in this essay.

6. Thompson, *Ideology*, 4.

7. Marc Ferro, *The Use and Abuse of History: Or How the Past Is Taught* (London: Routledge, 1984), *passim*.

8. The brilliant summary of the extensive literature by William M. Reddy in *Money and Liberty in Modern Europe: A Critique of Historical Understanding* (Cambridge: Cambridge University Press, 1987), is the more impressive since the author is a Marxist.

9. These reflections came to point of precipitation as I read *The Past Before Us: Contemporary Historical Writing in the United States*, ed. Michael Kammen (Ithaca, NY: Cornell University Press, 1980); and *The New Cultural History*, ed. Lynn Hunt (Berkeley: University of California Press, 1989).

10. *The Writing of History: Literary Form and Historical Understanding*, eds. Robert H. Canary and Henry Kozicki (Madison: University of Wisconsin Press, 1978), xi.

11. Accordingly I am in agreement with the arguments presented by Canary and Kozicki, ix–xv.

12. Including *Seventeenth-Century England: A Changing Culture*, *The Enlightenment*, and *Culture and Belief in Europe 1450–1600* (Milton Keynes: UK, Open University Press).

13. The print elements are available as *War, Peace, and Social Change: Europe 1900–1955*, 8 vols (Milton Keynes, UK: Open University Press, 1990).

14. Pieter Geyl, *Debates with Historians* (London: Batsford, 1955), 1.

15. Pieter Geyl, *Napoleon: For and Against* (London: Jonathan Cape, 1949), 15.

16. R. G. Collingwood, *The Idea of History* (Oxford: Clarendon Press, 1946).

17. See my *Nature of History*, 291–95.

18. G. R. Elton, *Political History: Principles and Practice* (New York: Basic Books, 1970), 133.

19. E. H. Carr, *What is History?* (1961; rpt. Harmondsworth: Penguin, 1964), 54, 142 (Carr writes of man being "enabled to harness nature and transform his environment").

20. What follows is both an abbreviation and an elaboration of pages 208–16 of my *The Nature of History*, where I list twelve types of sources.

21. My *Class: Image and Reality in Britain France and the USA Since 1930*, 2nd edn (London: Macmillan, 1990) makes substantial use of film material, as does my chapter "Room at the Top, the Novel and the Film" in Marwick (ed.), *Arts, Literature and Society*.

22. See *The Independent*, 26 February 1990.

23. E. H. Gombrich, *Art and Illusion: A Study in the Psychology of Pictorial Representation* (London: Phaidon, 1960), passim.

24. The point is made visually in Open University TV Programme *From*

Handicraft to Mass Production, Course A317, Programme 2 (Milton Keynes, UK, 1980).

25. Christopher Lloyd, *Explanation in Social History* (Oxford: Blackwell, 1986), 60–61.

26. Gregor MacLennan, *Marxism and the Methodologies of History* (London: NLB, 1981), 97–103.

27. Derek Attridge, Geoff Bennington, and Robert Young, *Post-structuralism and the Question of History* (Cambridge: Cambridge University Press, 1987), 5.

28. Barry Hindess and Paul Q. Hirst, *Pre-capitalist Modes of Production* (London, Routledge, 1975), 1.

29. Paul Q. Hirst, *Marxism and Historical Writing* (London: Routledge, 1987), viii.

30. Hirst, *Marxism and Historical Writing*, ix.

31. E. P. Thompson, "The Poverty of Theory: or an Orrery of Errors," in *The Poverty of Theory and other Essays* (London: Marlin, 1978), 193–397.

32. Anthony Easthope, *British Post-Structuralism Since 1968* (London: Routledge, 1988), 81.

33. Anthony Easthope, *Poetry as Discourse* (London: Methuen, 1983), 20, citing, Marx and Engels, *The German Ideology*, ed. C. J. Arthur (London: Lawrence Wishart, 1970).

34. Alan Sinfield, *Literature, Politics, and Culture in Postwar Britain* (Oxford: Blackwell, 1989), 40, 212, 233, 240, 260, 288, 290.

35. See my *Class: Image and Reality*, 11–24.

36. Anthony Giddens, *The Class Structure of the Advanced Societies*, new edn (Cambridge: Cambridge University Press, 1980), 110. I intend no general criticism of Giddens, a justly renowned sociologist with a strong sense of history.

37. Thompson, *Theory of Ideology*, 5.

38. Lewis Wolpert, *A Passion for Science*, eds. Lewis Wolpert and Alison Richards (Oxford: Oxford University Press, 1988), 6–7.

39. Peter Novick, in his immensely rich and rewarding *That Noble Dream: The "Objectivity Question" and the American Historical Profession* (Cambridge, Cambridge University Press, 1988), writing of the current state of "crisis" over the issue of objectivity, notes that: "At least for the foreseeable future there appeared no hope that historians' work would converge to produce the sort of integrated synthesis which had long been the discipline's aspiration" (590). For myself, I have little enthusiasm for this idealist, anthropomorphic (and very American!) construct, "the discipline"; I prefer to focus attention on the activities of individual historians, each with his / her own limited aims, and, as I see it, rather high levels of "objectivity."

40. "Fact" – a difficult word, of course: see my *Nature of History*, 193–97, esp. 197: "'facts' . . . are of considerable variety in nature, and in complexity."

8 Marxism and Historians of the Family

Richard T. Vann

> Just now we must really give priority to problems other than
> the forms of marriage prevalent among Australia's aborigines, or
> marriage between brother and sister in ancient times.
>
> Lenin to Clara Zetkin, 1920[1]

"Eventually," Gayle Rubin wrote in 1975, "someone will have to write
a new version of *The Origin of the Family, Private Property, and the
State*, recognizing the mutual interdependence of sexuality, economics,
and politics without underestimating the full significance of each in human
society."[2] But historians of the development of the family, if not of its
origin, have for the most part passed the last fifteen years without paying
much attention to this challenge; and in these days it perhaps sounds
somewhat quaint. Is there anything profitable for historians of family life
in the Marxist tradition? And if so, how might it best be appropriated?

History of "the family" – if we may for the moment accept that
hypothesized term – entered the Marxian canon proximately through
Engels' *Ursprung der Familie, des Privateigenthums und des Staats*
(Zurich, 1884)[3] but ultimately from Marx's own late-blooming anthropological interests.[4] Engels says in his preface that he has drawn heavily
on Marx's ideas, and there is certainly a strong family resemblance; what
Marx might have made of the subject had he produced a coherent text
can only be surmised from the jottings in his notebooks. The other major
Marxist work touching on the family, August Bebel's *Die Frau und der
Sozialismus*, predated the work of Engels, since its first edition appeared
in 1883. It was something of a best-seller – Daniel DeLeon's English
translation of 1904[5] was made from the thirty-third edition of the German
original – and has a good deal of sociological material which Engels lacks,
but adds almost nothing in theory. Bebel shared Engels' view that only the
full incorporation of women into productive labor would bring about their
emancipation. This implicitly calls for the eventual abolition of anything
like a monogamous nuclear family, although these implications are not
spelled out. With the triumph of socialism, Marxists believed that women

would be liberated along with all other oppressed people. Furthermore, they were explicitly told to await their turn; as Lenin berated Clara Zetkin in the autumn of 1920: "I have been told that at the evenings arranged for reading and discussion with working women, sex and marriage problems come first. . . . I could not believe my ears when I heard that. The first state of proletarian dictatorship is battling with the counter-revolutionaries of the whole world."[6]

Given the view that the problem of family life had been solved or at least subordinated in theory and would shortly be so in practice, it is not surprising that in Soviet historical scholarship, as David Ransel wrote in 1978, "Family history . . . has usually been seen as a secondary, even incidental problem."[7] Ransel attributed this in part to the fact that there was a rigid division of labor in Soviet academic life which had assigned family life to ethnography rather than history. The Soviet historical studies that have appeared generally have treated family history as an aspect of the history of the exploited peasantry or in the context of demographic developments.[8] There has been considerable interest in the size and organization of households in eighteenth- and nineteenth-century Russia, but the work on these has been done almost entirely by Western historians.[9] Somewhat the same could be said of other countries which until recently had communist governments. Yugoslavia, in particular, has an important pre-census household listing (Belgrade in 1734) and the remarkable joint family arrangement known as the *zadruga*; but the study of these has been largely left to Western scholars working outside any Marxist framework.[10] However interest in history of family life (again, largely mediated through historical demography) seems markedly greater in some parts of Eastern Europe; perhaps it is no coincidence that the leaders appear to be Hungary and Poland, which are also currently the most enthusiastic pursuers of capitalism.[11]

The work of Engels was much of its time. It shared not only some of the presuppositions of the works on which it partly rests, notably Lewis Henry Morgan's *Ancient Society* (New York, 1877) and Johann Jakob Bachofen's *Das Mutterrecht* (Basel, 1861) but also of Sir Henry Maine's *Ancient Law* (London, 1861) and John F. McLellan's *Primitive Marriage* (Edinburgh, 1865). And it has been involved in the common wreck of late nineteenth-century social theorizing and speculative history on the grand scale. Its framework was evolutionary; and the conventional wisdom is that "broad evolutionary syntheses of family change are linear, too simplistic, and rooted in ideological preconceptions."[12] (We are, alas, not given directions to the happy land where utterances are made entirely without ideological preconceptions.) Engels' work certainly was, in Marxian terms, "economistic," in that its emphasis fell mainly – though not exclusively – on family forms as an epiphenomenon of the forces and relations of production. It assumed that existing kinship terms can only have come into existence as unproblematic descriptions of past social relationships. Engels (here following Bachofen) attributed to primitive women a positively Victorian concern for chastity of which there is no evidence. For these and other reasons the book was all but forgotten until its rediscovery by Marxist feminists in the wake of the American and European women's movement.

I

In the meantime, proceeding almost entirely in an empiricist mode, "history of the family" was becoming in the 1960s and 1970s one of the great growth industries in Western historiography. In *An International Bibliography of the History of the Family*, whose comprehensive coverage stopped with the entries for 1976, about twenty-five percent of the entries were published in the 1960s and around forty-three percent from 1970 to 1976; since then the volume of publications in this broad area has become even greater.[13]

The historiography of the family has a somewhat peculiar family history. Although it came to form a substantial part of the boom in social history inspired in large part by the work of the French, it did not originate in the mainstream of historiographical practice. From the beginning it was interdisciplinary; in fact in some respects it was a kind of backward emanation of other social sciences. The first impulse to empirical work came from the French school of historical demography (often misidentified with *Annales: Economies, Sociétés, Civilisations* but actually primarily the achievement of the Institut National des Etudes Démographiques). The two fathers of the field, if the research into paternity can be allowed, were Louis Henry and Philippe Ariès. Henry of I.N.E.D. wished to compare the fertility of contemporary populations with some where there was no family limitation; since there were no modern European populations where this was the case, he decided to investigate French populations of the seventeenth and eighteenth centuries. To do this he invented the technique of "family reconstitution," a laborious technique of copying the entries in a parish register on individual slips of paper and assigning them to the individual families living in the parish at the time. The result is a "family reconstitution form" which gives all the available details of the baptisms, marriages, and burials which took place in the family. The advantages of these data for the demographer go well beyond providing evidence of what a population with "natural fertility" would look like.[14] They can be illustrated by looking at the other major technique for historical demography, the aggregative approach, which relies on simply counting the number of vital events in a large number of parishes.[15] With aggregative techniques, and sufficiently robust guesses about how representative the parishes are, estimates of a national population at various dates can be made;[16] but we know most precisely about the underlying processes of population change when we know what life expectancies were, how old people were when they married, and how they spaced their children throughout their child-bearing years. This is the sort of information which only family reconstitution can reliably supply.

Although most historical demographers plugged away with their refined techniques, convinced that they were discovering facts uncontaminated by theoretical preconceptions, there was an over-arching theory in which most of them believed: that of the "demographic transition." This held that the transition to modern populations (which presumably would in due course be traversed by all "developing" countries) was in three stages. The first, typical of pre-industrial populations, was one of high fertility balanced by high mortality, keeping population levels more or less stationary over prolonged periods of time. Then mortality began to fall, while fertility remained at its previous heights, resulting in a rapid rise in numbers. (This began to happen in most parts of Europe around 1750.) Finally, as family limitation began to be widely adopted, fertility began to fall to a level commensurate with that of mortality, producing the characteristic small families of Central and Western Europe and the United States.

An ingenious, now unjustly neglected, attempt was made by David Riesman to deduce the psychological consequences of these three demographic regimes. The personality type characteristic of the era of rapidly rising population, he claimed, was "inner-directed" – that is, responsive to an "internal moral compass" set in childhood by parents, which provides decision rules and supports entrepreneurial behavior. In the period of low-fertility, low-mortality equilibrium, the typical personality is "other-directed." Instead of a moral compass, Riesman's image for these is a gyroscope, constantly taking its direction from its surroundings – the peer group instead of the parents.[17]

Just how these personality traits were produced by, and not merely associated with, demographic patterns was left unspecified by Riesman, and nobody has followed up his speculations. His theory – and that of the "demographic transition" – was a variant of the modernization theory which generally held the field in post-World War II American social science. When applied to the history of the family, modernization theory stressed the loss of productive and educational functions in the modern family. It was, however, supposed to have acquired a new and, in capitalist and bureaucratic societies, a vital task: the provision of a "haven in a heartless world" – the one social institution where status was ascribed and did not have to be earned, and where love and emotional solace would always be available (chiefly from the mother, of course) for the family members who were otherwise engaged in the Hobbesian world of competitive capitalism.[18] Modern families were small and almost always composed only of parents and their offspring; it was thought that in contrast to these privatized modern nuclear families, families before the "demographic transition" had characteristically been extended, with more children but also with co-resident kin.

As empirical work in demographic history proceeded, it soon became apparent that the idea of a transition from large extended medieval and early modern families to small nuclear modern ones was hard to reconcile with newly-discovered facts. It was evident as early as 1965 that in northwestern Europe, at least, families had been small since the sixteenth century, if not earlier. Besides the high infant mortality, couples simply weren't married long enough to produce vast numbers of children. The age at first marriage in the seventeenth and eighteenth centuries was usually around twenty-five for women and a year or so older for men. The earlier impression that very early marriage was more typical rested mainly on Juliet's age at first marriage. Although Juliet's mother chides her for remaining unmarried at fourteen when she had herself borne Juliet at about that age, such early marriages (although they may not have been quite so unusual in aristocratic circles in Renaissance Verona) almost never happened in most Western European populations. Women would have had to marry in their early teens to be able to bear the dozen or so children which were supposed to typify the pre-industrial family; but the impression of great family size, like that of the typicality of early marriages, also rested on a common kind of sampling error, taking the exceptional family sizes of a few famous men – the twenty-two children of Johann Sebastian Bach or Samuel and Susannah Wesley – as norms. Families with more than twelve children were almost unheard of in pre-industrial Europe; few couples had more than eight.

Large extended families – three generations living together under one roof, with perhaps a celibate aunt or uncle thrown in for good measure – were also much less common in pre-industrial Western Europe than modernization theory required. They could never have been the predominant form, and it appears that in Northwest Europe, at least, they were quite atypical.[19] Furthermore, the conclusion of the first comprehensive survey of household surveys was that although there were marked variations among the various parts of Europe, there was very little change in size over time.

The findings indicating a relatively invariant household structure were disconcerting to historians of family life. They not only found that the reigning paradigm had collapsed, but also that they had not very much change to explain, unless they ventured speculatively back into the Middle Ages, where there was less chance of discovering inconvenient evidence.

At the same time the limitations of an approach to family history based entirely on quantitative series were becoming apparent. If there had been many extended families in the *ancien régime*, family reconstitution could scarcely have detected them. The families represented on family reconstitution forms are all nuclear, and they are purely reproductive units. It would be possible occasionally through linkage between family reconstitution forms to show how the reproducing pair was set in a wider kinship context, or how quickly the survivor might have remarried; but no study systematically doing this has yet been published. Of course no history of family life would be very convincing without basic demographic information, and an approach that places emphasis on events which befell, and decisions taken by, a couple and their offspring is particularly pertinent. But perhaps seductively pertinent; it is easy to focus entirely on the nuclear family and efface the neighbors, kin, work environment, and community which surrounded it. This temptation is reinforced by the fact that most parish registers did not provide very good information about the occupations of the men and women who lived there; and, true to the original concerns of Louis Henry, most studies of local populations have aimed at comparability of their age-specific vital rates with those of other populations, often quite remote in time and space, rather than at an intensive study of the parish register in the context of other documents that might illuminate the social milieu in which the families lived.[20]

For a time it appeared that parish registers were the only reliable quantitative source for the history of population in the pre-census era. (The census era began in Sweden in the mid-eighteenth century; by the end of the century the infant American republic had taken its first census, and such enumerations were common in Europe by the middle of the nineteenth.) In the early 1960s many local census-type listings, some of which date as far back as the late sixteenth century, were discovered in England (and later in France, Germany, and other countries). These are without doubt the single most important sources for a history of family life; and of course historians of the family are just as tethered by the available evidence as any other historians.

However, we often speak of "evidence" as though it were brutally *there*, just as solid as the pieces of paper or parchment that can be fetched out of a library or archive. But evidence is evidence *of* something; it has no meaning unless it is produced to help answer some sort of question, and it gives its answer only when the historian employs an appropriate technique of construing it. All historical sources demand a hermeneutics from their readers, although this hermeneutics usually emerges into consciousness only when the reading is contested. One of the reasons for the appeal of parish registers and household listings for historians of the family is that superficially they do not require the kind of interpretation that would be demanded by, let us say, a file of correspondence from one family member to another. Part of the intellectual baggage which social historians bring is a distrust of such "literary" sources – that is, those which most obviously demand hermeneutical skill. Instead, they prefer sources which can be coded and counted. The family reconstitution form does this job in the most detailed way for the parish register; once the array of local household listings had been discovered, the search was on for some equivalent form which could be codified, counted, and compared. We need not enter into the niceties of the most influential system of categorization which has been proposed;[21] the point is that the initial stage of treatment of the material was to abstract from all their particulars, including their immediate historical context, so as to yield data which would support cross-cultural and trans-temporal comparisons.

If the family which can be "reconstituted" is purely reproductive, that which can be censused is purely co-residential. Though we know that real families have many more dimensions than these, the temptation to elide the distinction between families and households is difficult to resist. As Michael Mitterauer and Reinhard Sieder point out in their general work *The European Family*, "It is only in the context of the house or household that the family may be placed within the scope of a quantitatively defined social group. The network of family connections differs for each person concerned and cannot be statistically defined."[22] But even if we grant that the family may best (or perhaps only) be studied as a "quantitatively defined social group," local household listings or census enumerators' handbooks pose hermeneutic problems of their own. A parish priest may forget to record some of the baptisms, marriages, or burials he performs, but at least it is clear what those actions were. However, as E. A. Hammel points out, "in stratified societies of the kind that leave records of households for historians, we would not be surprised to find differences of view on the definition of households between inhabitants and census takers."[23] Furthermore, household listings are seldom without their ambiguities in kinship terminology, designation of marital status, or even in distinguishing one household from another. Hammel shows that the difference between strongest and weakest assumptions about such matters would cause a thirty percent variation in the number of households which are considered nuclear. A similar change in assumptions could cause the impression that fewer than half of households were *zadrugas*, rather than eighty percent. Furthermore, apparent changes from a predominance of one household type to that of another can be the result simply of random demographic variations over a period of time (36–39).[24] These disconcerting observations led Hammel to conclude that "the household is simply not a very good unit of observation" and that "what we really study most of the time in investigating households (particularly as historians) is the classificatory habits of census takers but without any Linnaean system of our own against which to measure their decisions" (40).

Hammel is an anthropologist; many historians would probably say that comparison of the community listings with other documents from the same community would be necessary before rushing to use them in a comparative manner. But this moves us even more urgently from the comparatively safe haven of the social scientist's statistical techniques, and the important findings they have given us, into the polysemous thicket of heterogeneous texts.

These are, above all, the texts which are required to capture the emotional tenor of family life in the past. Here again history of the family has followed the lead of French social history generally as it moved somewhat away from the high statistical moment when Emanuel Le Roy Ladurie admonished all historians: *il faut compter!* As the attitudes, habits, and value structure of ordinary people in the past – all that the French mean by *mentalités* – came under scrutiny, it was inevitable that the sentiments and psychological formations underlying family life should move to the fore.

This was already apparent in the work of the other founding figure, Philippe Ariès, whose *L'Enfant et la vie familiale sous l'ancien régime* (Paris, 1960), familiar to Anglophone readers in Robert Baldick's translation, *Centuries of Childhood* (New York, 1962), was for many the book that opened up the whole subject. Ariès was not an academically educated historian – in fact he was by profession a curator of tropical plants – which probably accounts for the freshness with which he ranged through French (and a little English) history from the Middle Ages to the end of eighteenth century (with a number of reproachful glances at the sad state of family life in the twentieth century). The trajectory of his historical interests was again from historical demography (a history of French populations, work on the history of contraception) to *mentalités* (his classic work on childhood and family life and his final equally monumental study of Western attitudes towards death). Ariès is best known for his claim that the whole idea of childhood is a relatively modern one; that in the Middle Ages, once they were past infancy, children were simply treated as little adults. Parents in the seventeenth century began to coddle their children, but before then, high infant mortality discouraged any premature emotional investment in them.

Conceived on an even grander scale, although covering a shorter time-span, was Lawrence Stone's *The Family, Sex, and Marriage in England, 1500–1800* (New York, 1977). Stone proposes a typology and historical sequence of family types, based not on coresidential patterns, but on the structures of sentiment, from open-lineage (1450–1630) to restricted patriarchal nuclear (1550–1700) to closed domesticated nuclear (1640–1800 and presumably thereafter). Stone uses an even greater variety of evidence than did Ariès, but – as he grants – almost all of it comes from the upper strata of English society. Because the middle and working classes were not producers of such texts, we do not know whether their families had similar forms or developed in analogous ways.

Besides the difficulties posed by the unrepresentative character of literary sources, it is of course extremely hard to fit them into a coherent picture of something so vague and vast as "the family" over a span of a couple of centuries. Something of the difficulty is suggested by two studies which treat some of the same ground traversed by Stone. One, Randolph Trumbach's *The Rise of the Egalitarian Family: Aristocratic Kinship and Domestic Relations in Eighteenth-Century England* (New York, 1978), found the aristocracy to be increasingly forming "egalitarian families" which shared most of the characteristics of Stone's "closed domesticated nuclear family." The difference is that Stone sees the "closure" as marginalizing kinship relations, whereas Trumbach claims that aristocratic families were enthusiastically exploiting both their patrilineage and their kindred: the former for the benefits of inheritance, the latter to promote the interest of their class as a whole. It would appear that this apparent disagreement stems from the basically sociological approach of Trumbach as compared to Stone's emphasis on psychological configurations and *mentalités*.

While Trumbach would seem to have corroborated Stone, Linda Pollock totally disagreed with Stone's bleak picture of parent-child relationships prior to the eighteenth-century affectionate family. Through an extensive study of correspondence, journals and autobiographies, conduct books, and pediatric literature, she was unable to find any major change in parental attitudes from the sixteenth through the nineteenth centuries.[25] If Pollock's contentions are essentially correct, they, like the apparently invariant size of households, would suggest that a sequence of types and a minimum set of transformational rules governing their development such as Stone proposes is an inappropriate approach to the history of family life; but they sharply pose the question how such a history might proceed otherwise.

Although *mentalités* obviously proceed from minds, the history of *mentalités* is not psychohistory. Most historians have approached them in the way that a sociologist or anthropologist, rather than a psychologist, might do. Any borrowings from psychology have been mostly implicit ones from social psychology. The most ambitious attempt to use depth psychology, and on a timescale rivalling Freud's speculative historical reconstructions, is Lloyd deMause's edited volume *The History of Childhood*. This is, even for collaborative volumes, an unusually motley collection, and in fact most of the contributors pay scant attention to psychohistory. DeMause, however, proposes an evolutionary schema of six modes in the history of childrearing: infanticidal, abandonment, ambivalent, intrusive, socialization, and finally a "helping mode" beginning in the mid-twentieth century. The helping mode "results in a child who is gentle, sincere, never depressed, never imitative or group-oriented, strong-willed, and unintimidated by authority."[26] Unfortunately there seem to be only four of these paragons, including DeMause's son.

Histories which explore a new range of problems, and which propound such sweeping solutions to them, are sometimes initially ignored, especially when they are written by people who are not professional historians.[27] They are also likely to be exposed to peculiarly harsh criticism, which none of these volumes has escaped. Their treatment of parent-child relationships, in particular, is highly contested. Most historians have treated the eccentricities of DeMause's contribution to *History of Childhood* as beneath serious comment.[28] The claim that there was no conception of childhood in the Middle Ages has been refuted by a number of medievalists, and it has been pointed out that if parents were as indifferent to their children as Ariès contended, very few would have had sufficient nurturance to survive childhood.[29] As we have seen, Stone and Pollock utterly disagree on the character of parent-child relations. These are not routine disagreements that might in principle be resolved by an appeal to "the evidence," because there is no agreement on what the relevant evidence is, or what principles of interpretation ought to be invoked. The emotional configuration of a family must be in a complex interrelationship with the reproductive behavior which is reflected in demographic statistics and with the residence patterns which may be caught by local censuses. Yet the sources for interpreting it are so different from parish registers and household listings, and the techniques required so unlikely to be combined with statistical and computing expertise, that no historian has yet made a convincing attempt to explicate this interrelationship. Finally, the deeper structures of *mentalité* are what in a culture remains unsaid, or what cannot be said; but this is precisely what leaves no evidence of itself. Historians are thus forced to construe silences – an even trickier proposition than construing words.

The difficulties here go beyond what is commonly taken to be "methodology." There is, notoriously, no single theory which explains both social and psychological facts. We are in an analogous position to that of physics, which has not succeeded in finding a "unified field theory" which will account for both the strong forces and both the weak forces. Perhaps it is utopian to expect the human sciences to accomplish a task of comparable or even greater difficulty; but the first stage in getting what we lack is always to remind ourselves what we lack.

II

There are at least some theories which purport to provide an all-encompassing explanation of social facts. It is now time to evaluate the various ones, including Marxism, which might help us to grasp all the functions that humans have invested in their families and the way that these have fitted into the social whole. Thus far, materials for the sequel to Engels' *Origin of the Family* which Gayle Rubin projected have clustered around the nexus of marriage, property, and – to use a convenient but ill-defined concept – "patriarchy." Like Engels, historians who have gathered them have tended to reduce the history of family life to the history of family formation – the ritual practices surrounding marriage, the power that parents exerted in determining the timing and choice of partners, the rules of residence for the new couple, the opportunities for remarriage by widows and widowers, and the eventual family size. Marxists, unsurprisingly, see the proximate levels of causation in the exchange of property among family members (as dowries or jointures, inheritances or *inter vivos* settlements), and seek to ground these in a mode of production.[30]

A good sample of the best Marxist, or at least *marxisant*, efforts being made in this direction can be found in the work of David Levine.[31] Since his focus is mainly on the history of English population – he disclaims any effort at a comparative perspective[32] – and since the percentage of people who married and the age at which families were formed are the principal cultural factors in population change in England, Levine tries to explain these by changes in the composition of the labor force, from one comprised predominantly of peasants or family farmers to one comprised primarily of industrial workers. The population of peasant communities, he argues, would have increased comparatively slowly, because sons and daughters would have to wait until their parents were ready to hand over farms or could set them up in an independent living as artisans. In families of wage-earners or proletarians, on the other hand, there was no patrimony to transfer to the younger generation, and wages were likely to be as high or even higher for the young as for older people. Thus there was no financial incentive to delay marriage, and women who married earlier would bear more children.

Levine and his sometime collaborator Charles Tilly have been chided for being influenced by Marxism,[33] but the nature of this influence is not immediately obvious. At first glance the work of Levine and Tilly fits comfortably into what has been given the name of "the new home economics" – an effort by economists to understand decisions about what size family to have as if they were made like other consumption and investment choices. (One of the earliest articles in this genre was called "Are Babies Consumer Durables?"). Naturally this approach, conceived in an era when means of contraception and abortion are freely available in almost all the developed countries, is most powerful when it treats modern families; but it is by no means limited to them. This is because decisions which enable populations to keep in rough balance with the resources available to them need not be confined to what have come to be called "Malthusian" ones (that is, for limiting fertility within marriage). Malthus himself regarded delaying marriage as the principal "preventive" check, as opposed to famines, wars, and plagues, the "positive" checks. For almost all families prior to about 1850 contraception was inhibited both by moral restraints and technical difficulties. Family formation, or at least the opportunity to begin procreation, was thus the hinge in the impact of economic conditions on family size, and perhaps on other aspects of family life.

Levine's hypothesis about proletarian and peasant families is thus in that sense an application of the "new home economics," and is Malthusian, or at least contains no reasoning that would have been foreign to Malthus and his modern followers.[34] Levine's avowed intent is to "force a Marxist concern with the social relations of production against a Malthusian emphasis on the cumulative characteristics of population growth."[35] The idea that these theories have to be forced against one another is not surprising, considering the abuse which Marx invariably poured on "Parson Malthus"; but there is considerable congruence between neo-Malthusian and some Marxist approaches to the history of the family. Both have focused on family formation, and specifically the age at marriage, as the key events; both figure nuptiality and fertility decisions in the context of changes in occupational structure, which are regarded as causes. This however should not be astonishing, since Malthus's analysis of the demography of his own period is integrated, via Ricardo, into Marx's model of the dynamics of capitalism. What Marx chiefly denied was that Malthus had discovered any natural law of population such that the possibility of abundance for all was precluded by any inexorable tendency of population growth to outstrip available food. Each historical epoch, defined by its distinctive mode of production, would have its own law of population, so that at most what Malthus claimed would be valid for the capitalist mode of production.

Thus in a static or synchronic analysis a Marxist and a Malthusian may reach the same conclusions. What sets the Marxist apart is – or should be – a sense of radical historicism and a belief that conflict between those with different roles in the productive process is ultimately the motor that drives the historical process. For example, Charles Tilly, on the origins of the European proletariat: "*Cherchez le capitaliste*. The activity of capitalists, not the abstract mechanics or population growth, lay behind all the components of the proletariat's growth." Now such a conclusion, as Tilly himself grants, neglects "all the graceful refinements that make the problem interesting."[36] He mentions in particular the difficulty in specifying the timing of the growth of the proletariat (in sixteenth-century England there may have been a *de*proletarianization) and charting regional variations. In a somewhat similar fashion, Levine rests a crucial part of his argument on the concept of "proto-industrialization"; yet, as he admits, "it has proven to be almost impossible to specify what proto-industrialization was." In fact, far from being a dogmatic adherent of theory, Levine regards himself as an historian who seeks to "produce answers which lead to knowledge" rather than to theory. "Historical knowledge," he claims, "is anti-theoretical in the sense that it is non-predictive." He believes that he has only to account for "proto-industrialization" in England and its relation to the Industrial Revolution there, rather than explain why similar "pre-industrial" social formations elsewhere did not lead to the same consequences. "As an historian of England," he concludes, "the issue of comparison is interesting and sometimes illuminating but it is also essentially beside the point."[37]

Theory, it would thus seem, is not only not knowledge, it is even opposed to knowledge; and concepts can be picked up out of any theory so long as they seem to apply to the case at hand. Since comparison is "beside the point," we need not worry if our "theory" applies only to one case. On this showing, no theory can ever be discredited, or shown to be useless, since a case might arise for which it seemed to be fitted. The historian would therefore be well advised to be as utter an eclectic as she or he is an empiricist, carrying in the intellectual tool kit the whole array of social theories. One might always come in handy.

In this conception of the uses of theory for history – which, it must be said, legions of historians share with Levine – Marxism would seem a rather refractory and specialized tool. Its greatest weakness is that it is primarily a theory of the relationship between capital and wage labor, whereas the family is above all the domain of subsistence reproduction. In other words, the family is where the human capacity for labor is produced and reproduced. While all of its members, occasionally, might be working for wages, the services exchanged among family members are not paid for or commodified. As Veronika Bennholdt-Thomsen has pointed out, "The lack of understanding which renders subsistence reproduction something like a black box in present marxist analysis, can be partly traced back to Marx's own thought."[38] And that of Engels, we might add, since Engels declared that "within the family he [the husband] is the bourgeois; and the wife represents the proletariat"[39] – an appealing analogy, but one which hardly analyzes the extra-economic exploitation all but universally visited by husbands upon their wives.

This deficiency in Marxism need not be irreparable. Rosa Luxembourg, for one, has made a start in the analysis of non-capitalist forms of production – which of course include the work of peasant proprietors as well as of wives and children.[40] But if it is to address extra-economic exploitation, or domination not based on the extraction of surplus labor, a Marxist theory of the history of the family would have to address all those areas of family life determined by sentiment and the unconscious structures of the psyche.

For Marxist historiography of the family, the key to this realm has been Freudian depth psychology rather than the history of *mentalités*. It would seem that reconciliation of Marx and Malthus to explain the process of family formation, as attempted by writers like David Levine, would be simple compared to the effort to make an amalgam of Freudianism and Marxism. Yet it is not hard to see why some Marxist historians have felt the inadequacy of Marxism without a systematic theory of the psyche. As Christopher Lasch has written, sociology cannot do without a theory of socialization, and such a theory must "rest on psychoanalysis, the most impressive body of insights into the internalization of culture."[41] Furthermore, as Paul Robinson has observed, "The mutual antagonism of psychoanalysis and revolutionary socialism is one of the as yet inadequately explained mysteries of twentieth-century intellectual history."[42]

These two great exemplars of the "hermeneutics of suspicion" have a good deal in common. Both are in a way materialistic – and can even lend themselves to mechanistic formulae. They are both dialectical, which should inoculate them against the danger of slipping into mechanism or into a facile assumption of harmony within the psyche or the social world. Finally, both require a theory of the unconscious (in Marxism, "false consciousness") to explain the manifest content of political and cultural life.

The project of bringing Freud to bear on Marx was a dominant concern of the Frankfurt Institut für Sozialforschung, and it also attracted the attention of one of Freud's own inner circle of analysts, the brilliant therapist Wilhelm Reich, who is doubtless the only person in the twentieth century to be expelled both from the German Psychoanalytic Society and the German Communist Party.[43] During his fairly brief period as an avowed Marxist, Reich devoted no fewer than six books to an attempted synthesis of the ideas of Freud and Marx.[44] He focused on sexual repression and the domination of the patriarchal family as an autonomous force perpetuating and intensifying capitalist exploitation. Sexual repression, to be sure, originated for economic reasons, in the power of males to accumulate vast amounts of property through dowries and their need to be certain of the paternity of the children born to the woman with whom they consorted. In this respect Reich's account resembled that of Engels; and he also reverted, in an even more enthusiastic manner, to the myth of primitive matriarchy – regarded by him as a demonstrated historical fact and dated at around 4000 B.C. This was the familial equivalent of "primitive communism"; its overthrow was the single overriding fact in the history of the family, and the task of revolution was not just to expropriate the expropriators, but to abolish the nuclear family and all inhibitions of heterosexual genital intercourse.[45]

While Reich's theory marked some advance over the position of Engels, it still offered little concrete assistance to historians of the family. If there ever was a period of universal matriarchy (which seems doubtful) it was lost in the mists of prehistory, and the idea of an omnipresent "patriarchal" sexual repressiveness which is supposed to have replaced it is insufficiently sensitive to the changes in family life which must have occurred in the interim between the golden age of matriarchy and the epoch of advanced capitalism. Like Freud, Reich has little to say about this rather extended period of transition. Insofar as he deigns to consider a real historical problem, it is the one which also preoccupied the Institut für Sozialforschung: why, when conditions appeared so favorable for the general socialist revolution after World War I, the working class – especially

in Germany – failed to take power. This led Reich to a consideration of
the psychological traits that produced deferential workers, and the types of
family that produced these traits. It was, he thought, the peasantry and *petite
bourgeoisie* which were especially susceptible to the appeal of Nazism;
and the reason for this was that fathers controlled their children's access
to small family farms and businesses. Control of the means of production
was, as always, linked to sexual repression; these fathers could delay their
children's marriages and prevent their sexual experimentation, whereas the
children of factory workers who had no patrimony to pass on were much
freer to initiate sexual relationships.[46]

This explanation of course is of a piece with the Malthusian ones for
the increase of population during the Industrial Revolution. What makes it
distinctively Freudian is the mechanisms employed for sexual repression.
It is not just a matter of explicit or even implicit cost-benefit analysis by
parents and children about the trade-offs between earlier access to property
and earlier indulgence of sexual instincts. Instead, sexual urges are truly
repressed – driven into the unconscious, or, as Reich put it, incorporated
into the "character armor" of both parents and children. Thus is transmitted
from generation to generation a disposition to dominate children and those
lower in the social order, while identifying with and willingly accepting
subordination to authority of all kinds. The unconscious elements of the
Weltanschauung that fits this character structure prevent peasants and *petits
bourgeois* from seeing that they are colluding in their own exploitation.
Marx's notion of "false consciousness" is thus given a psychodynamic
explanation.

Reich's analysis of the characteristics of German families that made the
nation submit to Hitler is an intriguing hypothesis; but he left it merely
as an hypothesis, without attempting any historical investigation to see
whether it could be confirmed. Furthermore, even in *The Mass Psychology
of Fascism* it plays a relatively insignificant role, for Reich quickly moved
to a treatment of fascism so broad-scaled and abstract as to empty it of any
specific historical content.[47]

In *Studien über Autorität und Familie* (1936), by members of the
Frankfurt Institute, understanding the family was conceived as the essential
psychoanalytic supplement to Marxism, for, again, it was the socializing
agency which inculcated the personality traits necessary to maintain oppressive social relationships. Exactly how this was accomplished, however, was
left somewhat uncertain; paternal authority was the principal villain, and
control of property the main mechanism, but there was comparatively little
effort to specify how this differed among social classes, and still less to
trace the historical development of these family patterns. Once they had

emigrated to New York, where they became the nucleus of the New School for Social Research, Theodor Adorno and Max Horkheimer collaborated in a massive study of *The Authoritarian Personality* (New York, 1947); but this survey, focused specifically on what personality types were likely to be anti-Semitic, was based on questionnaires administered by American social psychologists and some depth interviews. It had no historical scope and few, if any, traces of the Marxism which had been dominant in the Institut für Sozialforschung. Meanwhile the member of the Frankfurt Institute who was most successful in producing a philosophical treatment of Freud and Marx, Herbert Marcuse, did so with scarcely a mention of the role of the family.[48]

In sum, then, a Freudian history of the family remains an unfulfilled research program. It is generally recognized that Freud mistook the psychological products of middle-class Viennese families at the turn of the twentieth century for universals of the human species; but it has been much more difficult to specify what sort of children's psyches would be produced in an aristocratic family of the seventeenth century, where children might not see their parents for days at a time, or in a peasant family scarcely distinguishable from the village in which it lived. Nor do we have any convincing analysis of the effects in depth psychology of the transitions produced when a peasant family moves to the city and factory work replaces the old domestic economy. Some historians, as we have seen, have pronounced these problems insoluble, because the appropriate evidence has disappeared; but psychoanalytically trained historians, like Freud himself, see evidence in what others dismiss as trifles. They also seize upon single utterances or isolated but symptomatic actions as clues to the underlying psychic structure, whereas most historians tend to weigh up the total record of actions and speech, having recourse to psychological explanations only when common sense suggests that the agent was obviously irrational.[49] Because Freudian theories most obviously fit modern bourgeois families, most psychohistorians have worked only on these. It remains to be seen whether if there were many classicist, medievalist, or early modern psychohistorians, they would be able to throw equivalent light on character structures in those periods. So far, however, most psychohistorical interest, at any period, has fallen on individual character (Erik Erikson's studies of Luther and Gandhi being only the best-known examples); there has been much less effort to explicate the typical psychological configurations of particular family types, much less any theory, no matter how tentative, of how these psychological configurations are rooted in the social structure. Of course the even more ambitious project of accounting for the transition between one sort of family and its historical successors has hardly been attempted.

Almost all variants of contemporary Marxism understand that the crude model which relegates ideas and sentiments to a "superstructure" responding more or less automatically to changes in the forces and relations of production must either be abandoned or enriched. As Freud himself noted, "materialistic views of history sin in underestimating" the fact that "a child's super-ego is in fact constructed on the model not of its parents but of its parents' super-ego." Thus although it is "true" that "human 'ideologies' are nothing other than the product and superstructure of their contemporary economic conditions," this is not the whole truth, since the super-ego, in rooting and passing on tradition, guarantees that "mankind never lives entirely in the present."[50] The notorious problem in Marxist interpretation of contemporary history, failure of the socialist revolution to occur in the most developed countries, can be addressed by the invocation of Freudian theories which give a more plausible account of "false consciousness" – but it can also be addressed through Lenin's theory of imperialism as the highest stage of capitalism. For the Marxist historian of the family, of course, there is much more, potentially, to be learned from Freud than from Lenin; but the Freudian historian of the family may well have even more to learn from Marx.

But why should the historian of the family learn from either Freud or Marx? One-sided, speculative, often only loosely connected, if at all, with the results of contemporary research, such grand theories may be entirely premature, or objectionable in principle. Since modernization theory has been to some degree discredited and its ideological character exposed, most historians of the family are prepared to be historians only of family life – that is, to accept that there is no perdurable human institution called "*the* family" which could appropriately serve as the central subject of any master historical narrative. Instead there were all kinds of families, defined quite variously in different societies, assigned a wide variety of functions, and treated in some as extremely important, in others not. As Mark Poster put it in his prescription for historians of the family:

> the history of the family is discontinuous, involving several distinct family structures, each with its own emotional pattern, and . . . these family structures cannot be correlated, in their development, with any single variable, such as modernization, industrialization, patriarchy, capitalism, urbanism or empathy.[51]

Furthermore, empirical research is very far from discovering any reason internal to family life why one form of family should be succeeded by another, or even if there is any typical sequence. (For example, it appears that among those typical modern workers, English factory hands, extended families were more common than in the small farms and villages from which these people had emigrated to the industrial cities; and they did not retreat into the sort of private family life supposedly created by industrial capitalism.)[52] And as if historians needed further encouragement to revel in particularity and detail, the post-modern mood assures them of the inscrutability and undecidability of the social text.

Against this position no conclusive argument is possible. One way of evaluating theories is to test them against evidence, and propose other, better theories; but no amount of evidence will convince someone who believes that there can be no theory explaining it. Indeed, no theory will explain every particularity of the evidence; that is not what theories are for. But there is reason to believe that even the most dogged empiricist carries around a rag-bag of (often competing and even incoherent) theories. In the classic words of Hegel:

> Even the ordinary, the "impartial" historiographer, who believes and professes that he maintains a simply receptive attitude; surrendering himself only to the data supplied him – is by no means passive as regards the exercise of his thinking powers. He brings his categories with him, and sees the phenomena presented to his mental vision, exclusively through these media. And, especially in all that pretends to the name of science, it is indispensable that Reason should not sleep – that reflection should be in full play. To him who looks upon the world rationally, the world in its turn presents a rational aspect.[53]

The issue, then, is *what sort* of theory. And here, surely, the view that social institutions, including the family, form some sort of coherent and intelligible complex and that human history as a whole makes some kind of sense cannot be ruled out *a priori*. It is a presupposition; but so is the opposite view. Furthermore, the more fragmentary the theories which historians use, the more they risk falling into "a historical practice which, however far removed from traditional canons, confines itself to specialist areas, partial problems, and tentative technical innovations, and thereby remains loyal in fact to the least creative kind of empiricism."[54]

Plenty of examples of this sort of historical practice can be found in the historiography of the family. But, as we have seen, modernization theory and the theory of demographic transition have informed – not always consciously – much of the work which has been done in the field.

And, if one judges by counting up how many "facts" that have turned up in the researches of historians of family life can be explained, modernization theory probably leads the field. But these "facts" are never completely theory-free, and the comparative success of modernization theory can be explained by the fact that more historians have wanted to find the facts that fit that paradigm, and so have been unusually alert to them. An historian who believes that wealth creation is the primary task of an economic system and that the family is a harmonious refuge in a competitive economic system will probably be impressed by the accomplishments of capitalism, and predisposed to the argument that the worldwide spread of capitalism will entail the worldwide spread of the small nuclear family, just as modernization theory predicts. Those who place a higher value on more equitable wealth distribution and see the family, like the capitalist economic system, as an arena of conflicting forces, will likely be drawn to Freudian and Marxian approaches. Despite the inability of scholars thus far to bring the two together in an illuminating way for the history of the family, the juxtaposition of Freud and Marx does give some promise of a convincing linkage between psychological and economic configurations, just as the juxtaposition of Marx and Malthus has made some advances in linking stages of economic history and family history. Thus the effort to follow up these lines of inquiry is not simply a matter of "looking upon the world rationally"; there is an irreducible element of will or desire. This does not mean that the historian is excused from the task of archival research and responsible writing; but the deepest theoretical commitments, as Hayden White has observed, are at bottom moral.[55] It is these which may, even in the world of late communism, invite the historian to accept the challenge Gayle Rubin has thrown out.

Notes

1. Clara Zetkin, "My Recollections of Lenin," in *The Emancipation of Women from the Writings of V. I. Lenin* (New York, 1934), 103.
2. "The Traffic in Women," in *Toward an Anthropology of Women*, ed. Rayna R. Reiter (New York, 1975), 210.
3. Two modern paper-back editions of the English translation by Alec West, *The Origin of the Family, Private Property, and the State*, appeared in 1972 from two New York publishing houses espousing different flavors of Marxism: one from Pathfinder Press with an introduction by Evelyn Reed and the other from International Publishers with a (considerably superior) introduction by Eleanor Burke Leacock.

4. See *The Ethnographic Notebooks of Karl Marx*, ed. Lawrence Krader (Assen, 1972).

5. *Woman Under Socialism*, trans. Daniel DeLeon (rpt. New York, 1971).

6. "My Recollections of Lenin," 101.

7. *The Family in Imperial Russia*, ed. David Ransel (Urbana, 1978), 5. This collection contains a valuable annotated bibliography which gives a good idea of the work Soviet and western scholars have done on Russian family life.

8. As does M. Ia. Fenomenov in *Sovremennaia derevnia*, 3 vols (Leningrad, 1925). I do not read Russian, and am heavily dependent on Peter Czap of Amherst College and David Ransel of Indiana University for information on Soviet historiography of the family. Fenomenov's book is cited in Czap's article "'A large family: the peasant's greatest wealth': Serf Households in Mishino, Russia, 1814–1858," in *Family Forms in Historic Europe*, ed. Richard Wall, with Jean Robin and Peter Laslett (Cambridge, 1983), 106 n.9.

9. Particularly important are Czap, Ransel, and Andrejs Plakans, although Plakans has worked primarily with non-Russian peoples in the Baltic provinces. Estonian historians have recently begun an active research program on their own rich sources. See for example Heldur Palli, "Estonian Households in the Seventeenth and Eighteenth Centuries," in *Family Forms in Historic Europe*, 207–16, and his *Estesvennoe dvizhenie selskogo naseleniia estonii 1650–1799* [*Natural Increase of the Rural Population of Estonia 1650–1799*] (Talinn, 1980). There is however no indication of any discernible Marxist influence.   The philosopher I. S. Kon has recently published *Rebenok i obshchestro* [*Child and Society*] (Moscow, 1988), which is a review of Western works on the history of childhood. It has very little on Russia itself, but does introduce western historiography to Russian scholars. A sign that Russian historians are turning to this field is a candidate dissertation at the Institute of History of the Academy of Sciences, Leningrad, in 1989: *Reviskie skazki kak istochnik no sotsial'no-demografischeskoi istorii. Opyt obrabotki na EVM reviskikh skazok moskovskogo kupechestra XVIII–pervaia polovina XIX v*, by Natalia Leonidovna Iurchenko. This is an attempt at computer-assisted analysis of soul tax lists for the Moscow merchant class in the eighteenth and first half of the nineteenth century. (I particularly thank David Ransel for supplying this information.)

10. See, for example, Peter Laslett, "Age at Menarche in Europe since the Eighteenth Century," *Journal of Interdisciplinary History* 2 (1971–72):221–36; E. A. Hammel, "The *Zadruga* as Process," in *Household and Family in Past Time*, ed. Peter Laslett and Richard Wall (Cambridge, 1972), 335–74.

11. Among the contributors to *Family Forms in Historic Europe* were Jacek Kochanowicz, "The Peasant Family as an Economic Unit in

the Polish Feudal Economy of the Eighteenth Century" (153–66), and
Rudolf Andorka and Tamás Faragó, "Pre-industrial Household Structure in Hungary" (281–309). In both countries serious and extensive
work in historical demography has been going on at least since the
mid-1960s.

12. Robert McC. Netting, Richard R. Wilk, and Eric J. Arnould, "Introduction," *Households: Comparative and Historical Studies of the Domestic
Group* (Berkeley, 1984), xviii.

13. Edited by Gerald Soliday, Tamara K. Hareven, Richard T. Vann, and
Robert Wheaton (Millwood, NY, 1980). At a conservative estimate,
three-quarters of the scholarship on the history of the family has been
produced since 1970. Of course, this fertility must be seen in the
context of the increasing numbers of historians, sociologists, etc., at
risk of producing such scholarship.

14. In fact, Louis Henry found some of the historical populations he studied
to be "pre-Malthusian" rather than "non-Malthusian" – that is to say,
they had customs like prolonged breast feeding of infants or taboos on
intercourse during lactation which, although not consciously intended
to reduce fertility, did have that effect: "La Fécondité des mariages au
Japon," *Population* 8 (1953):711–30.

15. Both approaches can conveniently be studied in *An Introduction to
English Historical Demography*, ed. E. A. Wrigley (London, 1966).

16. The masterpiece of this genre is E. A. Wrigley and R. S. Schofield,
The Population History of England 1541–1871: A Reconstruction
(Cambridge, MA, 1981).

17. David Riesman, with Reuel Denney and Nathan Glazer, *The Lonely
Crowd: A Study of the Changing American Character* (New Haven,
1950).

18. This is a very schematic and doubtless oversimplified representation of
the position of Talcott Parsons; see Parsons and Robert Bales, *Family,
Socialization and Interaction Process* (Glencoe, IL, 1960).

19. See Peter Laslett, *The World We Have Lost* (London, 1965), especially
ch. 2.

20. The extraordinary laboriousness of family limitation may account for
this. A regional study which does exploit a wide variety of sources,
Albion Urdank's *Religion and Society in a Cotswold Vale* (Berkeley,
1990) did not make any effort at family reconstitution. An interesting
study could be made of the effects on American historiography of
the timing of expiration of graduate school fellowships and tenure
decisions.

21. E. A. Hammel and Peter Laslett, "Comparing Household Structure
over Time and between Cultures," *Comparative Studies in Society and
History* 16 (1974):73–109.

22. Michael Mitterauer and Reinhard Sieder, *The European Family:
Patriarchy to Partnership from the Middle Ages to the Present*
(Oxford, 1982), 27; this is a translation by Karla Osterveen and

Manfred Hörzinger of a revised version of *Vom Patriarchat zur Partnerschaft: Zum Strukturwandel der Familie* (Munich, 1977).

23. E. A. Hammel, "On the *** of Studying Household Form and Function," in *Households*, ed. Netting, Wilk, and Arnould, 31.

24. From a series of simulations based on English household listings and demographic rates, Hammel suggests that a change in the rules for household formation would indeed make the largest difference in the types that show up in a local census, followed by random demographic variations, with changes in basic demographic behavior such as nuptiality and mortality accounting for the least variation (40).

25. Linda Pollock, *Forgotten Children: Parent-Child Relations from 1500 to 1900* (Cambridge, 1983).

26. Lloyd deMause, "The Evolution of Childhood," in *The History of Childhood*, ed. Lloyd deMause (New York, 1974), 51–54.

27. This happened to *Centuries of Childhood* (see Richard T. Vann, "The Youth of *Centuries of Childhood*," *History and Theory* 21 [1982]:279–97), and also to DeMause's *The History of Childhood*.

28. For example, Michael Anderson, noting that "de Mause's introduction shows the limitations [of psychohistory] and one or two papers some strengths," says of psychohistory that it has already run into insoluble problems of evidence and "involved its practitioners in so much anachronistic judgement and blatant disregard for many of the basic principles of historical scholarship" that he did not think it worth detailed consideration: *Approaches to the History of the Western Family 1500–1914* (London, 1980), 90–91, 15.

29. David Hunt, *Parents and Children in History: The Psychology of Family Life in Early Modern France* (New York, 1970); Adrian Wilson, "The Infancy of the History of Childhood: An Appraisal of Philippe Ariès," *History and Theory* 19 (1980):132–53.

30. Here I follow Martha C. Howell, "Marriage, Property, and Patriarchy: Recent Contributions to a Literature," *Feminist Studies* 13 (1987):204.

31. Especially *Reproducing Families: The Political Economy of English Population History* (Cambridge, 1987) and a volume which he edited, *Proletarianization and Family History* (Orlando, 1984).

32. *Reproducing Families*, 95.

33. Specifically, for being "less concerned with demonstrating the many complexities of historical reality than they are with establishing the correctness of their own particular versions of Marxist truth": R. B. Outhwaite, "Keeping it in the Family," *Historical Journal* 29 (1986):467.

34. For a good sampling of these, see *The State of Population Theory: Forward from Malthus*, ed. David Coleman and Roger Schofield (Oxford, 1986).

35. *Reproducing Families*, 5.

36. Charles Tilly, "Demographic Origins of the European Proletariat," in *Proletarianization and Family History*, 53.

37. *Reproducing Families*, 94–95.
38. "Subsistence Production and Extended Reproduction," in *Of Marriage and the Market: Women's Subordination Internationally and its Lessons*, ed. Kate Young, Carol Wolkowitz, and Roslyn McCullagh, 2nd edn (London, 1981), 48.
39. *The Origin of the Family, Private Property, and the State* (London, 1972), 137.
40. Bennholdt-Thomsen reminds us that "worldwide there are more unpaid subsistence producers than wage workers" even though "there is no country today where wage work has not become the dominant social relation, even in those cases where it does not prevail quantitatively" (49).
41. *Haven in a Heartless World: The Family Besieged* (New York, 1977), 150.
42. *The Freudian Left* (New York, 1969), 127.
43. On these writers see Robinson, *Freudian Left*, and Mark Poster, *Critical Theory of the Family* (New York, 1978), ch. 2.
44. Robinson, 40–52, has a good account of these.
45. Poster, 46–52. Reich's speculative history of the origin of sexual repression is Part I of his *Der Einbruch der Sexualmoral* (1932), trans. anon. as *The Invasion of Compulsory Sex-Morality* (New York, 1971). Unlike Herbert Marcuse and N. O. Brown, Reich was intolerant of homosexuality and the so-called sexual perversions. These, along with pornography and dirty jokes, would presumably wither away once the root of sexual repression has been extirpated.
46. Robinson, 47–48. Reich's *Die Massenpsychologie des Faschismus* (Copenhagen, 1933) was originally translated into English in 1946. A new translation by Vincent Carfagno was published as *The Mass Psychology of Fascism* (New York, 1970).
47. "[M]y medical experiences with men and women of various classes, races, nations, religious beliefs, etc., taught me that 'fascism' is only the organized political expression of the structure of the average man's character, a structure that is confined neither to certain races or nations nor to certain parties, but is general and international": *Mass Psychology of Fascism*, xiii.
48. *Eros and Civilization* (Boston, 1955).
49. See Gerald Izenberg, "Psychohistory and Intellectual History," *History and Theory* 14 (1975):139–55.
50. *New Introductory Lectures on Psychoanalysis*, trans. John Strachey (New York, 1964), 67. It might be noted that Strachey was for a time a Marxist; see his introduction to *Marxism and Psycho-Analysis* by Reuben Osborn [pseudonym of Reuben Osbert] (London, 1965), vii–xvi.
51. *Critical Theory of the Family*, xvii.
52. On this see Michael Anderson, *Family Structure in Nineteenth Century Lancashire* (Cambridge, 1971), and Levine, *Reproducing Families*.

Eli Zaretsky argues that "the rise of industrial capitalism, while destroying the traditional form of family life, gave rise to a new search for personal identity which takes place outside the division of labour. In a phrase: proletarianization gave rise to subjectivity": *Capitalism, the Family, & Personal Life* (London, 1976), 9–10. Little evidence is produced in support of this claim. Levine's reading of nineteenth-century working-class autobiographies suggests that, on the contrary, working-class life was built on "a communalism in which mutual-aid complemented self-help" (200).

53.   G. W. F. Hegel, *The Philosophy of History*, trans. J. Sibree (New York, 1956), 11.

54.   Pierre Vilar, "Marxist History, a History in the Making: Towards a Dialogue with Althusser," *New Left Review* 80 (1973):101.

55.   "It is fruitless, then . . . to try to arbitrate among contending conceptions of the nature of the historical process on cognitive grounds which purport to be value-neutral in essence, as both Marxist and non-Marxist social theorists attempt to do. The best reasons for being a Marxist are moral ones, just as the best reasons for being a Liberal, Conservative, or Anarchist are moral ones": *Metahistory: The Historical Imagination in Nineteenth- Century Europe* (Baltimore, 1973), 284.

9 "They Were Not Quite Like Us": The Presumption of Qualitative Difference in Historical Writing"

Eero Loone

I

The epistemology of history has been ridden by *one-property-essentialism*. Many philosophers and some historians have tried to reduce historical writing to one and only one trait that has been treated both as the signifier of the fundamental difference between history and all other forms of inquiry, and as the essential mechanism generating all epistemologically interesting properties and structures of historical writing (or historical knowledge). Historical inquiry has been essentially reduced by past philosophers to *Verstehen*, or to ideographic treatment of valued individuals (persons or states-of-affairs), or to re-enactment. The numbers of writers who have been opposed to simplistic reductionism, either explicitly or implicitly, have been few.[1]

This strategy has been effective in discovering some traits present in actual historical writings of the past two centuries. Nevertheless, as a strategy, it is insufficient and can degenerate into imposing Stalinist, dogmatic, pre-set limitations on a free inquiry. First, the elucidation of a specific trait present in historical writings does not provide a necessarily exhaustive network of concepts for analyses of historical thought. To compare history and, for example, biology, one needs to discover both the common traits and the traits that belong to each discipline alone. To talk only of the specific and not to discuss the common is to commit Hegel's conceptual sin of historical and non-historical nations. Moreover, it is quite possible that there is more than one specific trait or property. It is also possible that there exists a set of traits or properties which is specific to history, while each element of that set can be found in some other set of traits which is representation of some other discipline. And if the fabric of historical inquiry is woven from a multiplicity of threads, then one-property-essentialism will be patently wrong. Of course, it might be quite wrong in physics, too.

The currently fashionable one-property-reductionism is the *rhetorical reductionism* which assumes that history is a mode of rhetoric. For example, it looks at a narrative as essentially a rhetorical device. Thus, history is classified as a mode of fiction. To avoid succumbing to well-advertised fashions, one has to be aware that it is possible to bring extremely serious charges against rhetorical reductionism. Its anti-realism is introduced implicitly. At best, realism is dismissed with a few phrases. It provides implicit support for a research program that is not able to differentiate rhetoric from logic or from cognitive content. This implies a preemptive dismissal of inquiries about logic and cognitive systems of historical writings.

Certainly, historical writing is an exercise in communication. The rhetoric of history is a legitimate area of study. But is history only communicative rhetoric, a form of advertising without any reference to what is advertised? Many historians have viewed and are still viewing their discipline primarily as a cognitive enterprise. This constituent part of history must not get lost in implicit reductionism. Moreover, the reasons for anti-realism as it is currently applied to history are not specific for history. They are valid for any kind of anti-realism. The assumption is not that historical knowledge is impossible but that any knowledge is impossible. This equates to solipsism and assumes away everything outside the "I" (including limbs, heart, stomach, meals, and, of course, books). Solipsism might be right but, granted its assumptions, it would be wrong to set up a discourse about any discourse involving other human beings, or about any discourse written down in books. There would be no books, no other humans. Communication would be a meaningless enterprise or just a play within my mind.

Therefore, it is reasonable to assume within the limits of this essay that we can tell armies from windmills, people from crossbows, peasants from lords. I do also assume that, if we can tell our friends from electronic typewriters in the present, then we can also discover whether an entity in the past was our friend or an electronic typewriter, given that evidence is available and that there are methods of discovery accepted by professional historians. If one accepts any possibility of knowing what happened in the past, then *Quellenkritik* has been available since the beginning of the nineteenth century as a method of discovery and confirmation.

Given that one-property-essentialism is probably wrong, there arises a difference between a book and a paper or an article. In a book the author can discuss many threads and how they are woven into a fabric. In a paper, it might be good strategy to confine oneself to a discussion of one trait, without asking or answering questions about whether that trait is a uniquely essential or just a secondary one and which are its relationships to other traits in a pattern. The following is just a discussion of one such trait that I believe to be present in many historical writings.[2] The idea itself has been explicitly suggested by M. M. Postan.[3]

There is one more preliminary. This is an essay in Collingwoodian analysis. R. G. Collingwood did not confine himself to discussing merely the language (or even just the words of the language) of historical writing. He was interested in analyzing the thoughts that are conveyed and formulated by the language, and he wanted to discover something about these thoughts and the kind of reality they referred to. These forms of thought might not have had appropriate labels fixed to them within the mode of thinking that was the subject of his inquiry. His philosophy was not reduced to technical puzzles and the labeling could be done by the philosopher. At the same time, it did not avoid the increase in the precision of argumentation that has been an important trait of English-language philosophic writing as developed after his death under Wittgensteinian or positivistic auspices. The latter change has not been sufficiently understood by, and incorporated into, European continental philosophies.

II

Let us now consider some examples of conceptualizations in historical thought.

(a) Weather was a matter of grave concern in the everyday life of England in the seventeenth and early-eighteenth centuries. London was several times half-starved when ships bearing essential commodities failed to arrive because the wind blew persistently from the wrong quarter. Industrial activity had to be fitted in between the seasonal peaks of agricultural activities.[4] Although the weather still provides a useful neutral starting point for conversation in contemporary Britain, its status as a determining factor of short-term economic activities has certainly changed.

(b) Medieval knights or rulers in ancient Mesopotamia were quite proud of the number of human beings they had killed. Most Western Europeans at the end of the twentieth century do not ordinarily share that feeling and do not ordinarily consider somebody great because of the great number of their enemies they have killed.

(c) Accumulation of wealth did not make much sense to hunter-gatherers (and all human were once hunter-gatherers). They had to carry their wealth on them. It consisted of actual things. There was no money and there were no credit cards. In late-twentieth-century, free-market economies, it certainly makes sense to be wealthy and to go on accumulating wealth (at least from an individual's viewpoint).

(d) Between 1900 and 1910, the GNP of a country X grew by 4.9 percent.

(e) The median noon temperature at B was 1.9 degrees centigrade in January 1900, and 1.8 degrees centigrade in January 1901.

What the examples (a) through (e) have in common is that they deal with a trait or property or a state-of-affairs compared over time. In all cases, the comparison involves making distinctions. The differences fall into two kinds. In cases (a) through (c), the differences are somehow essential, qualitative, while in cases (d) and (e) they are quantitative, different values of the same variables. I am not suggesting that the cases referred to in (d) and (e) cannot be presented as cases of essential differences in at least one of the possible worlds, but they are not presented in that way in my examples.

Historians have to presume that past ways and rules of behavior, past sets of values, past economic, governmental, and other societal institutions, etc., were sometimes essentially or qualitatively different from those that are contemporary to an historian. It is possible to eliminate the reference to the historian's own time. The statement is then transformed into the following: Historians have to presume that there have sometimes been qualitative differences between ways and rules of behavior, sets of values, economic, governmental, and other societal institutions or entities located at different points or intervals of the time-dimension. The principle here is named the *Presumption of Qualitative Difference* (PQD, for short).

I have retained the traditional and somewhat old-fashioned philosophic concept of *quality* and *quantity* (or qualitative and quantitative differences) in the formulation of the presumption that is the object of this study. They seem useful labels. The terms are not meant to convey the impression that the author is an Hegelian or an Aristotelian or a dogmatic *diamatchik*. He belongs to none of these -isms. Certainly, human conceptual networks evolve and develop over time. Some notions are better to be discarded. But some parts of the older networks can be meaningfully retained and incorporated into later networks of concepts to preserve enough family resemblances to justify the retention of this or that older word.

Is the mode of knowledge and understanding that involves the PQD projectable into the future, for example, to make predictions? One has to presume that there might be qualitative differences between present and future happenings or institutions. It is trivial to say that nothing is eternal or, at least, that determinate entities (things, systems, etc.) are not eternal. But some systems and types of systems preserve essential qualitative unity while changing quantitatively over time. Thus, one kind of prediction is constituted by predictions within a given system, as often made in the natural sciences. A second kind of prediction deals with the breaking points of a system. It uses knowledge of a system to make assertions about a catastrophe within that system, if its variables assume certain values or if some entities or relations are removed from the system or added to it. Implicit in predictions about a catastrophe is a claim that some other system or entity will displace the existing one. A third kind of prediction tries to describe the entity that emerges after the "catastrophe." The second and the third kind of prediction involves the PQD; the first one deals with "quantitative" differences.[5]

Whenever historians write about periods, they imply qualitative differences. The name of the period is a means of elucidating some specific trait making that entity under study different from other entities. The comparison becomes implicit. Sometimes historians point at the specific traits at the beginnings of their studies. C. F. Richmond started a study on the history of the English Navy in the fifteenth century by pointing out that in that century, no country in Europe had either the resources or the motive to achieve naval superiority for much longer than a single summer. Moreover, superiority at sea was not determined by fighting as much as it fell to the first comer.[6] These statements are forceful enough to contain an implicit reference to later situations quite different from what obtained in the fifteenth century.

Sometimes it is the change itself that is studied. An account of a change involves references to preceding states and to the state of affairs that arises out of the change. Geoffrey Elton's study of the administrative change in the reign of Henry VIII provides an excellent example of this type of involvement of the PQD.[7]

The PQD is involved in tracing the emergence of some trait or societal system. Any statement about a trait or an entity being a new one implies a statement that there were systems without that property or without that particular entity (or type of entities). Sometimes the tracing might involve a relatively simple entity. For example, a study of enclosures might build up a series of statements about the proportion of arable land (or total land) enclosed at a particular date, like the following imaginary data:

1520 – 2% enclosed
1650 – 20% enclosed
1780 – 87% enclosed

Obviously, the structures of land-use in the period 1520 through 1780 in that country were qualitatively different.

Tracing the rise of a system is more difficult. It involves finding out when the component parts and relations came into existence. The emerging picture can be described like this (the letters stand for parts or relations, the time flows from bottom upwards):

abcdef
ab def
ab ef
a   ef
    e

If we mention the units only when they come into existence, then we can construct two narratives (timeflow is from left to right): eafbdc or efabdc. Tracing the rise of a system is a proper historical activity. For example, an historian might be interested in tracing how the economic and political institutions of England at the beginning of the eleventh century had come into existence. Any problem about the origins of a societal system involves tracing.[8]

Parts of historical writing that involve the PQD provide *relational knowledge*. In that kind of knowledge, a useful distinction can be made between the *core area* and the *referential area*. The core area is the one that is actually mapped by the historian. The referential area is deemed to be different from the core area; it is not a central object of study. Sometimes references are made to the time-grid (the fifteenth century, the third millennium B.C.). The time assumed is probably Newtonian. It is not an object of study in history; it is a grid locating humans and their societies. References to time-intervals are convenient shorthands. Historians usually agree about much that went on within a given time-interval, although they still might disagree about some essentials of the unit under study. Reference to the time-interval delineates the unit under study and makes communication between historians possible by means of separating references from understanding and description.

Relational knowledge can be *contrastive* ("We and They," "Present and Past"). Contrastive reference is often implied. With the changes in the reference area, history comes to be re-written. The "Present" of early-nineteenth-century United States was somewhat different from the present of late-nineteenth-century or of late-twentieth-century United States of America. This does not mean a loss of objectivity. The core area remains the same. What is studied is its differences with another reference area.

Relational knowledge can be *sequential*. The reference area in sequential history either immediately precedes or immediately follows the core area on the time-grid. Elton studied Tudor administration but he did this with reference to a preceding area and a later area. Marxism sets up a system of sequentially ordered societal types. Thus, discovery and discussion of the sequences form an important part of the fabric of historical thinking. Of course, the past cannot be reduced to the differences. There were similarities as well as differences between core areas and reference areas. Similarities are usually assumed if the reference area is contemporary to the historian. In cases of sequential reference, it is sometimes better to state them explicitly. This is strongly recommended for inquiries dealing with contested separation of phenomena into differing entities.

The distinction between a core area and a reference area make sense for certain short sequences. A minimal sequence is a sequence of two entities, and one of them can be chosen to be a core area. In a three-entity linear sequence, the middle entity provides the core area. In some other sequences, this pair of concepts is no longer applicable. Given, for example, a seven-entity nonlinear sequence, minimal comparative descriptions have to deal with all pairs of entities that stand in immediate evolutionary relations between them. What is studied in this case are the differences within the sequential entity and not just its parts.

The historians in nineteenth-century Europe developed a special language, the *Historismus-language*, which implicitly involves the PQD. The Historismus-language uses for its technical terms words from the language of the society under study. Historians write about *polis, manor, smerd, beneficium, pronia*. Historismus-language is useful as a means of naming past entities that exist no more in the historian's present. With the help of Historismus-language it is possible to refer to imperfectly known entities and, therefore, to build up discourse about these objects while avoiding the trap of a possible unwarranted identification of these past entities with some present entities. A treatise about the ideal government for a *polis* is not necessarily a treatise about the ideal government for the *barbarians* (maybe the barbarians could never hope to have an ideal government).

But a treatise about the government of a *polis* is not a treatise about any kind of government. Whether the knowledge gained in the study of the government of a *polis* is exhaustive (as knowledge about any kind of government) is something that can only be determined *a posteriori*. Moreover, the Historismus-language precludes the inadvertent transference of historian's own value judgments to the persons and societies within the core area of his study. This is different from the deliberate and explicit introduction of values by historians. I am not advancing the claim that the Historismus-language is a solution to all ills of historical writing. It can become very dangerous because of its implicitness. Its use can preclude explicit comparisons and replace proofs with intuitions. But it is certainly a trait of a level of historical knowledge. Troubles start to emerge if it is accepted as the only language of historical thought.

III

Which kinds of conceptual means are available to thinking and writing about differences between societal entities or situations? Traditionally, historians have relied on an intuitive understanding of separateness and sequential interrelationships. Nineteenth-century *Verstehen*-techniques provided the means, coupled either with *Historismus-language labeling* of entities or with *Historian-labeling* (i.e., different labels attached to different entities were made from the words that were either invented by the historian or drawn by him from the ordinary vocabulary contemporary to him). The rhetoric of history had its purpose in communicating this understanding and, obviously, *Verstehen*-techniques are amenable for providing good rhetoric. A certain core-content of understanding can be expressed by varied rhetorical devices and texts; on the other hand, the discovery that there is a rhetoric of history cannot be used to prove that historical writing can be reduced to its rhetoric.

Verstehen-type techniques also provide good substitutes for ostensive definitions and identifications. Nobody in 1990 A.D. can be present at a meeting of the Roman Senate and describe his impressions of that meeting. Nobody can point a hand toward a person and say: "This is Ivan the Terrible, ruler of Russia." It is not easy, in any case, actually to touch an entity like the "state" or the "police" with one's hand and name it, although it is possible to point at individual civil servants or police officers. Historismus-language provides historians with a source of ready-made names for various entities that had existed before historians started writing about these entities. They do not have to invent a primary language.

The articulation of concepts used in modern social sciences to account for human behavior and human societies is somewhat different from the methods available with the help of the Historismus-language. These concepts (and words) are introduced by an author to be his notions and names for types of entities. They are introduced *a priori*, before any token of that particular kind has been identified. Indeed, investigation might lead social scientists to a conclusion that some notions were empty, there having been no token of that particular kind. Possible entities are not always actual entities. Social science terms can be arbitrary inventions. Even if they are derived from an ordinary language, they are expressions of, or otherwise restrictions on, the family of the ordinary, everyday meanings of the word that is transformed into a term (and a concept). In some social sciences (for example, economics), the use of concepts is rather similar to that of the natural sciences.

Historians have been wary of *a priori* notions but there is no reason to be afraid of inventing concepts before the start of some particular inquiry. Everyday concepts are always *a priori* relative to the assertions formulated with their help. Social science-type concepts are only relatively *a priori*; they are not Kantian forms of all thought. If the utility and applicability of the concepts that have been introduced as relatively *a priori* are to be determined in particular cases to be, in fact, *a posteriori*, then the method of so introducing concepts *a priori* to an investigation is epistemologically sound. To find out whether there was a war, we need a concept of war, rules of evidence, rules of identification, and evidence itself. To find out whether the Ruritanian society was a male-dominated society, we need a concept of domination (and maleness, and society). To find out whether there has been at least one society belonging to the Asiatic Mode of Production, we need a concept of a mode of production along with a concept of the Asiatic Mode of Production.

There are certain logical forms appropriate to any investigation which involves the PQD and employs social science-type concepts. First, a minimal language L is necessary. The latter has to include in its vocabulary at least two terms referring to different "real" entities. Second, there is an underlying question for any research program within this type of inquiry. This is the identification problem.

Let us have a language L that includes in its vocabulary social science-type concepts "A", "B", "C", "D" . . . These concepts refer to kinds or sets of entities (the distinction between kinds and sets is unimportant here). They are used as labels for any token of the appropriate kind (any element or part of the appropriate set). Let **a, b, c, d** . . . stand for some entities and let → denote a relation "is labeled by." The basic identification problem, then, has the form:

$$\textit{Either } \mathbf{a} \rightarrow \textbf{"A" } \textit{or } \mathbf{a} \rightarrow \textbf{"B"?} \qquad (1)$$

(Read: Is entity **a** labeled by type concept **"A"** or by **"B"**?)

Let **A, B, C, D** . . . stand for sets or kinds labeled by **"A", "B", "C", "D"** . . . Then (1) can be transformed into:

$$\textit{Either } \mathbf{a} \in \mathbf{A} \textit{ or } \mathbf{a} \in \mathbf{B?} \qquad (2)$$

(Read: Is entity **a** member of a kind **A** or a kind **B**?). Or into:

$$\textit{Either } \mathbf{a} \subset \mathbf{A} \textit{ or } \mathbf{a} \subset \mathbf{B?} \qquad (3)$$

(Read: Is entity **a** part of a set **A** or a set **B**?) The entity **a** can be designated with the help of the Historismus-language, or by extensive description without any labeling at all, or by setting up boundaries to delimit it from any relevant non-**a**, or by any other means.

Let us consider an example. The agrarian structures in Eastern Europe during the eighteenth century were based on peasant serfdom. In some cases (e.g., in Estonian) the proper Historismus-language word even translates as "real slavery" ("pärisorjus"). The peasants could be sold and bought, although there were some restrictions on the sale of these not-quite-human beings. For an historian using Marxist language, the problem of identification in this case is:

> Did eighteenth-century Eastern Europe have a slave or a feudal
> mode of production? (E1)

Were we to restrict the use of the word "feudal" for a specific type of political hierarchy, it would be possible to rephrase (E1) as:

> Did eighteenth-century Eastern Europe have a slave or a
> seigniorial economy? (E2)

Let **L** be a language with a social science vocabulary $\mathbf{V_L}$. The language **L** is said to be *adequate* if:

> (D1) any entity in the reference area can be labeled by a referring
> term from $\mathbf{V_L}$.

The reference area is assumed not to contain just anything within some spatio-temporal boundaries, but to be a particular slice of the spatio-temporal segment under investigation (politics, family, etc.). The concepts of natural kinds and natural differences between entities make empirical sense, given this slice.

The language **L** is said to be *just adequate*:

> (D2) 1) if (D1), and
> 2) if any referring term from V_L refers to at least one entity within the reference area.

The language **L** is said to be *loosely adequate*:

> (D3) 1) if it is adequate, and
> 2) if it includes social science-type referring terms that have no relevance to the reference area.

The language **L** is said to be *vacuous*:

> (D4) if no entity in its reference area can be labeled by a referring term from V_L.

The language **L** is said to be *inadequate*:

> (D5) if some entities from its reference area cannot be labeled with the V_L.

Let us consider a case of a language **Q** which has a V_Q that includes four social science-type terms, "A", "B", "C", "D". The respective kinds or sets are designated **A, B, C, D**. Let us have:

$$a \subset A, \ b \subset B, \ c \subset C, \ d \subset D \tag{4}$$

and

$$x \not\subset A, \ x \not\subset B, \ x \not\subset C, \ x \not\subset D \tag{5}$$

Now we can assert that:

> if (4) & (5), then **Q** is inadequate. (T1)

The proof is obvious from (D4).

Let us build a language Q' which has a $V_{Q'}$, that includes five social science-type terms "A", "B", "C", "D", "X", and the respective stand-ins for sets, A, B, C, D, X. Now we can assert that:

if (4) and

if $x \subset x$, then $V_{Q'}$ is adequate. (T2)

(Read: if (4), and if entity x is part of the set X, then the language $V_{Q'}$ is adequate.) The proof is obvious from (D1).

Let us consider an example. There is a famous controversy among Marxists (and among some non-Marxists) about the "Asiatic Mode of Production." If one accepts the Stalinist language of only five modes of production (primitive, slave-owning, feudal, capitalist, and communist) then historians encounter serious difficulties with labeling some societies of pre-Columbian America, pre-classical Greece, early Mesopotamia, China, etc. The Stalinist language is inadequate. If one extends the list of the modes of production by introducing another one (it was labeled "Asiatic" by Marx), then the problems disappear. Of course, one extension might still prove inadequate and another one might prove adequate. Brendan O'Leary has recently put forward a very good argument about the concept of the Asiatic Mode of Production as used by Marx. He has given reasons for saying that Marx's notion of the Asiatic Mode of Production is an empty one. He also has accepted the Stalinist language as inadequate.[9] His argument does not preclude any other extensions which might even retain the words "Asiatic Mode of Production" (though the choice of words is, indeed, somewhat unfortunate) but give them a different reference from that of Marx.[10]

Using vacuous language is certainly wrong. True, vacuous language lends itself well to building speculative systems. But the latter have little interest or practical value to actual historians, although they have been, and are liked by some philosophers. Of course, we cannot know *a priori* whether a language is vacuous. Thus, using a language becomes wrong only after it has been shown that it is vacuous. Until that moment is reached, it can be used in a research program which has later to be abandoned although some of its results could be salvaged.

Using inadequate language is not just wrong. The language Q was adequate for purposes of dealing with a, b, c, d. It was inadequate over the whole area of reference, but it was adequate for a part of it. Adequacy can be partial. Languages and thoughts which are capable of being extended or developed are not to be condemned off-hand. It is a Philosophical Stalinism to accept an all-or-nothing approach. Although Philosophical Stalinism lends itself seemingly well to precise formalization, it is better to abandon it and to replace this kind of naive dogmatism with a more sophisticated approach.

Differences have to be ascertained before they can be explained. Let the asterisk * stand for "is different from." Now let us write:

$$a * b, \text{ because } (a \subset A) \text{ and}$$
$$(b \subset B) \text{ and } (A * B). \tag{6}$$

(Read: a is different from b, because a belongs to A and b belongs to B, and A is different from B.) Statements conforming to (6) are not necessarily causal. Of course, I am using the word "explanation" here in a rather loose way and not narrowing down its meanings to strict Hempelianism. Nevertheless, a question remains: Do statements conforming to (6) explain anything at all?

If we read $\subset$ as "is an expression of an essence," then (6) is a form for essentialist explanations. I am not a supporter of essentialism but some philosophers are, or have been, essentialists and some Stalinist historiography has been essentialist.

If we read $\subset$ as "is a part of," then, first, it becomes possible to interpret (6) as a form of functional explanation. If a has a function M within A, and if b has a function M within B, then A * B explains a * b. Functionalism might be wrong but it is possible to build up rational support for it. Functional statements can be regarded as just shorthand for more complex conditional sentences (E. Nagel) or for feedback descriptions (G. Klaus), or for consequence explanations (G. A. Cohen). Moreover, on this reading of the sign $\subset$, formula (6) can be treated as a shorthand involving loose reference to something that is not precisely elucidated by the historian who is giving the explanation. In some cases, even causal relationships might be involved in the area of reference. Explaining differences of rationality of actions provides us with an example.

To describe an action as a rational one, we need to know about the conditions which obtained at the time of action. We need to know about the possibilities and impossibilities of actions (as well as about whether such conditions were known to the actors, and about the values and aims of the actors, etc.). Accounts of possibilities and impossibilities depend on theories. Strict theories are formulated on models (M) of the reference area. There are few such strict theories in social studies outside of economics. The latter is obviously a social science; thus, there are some strict theories in social sciences. Weaker forms are used in many other social sciences. They are formulated on quasi-models and model-sketches. A *quasi-model* (QM) includes a list of entities (or types of entities) and a sublist of pairs (or n-tuples) of entities allowed to enter into some relations. Relations in a quasi-model are indicated by means that do not allow for their quantification; thus, it becomes impossible to predict the values of variables. A *model-sketch* (MS) includes a list of entities and a list of relations between some of these entities, but some of the values involved are not operationalizable at a given level of knowledge. Quasi-theories are formulated on quasi-models and theory sketches are formulated on model sketches.

Let us now consider cases (7) and (8):

Action A was rational under M_c or $(QM)_c$ or $(MS)_c$, although it would not have been rational under M_r or $(QM)_r$ or $(MS)_r$.   (7)

Institution B obtained because it was compatible with the rest of society under M_c or $(QM)_c$ or $(MS)_c$, although it was not compatible with the rest of society under M_r or $(QM)_r$ or $(MS)_r$.   (8)

What is explained in both cases is a difference (between A and some other action or type of action, between B and some other institution). Of course, a full explanation in both cases involves not just naming the individual models and theories (or quasi-models and quasi-theories, or model-sketches and theory-sketches) but also setting out their relevant parts. Quasi-models and model-sketches might prove to be sufficient to explain differences even if they are not quite sufficient for the purpose of explaining everything within their reference area. To explain why some actions were rational in hunter- gatherer economies, although they are not rational in full market economies with developed financial institutions, one does not always need a formalized mathematical model of a hunter-gatherer economy. For the purposes of investigating qualitative differences, quasi-models and model-sketches may be sufficient. History can proceed without strict theories.

IV

Let *conceptualization* stand for a theory or a quasi-theory or a theory-sketch, or a model or a quasi-model or a model-sketch. Let *ahistorical* stand for "not involving the PQD." Let *historical* stand for "involving the PQD." Are valid ahistorical conceptualizations of human societies possible?

Suppose a conceptualization applies only to the society of its author. Then it avoids the PQD locally but involves the PQD globally. Such a conceptualization is locally ahistorical but it is historical globally. If the author of this conceptualization considers it to be universally valid, then the conceptualization is proposed ahistorically and, as such, is not valid. In this sense, it represents "ideology" or "false consciousness" (both terms are used in the sense introduced by Marx and Engels). If the field of applicability of this conceptualization is not indicated by explicit means, then we have a case of indeterminacy. This is cognitively less preferable than an explicit setting out of the boundaries of application of a conceptualization. Sometimes ideology or claims of universal validity are introduced implicitly, without sufficient empirical grounds. This has often been the case with economic theories.

Suppose there have been more than one type (or set) of human societies. Suppose there is a non-empty intersection of $\cap$ s of all these types. Then a conceptualization of $\cap$ s is ahistorical. To compare humanity with systems made up from non-human beings (dogs, bees, fir trees, or stars), the conceptualization of $\cap$ s might supply us with an adequate or at least nonvacuous language and thought. This is not necessarily true if our study is limited to humans, i.e., to human interrelationships with things as used by humans. To account for any actual type of society, complementary conceptualizations would be needed. And to account for a particular society belonging to one of these types, yet more complementary conceptualizations would be necessary. Hence the cognitive value of a global, ahistorical conceptualization might be quite low in most cases of dealing with individual societies or humans, particularly in cases involving the discovery and explanation of differences within human society.

Humans have been playing different games within different sections of the time-grid covering their existence. Some games have been replaced by other games; some have evolved into other ones; there have been sequences of games involving different kinds of players. There has been some evolution of human societies.

A problem for historians is that of discovering and explaining sequences of societies (social systems, institutions, modes of action or thinking, etc.). This means asking questions both about the stability of societal systems and about conditions for change and replacement of these systems. A conceptualization of a sequence involves the PQD and is, thus, historical. The sequence itself is not a part of the $\cap$ s. Therefore, any ahistorical conceptualization of the $\cap$ s is inadequate.

I am not putting forward a claim that it is possible to build a unified typology of all human societies which places each type in an evolutionary sequence, even if that sequence is multilinear. Many dogmatic Marxists have certainly committed this sin, but they have not been the only ones thus guilty. This does not mean that one has to avoid constructing any evolutionary sequences of any set of types or subtypes of societal systems. An argument that rejects universalistic systems does not necessarily condone the rejection of other kinds of systems. The assertion that some systems are wrong does not entail the assertion that all systems are wrong. One can even find something rational in Marxism, if it is stripped of a lot of nonsense. The result would not be a Marx-*ism* any more, but Marx and the Marxists certainly do not deserve to be excluded from the set of writers about history and historical sociology who have still something to say to us. It is the Stalinists who have at least as much to fear from deconstructing any -ism as they have from replacing their particular -ism with some other -ism.

V

The PQD is highly or moderately relevant to some issues in history or philosophy. What follows is a short outline of some of these implications.

(A)   The past is to be understood as past. "Past" is here a short-hand reference to past humans, their societies, their things, and their relations with their environment. Contemporary concepts are sometimes meaningless while dealing with the past, or are only members of various families of concepts. What is meant by "corruption" in late-twentieth-century Britain or the U.S.A. might be indisputable at least for a core area of meaning. Matters change if we start dealing with Medieval Europe, as has been already pointed out by historians.[11] Understanding the past means understanding what was similar to us and what was dissimilar. They were not quite like us.

(B)   Theories about the past might be different from theories about the present. Marshall Sahlins did not duplicate the economic theory of capitalism (the latter word is not necessarily a term of opprobrium; it can also be a term of praise) when he wrote about primitive economy.[12] Boris Porshnev did not duplicate theories of capitalism when he wrote his book on the economic theory of feudalism.[13]

(C)   Given differences in conditions (societal systems), standards of rationality differ. Philosophers discuss rationality as if there were only ∩ s in existence, but this presupposition is wrong. To be more exact, this presupposition is inadequate.

(D)   Modern theories of justice are certainly ahistorical. They might turn out to be ideologies in the Marxian sense of that word. In the past, some people considered hierarchies to be desirable. For them, justice was relational to social positions. In some Historismus-languages, the words "just" and "fair" might be absent or not differentiable. Values like "justice" and "fairness" might not have been central at all. There is certainly a case for additional historical investigation of the empirical claims and underlying assumptions of all modern theories of justice.

(E)   Hegel created a historical philosophy. Most philosophers have been inventing ahistorical systems or treatments. Nowadays, support for Hegel's system cannot rationally be justified any more, because it involved speculative statements about empirical matters. This does not mean that universalism has to be implicit in philosophy. If philosophers deal only with the ∩ s, then they have to say so in an explicit manner and thus delineate the boundaries of applicability of their treatises. If they deal only with the contemporary English language, although pretending to deal with the ∩ s, then they are, at least, ideologues and only seemingly rational.[14]

It is obvious from the examples (A) to (E) that the account of the PQD given above is an open one. Various paths for further research are open to be traversed. New paths that have not been charted in this essay can be found. It is my sincere hope that somebody will be moving on.

Notes

1.   A. Megill, "Recounting the Past: 'Description,' Explanation, and Narrative in Historiography," *The American Historical Review* 94.3 (1989):629–53; Rex Martin, rev. of *Historical Understanding* by Louis O. Mink, *The American Historical Review* 94.4 (1989):1057; E. Loone, *Sovremennaia filosofia istorii* [*A Contemporary Philosophy of History*] (Tallinn: Eesti Raamat, 1989): English trans. *Marxism and the Analytical Philosophy of History* (London: Verso, 1990).

2.   This statement is made to avoid implicit one-trait reductionism.

3.   M. M. Postan, "History and the Social Sciences," in *Fact and Relevance: Essays on Historical Method* (Cambridge: Cambridge University Press, 1971), 15–21.

4. See B. A. Holderness, *Pre-Industrial England: Economy and Society 1500–1750* (London: Dent, 1976), 2–4.

5. Predictions of a "catastrophe" under specific conditions are quite legitimate. It is still an open question whether we can predict some traits of the replacement system. Troubles begin if we start trying to predict all properties, parts, etc., of the replacement system.

6. C. F. Richmond, "English Naval Power in the Fifteenth Century," *History* 52.174 (1967):1.

7. G. R. Elton, *The Tudor Revolution in Government* (Cambridge: Cambridge University Press, 1969). Elton's arguments about the nature of administrative revolution are independent of his assessments of the roles of particular individuals in changing the governmental structures of England.

8. Tracing differs from describing a series of kinds or periods. The traits that got abandoned are not mentioned at all. The traits that are not traced are also not mentioned. There is a danger of formulating tracing in a teleological rhetoric. The latter development is cognitively unfortunate because tracing does not imply teleology.

9. Brendan O'Leary, *The Asiatic Mode of Production: Oriental Despotism, Historical Materialism, and Indian History* (Oxford: Blackwell, 1989).

10. Thus it is reasonably possible to reject Marx and still accept Marxism as a paradigm or a research program. This is, of course, only a statement about the logical issues involved in O'Leary's argument.

11. J. Hurstfield, "Political Corruption in Modern England: The Historian's Problem," *History* 52:174 (1967):16–34.

12. Marshall Sahlins, *Stone Age Economics* (London: Tavistock, 1974).

13. Boris F. Porshnev, *Ocherk politicheskoi ekonomii feodalizma* [*An Essay on the Political Economy of Feudalism*] (Moscow, 1956).

14. See V. A. Lektorski, *Subiekt, obiekt, poznanie* [*Subject, Object, Cognition*] (Moscow, 1980).

10 Strategies of Causal Explanation in History

Andrus Park

I

This article identifies some strategies of causal explanation in history, more specifically, the typologies of six common explanatory strategies: "summary," "description of causes," "emerging causes," "periodization," the "hierarchical typology of causes," and the "narrative of causes." In working out the concept of explanation, I use some ideas put forward by a number of both western and Soviet theorists.[1] The study of history is here broadly understood as sociological or political interpretation. Most writings by K. Marx, F. Engels, and V. Lenin are taken in this sense. I concentrate my attention mostly on the analysis of explanatory strategies in these three Marxist authors.

Perhaps some general comments about Marxism are needed in the current political context. I do not consider myself a Marxist in any accepted sense. Furthermore, I think that Marxist ideology has failed completely and, it is to be hoped, will never again emerge as an influential worldview. At the same time, it is obvious that Marxism will remain an interesting and important chapter in the intellectual history of mankind. Although it is useless as a vision of the future, historical materialism still has some value as an interpretative theory about the societies of the past. Therefore, it continues to be meaningful to analyze the epistemological structure of Marxist historical writings.

II

Explanation is a procedure of grasping the essence (or part of the essence) of the object under study with references to appropriate laws, causes, or other essential conditions.[2] Such terms are here understood in a dialectical, materialist sense, as they are, for example, in V. Lenin's *Materialism and Empiriocriticism* or *Philosophical Papers*. Such a liberal understanding to a great degree corresponds to historians' ordinary use of language. Historians almost never use the concepts "cause," "explanation," "essence," etc.,

182

in some strict sense. They usually do not draw a sharp line between causes and mere conditions, although mere conditions, as a rule, can be identified on the basis of intuitive expert judgment. The philosophy of historical understanding must take this vagueness and ambiguity into account. Philosophers should not work out artificially strict notions that cannot be applied in real historical thinking.

"Historical explanation" here means an explanation, offered in history as in any intellectual discipline. For instance, a sociological explanation is an explanation in sociology, and so on.

By "explanatory statements" I mean statements like "E is explained by L," where E marks an explanandum and L stands for some kind of explanans. "Causal explanation" is understood as an explanation where reference is made to causes. Some explanatory statements are causal statements, and I think that most causal statements are explanatory statements. Causal explanatory statements may have forms like "E because C," "E is caused by C," "E is caused by $C_1, \ldots, C_n$," etc., where E again marks an explanandum and C stands for cause.

Statements such as these may be taken as typical examples of explanatory causal statements: "The rise of the activity of Moscow's foreign policy in the West in the second quarter of the 17th century was caused by the fact that the tartar states of Astrakhan and Khazan were defeated in the 16th century"; "The Italian policy of the German Emperors was one of the most important causes of the decline of the German Empire in the 13th–15th centuries"; "The Barbarian pressure was the most important cause of the collapse of the Western Roman Empire." Comparable examples can be found also in current historical studies, for example: "The main cause of the economic decline of the USSR in the 1970s and 1980s was the dominance of Marxist-Leninist ideological dogmas in economic policy"; "The main causes of perestroika in the Soviet Union were the Soviet failure to cope with the technological arms race (in particular, the Soviet fear of the American Strategic Defense Initiative), the decline of Soviet hard-currency oil revenues, and the change of the leadership in the Kremlin in 1985."

I understand "cause" as a phenomenon which creates, determines, changes, produces, etc., another phenomenon called an "effect." Each concrete causal connection takes place against the background of some conditions that can be divided into: more important and less important, necessary and unnecessary, etc. There is a dialectical interplay between causes, effects, and conditions: a phenomenon which is a cause in one connection may be an effect in another, and a mere condition in a third. As I indicated above, mere conditions can usually, in each concrete case, be identified and separated from explanatory causes on the basis of intuitive judgment. For example, it is possible to assume that phenomena like the exact titles of the main Soviet newspapers before 1985 or the important place of black bread in Russian cuisine can be taken just as mere conditions and not as explanatory causes of the emergence of perestroika.

Causes and effects can be treated as aspects of the universal systemic causal order – as aspects of the universal mutual relationship – that can be abstracted from the complex, dynamic, causal order for some concrete cognitive task. Reasons can, within this framework, be taken as causes: the difference between them is not essential. Similarly, we can also see as nonessential the difference between individual causes (for example, the crop failures of 1845–46 as one of the causes of the February revolution in France in 1848) and more general causes (for example, the emergence of social stratification as one of the main causes of the formation of a state).

I will focus my attention not on the differences of possible meanings of the notions "cause," "effect," and others, but – as said – on some explanatory strategies. The basic terminology used here is presented by Figure 1. The notions "historical" and "synchronic" are used here in the following sense: in the historical approach, explanatory causes are presented as emerging one after another in time; in the synchronic approach, as existing at the same time (neglecting here the dynamic pattern of their emergence).

There is also a certain distinction between the strategies of the explanatory *study* and the strategies of the *textual presentation* of explanation. It is possible that the explanatory study may sometimes follow a different strategy than the final textual presentation of it. But this aspect of the problem is beyond the framework of this article. Here, I will take the

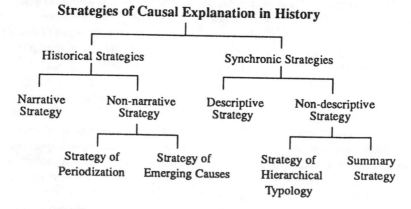

Strategies of Causal Explanation in History

Historical Strategies — Synchronic Strategies

Narrative Strategy — Non-narrative Strategy — Descriptive Strategy — Non-descriptive Strategy

Strategy of Periodization — Strategy of Emerging Causes — Strategy of Hierarchical Typology — Summary Strategy

Figure 1

textual presentation of the historical explanation as a basis for identifying the historian's explanatory strategy.

In following *synchronic* explanatory strategies, the historian puts a considerable emphasis on assuming (or demonstrating) that the causes $C_1, \ldots, C_n$ existed (or exist) practically at the same time, or that their chronological sequence is irrelevant for explanatory purposes. A *descriptive* strategy means that much attention in the textual presentation of the explanation is devoted to mere non-causal conditions of E. If we use the perestroika example again, we may again repeat that Russians eating a lot of black bread can be taken as a mere condition and not an explanatory cause of perestroika, whereas factors like the Soviet inability to cope with the arms race can be listed as one of the explanatory causes $C_1, \ldots, C_n$.

The systemic or *non-descriptive* strategies are divided in the table into two. In using a *summary* strategy, the historian does not attempt to give any significant information about E except a statement that $C_1, \ldots, C_n$ are some of the most important causes of E and exist at the same time. The strategy of *hierarchical typology* assumes also that $C_1, \ldots, C_n$ are similarly listed. But, in addition to listing $C_1, \ldots, C_n$ and assuming (or stressing explicitly) that they exist at the same time, the hierarchical-typology strategy aims at showing also that $C_1, \ldots, C_n$ are, in fact, groups of sub-causes. That is, if it is asserted that the Soviet failure to succeed in the modern arms race is one of the explanatory causes of perestroika, then an historian (following this strategy) attempts to show that the phenomenon "failure to succeed in the modern arms race" is itself a group of elements that function as explanatory sub-causes. Among these sub-causes, an historian may list factors like: "the failure to succeed in producing computers for military purposes," "the failure to compete successfully in developing space-based laser weapons," etc. We may mark these sub-causes as $C_{11}, \ldots, C_{1n}$. Similarly the application of the strategy of hierarchical typology requires that $C_2, \ldots, C_n$ should be also divided into sub-causes.

The use of the *historical* strategies of explanation assumes that a considerable effort is put on showing or assuming that the explanatory causes $C_1, \ldots, C_n$ exist in time, that C_1 existed before C_2, which existed before C_3, etc. In other respects, there is a great similarity between synchronic and historical strategies of causal explanation in history. The *narrative* strategy pays attention to non-causal conditions of E. The situation is similar to that with the descriptive strategy, except for the assumption about the chronological sequence of $C_1, \ldots, C_n$. Historical *non-narrative* strategies again come quite close to synchronic, non-descriptive strategies. The strategy of *emerging causes* is a rough diachronic equivalent of the summary strategy. If the emerging-causes strategy is followed, then an historian does not attempt to give any other significant information about E except a statement that $C_1, \ldots, C_n$ were the causes of E, and that C_1 emerged before C_2, C_2 emerged before C_3, etc. Suppose, for example, that E is the Soviet economic decline in the 1970s and 1980s and C_1 is Lenin's policy of creating a totalitarian party-state and C_2 is the Stalinist command-economy system. The historian who explains the Soviet economic decline in the 1970s–1980s through Leninist policy and the Stalinist system may then assume or show also that the Leninist policy was formed earlier than the Stalinist system.

The strategy of *periodization* differs from the strategy of the hierarchical typology of causes mainly, again, from the point of view of chronological assumptions. Like the hierarchical typology, the periodization strategy assumes that the explanatory causes $C_1, \ldots, C_n$ are, in fact, groups of sub-causes $C_{11}, \ldots, C_{1n}$, etc. In other words, the emerging causes are, in that case, themselves divided into sub-causes. For example, it would be possible to divide "Lenin's policy of creating the totalitarian party-state" into sub-causes like "destroying the democratically elected legislative body at the beginning of 1918," "establishing Cheka, i.e., the repressive security organs," etc.

There are, of course, almost endless different possibilities of building explanations according to the periodization strategy, which reflects, also, different objective combinations of historical causes. For example, $C_1, \ldots, C_n$ may strictly follow each other in time, so that C_1 ceases to exist when C_2 emerges. But there are also cases when C_1 continues to exist and even play an important role after C_2 has also occurred. It may be possible, also, to find similar patterns among the sub-causes $C_{11}, \ldots, C_{1n}$, $C_{21}, \ldots, C_{2n}$, and so on.

It seems to be obvious that the patterns of causal explanation in history are usually mixed. In real thinking, the outlined strategies appear in vague forms. Many components are not present explicitly but can be implicitly assumed. Still, from my point of view, the "ideal models" of different strategies of causal explanation are needed to understand the rationale behind the explanatory texts.

III

The analysis of a number of texts written by K. Marx, F. Engels, and V. Lenin shows that various causal explanations offered by them can be epistemologically clarified using the concepts of the strategies depicted.

The essential features of the *summary* strategy can be traced in numerous statements. Consider, for example, the following:

The present war has an imperialist nature. This war is created by the conditions of the epoch when capitalism has reached the highest stage of development; when not only the export of goods but the export of capital has the greatest importance; when cartels of production and the internationalization of economic life have reached considerable extent; when almost all the globe is divided as a result of the colonial policy; when the productive forces of world capitalism have overgrown the narrow frameworks of the national-state divisions; when all the objective conditions for the implementation of socialism are ripe.[3]

These lines are taken from the resolution of the 1915 conference of the Russian Bolsheviks in Switzerland and the statement refers, of course, to World War I. The text of the resolution was written by V. Lenin and the quoted passage is, in fact, the first paragraph of the resolution under the title, "On the Nature of the War." It is possible to interpret the given passage as a causal explanation according to the summary strategy, where World War I stands for E and the phenomena that Lenin calls the "conditions of the epoch" (the fact that capitalism "has reached its highest stage of development," the importance of the export of capital, etc.) stand for $C_1, \ldots, C_n$.

An example that has the features of the strategy of *hierarchical typology* can be found in the second part of Engels's *Anti-Dühring*. Here, he gives a causal explanation of the origin of social classes and relations based on domination and subjection. He says that they "arose in two ways." Within the framework of the "first way," Engels lists several causal factors that are connected with the need to safeguard common interests: creation of special organs allegedly representing these common interests, certain independence of these organs, transformation of the "servants of society" into the "lords of society," and so on. Speaking about the second way, he stresses that "the natural division of labor within the family cultivating the soil made possible, at a certain level of well-being, the introduction of one or more strangers as additional labor forces." Engels says that "the labor-power of a man could now produce more than was necessary for its mere maintenance," "the prisoners acquired a value," "slavery has been invented," etc.[4]

It seems to me that it is possible to interpret "the origin of social classes and relations based on domination" as E, and the "two ways" as groups of sub-causes C_1 and C_2. Now, several sub-causes $C_{11}, \ldots, C_{1n}$, etc., are identified by Engels within both C_1 and C_2: "the creation of special organs safeguarding common interest," "the emergence of slavery," etc. Generally, we may identify the given example as coming close to the hierarchical typology of causes.

An example which can be taken as representing the *descriptive* strategy of causal explanation can be found in Marx's *The Class Struggles in France 1848 to 1850*, which analyzes the causes of the revolution in France in February, 1848, when the July Monarchy was overthrown. The February Revolution itself, of course, can be identified as an explanadum E. There are several causal factors listed by Marx that can be taken as explanatory causes $C_1, \ldots ,C_n$: that it was not the whole French bourgeoisie that ruled under Louis Philippe but only one faction of it, the so-called finance aristocracy; the industrial bourgeoisie proper formed a part of the official opposition; the petty bourgeoisie of all gradations – the peasantry, the bourgeois ideological representatives and spokesmen (lawyers, doctors, etc.) – were also excluded from political power; the faction of the bourgeoisie that ruled had a direct interest in the indebtedness of the state and extraordinary state expenditure; the ruling class speculated with the building of railways; corruption; a series of foreign policy setbacks; economic events that accelerated the outbreak of the revolution (the crop failures, the potato blight, the general commercial and industrial crisis in England). The presentation of these main causal factors by Marx is mixed with several, more detailed accounts about various aspects of the main factors. But, although these more detailed accounts play an important stylistic role, it seems reasonable to classify them as non-causal conditions. Among these non-causal conditions may be mentioned the fact that a Rouen manufacturer, Grandin, was the most violent opponent of Guizot in the Chamber of Deputies; another politician, Bastiat, agitated in the name of the wine-producing France against the ruling system; the exact titles of some pamphlets circulating in Paris; etc.[5]

If we move on now to the historical strategies of causal explanation, we again can find examples in classical Marxist texts. Consider the following quotation from the point of view of the strategy of *emerging causes*:

> Bourgeoisie and proletariat both arose in consequence of a transformation of the economic conditions, more precisely, of the mode of production. The transition, first from guild handicrafts to manufacture and then from manufacture to large-scale industry with steam and mechanical power, had caused the development of these two classes.[6]

The structure of Engels's thought here can be interpreted in the following way. We may mark the emergence of the proletariat and the bourgeoisie with E. C_1, C_2, and C_3 may correspond, respectively, to the phenomena of the successive phases: guild handicraft, manufacture, and large-scale industry. The three causal factors C_1, C_2, and C_3 together can be taken as the causes of E, and, consequently, we have found here one of the forms of the implementation of the strategy of emerging causes.

There are also examples in Marxist studies that can be interpreted as the *periodization* of causes. Let us consider, for example, a passage from Marx's *The Eighteenth Brumaire of Louis Bonaparte*. After describing and analyzing in detail the process of the political development of France from the revolution of 1848 to the establishment of the rule of Louis Bonaparte, Marx summarizes developments in the form of a periodization of major events and the tendencies that result. Marx distinguishes three periods in this development. The second period is divided into sub-periods, and the third period is divided even into sub-sub-periods. Because the whole periodization is rather lengthy, I will present here only the description of the third period as an illustration.

Third period. Period of the *constitutional republic* and of the *Legislative National Assembly.*

1. May 28, 1949, to June 13, 1849. Struggle of the petty bourgeoisie with the bourgeoisie and with Bonaparte. Defeat of the petty-bourgeoisie democracy.
2. June 13, 1849, to May 31, 1850. Parliamentary dictatorship of the Party of Order. It completes its rule by abolishing universal suffrage but loses the parliamentary ministry.
3. May 31, 1850, to December 2, 1851. Struggle between the parliamentary bourgeoisie and Bonaparte.
    (a) May 31, 1850, to January 12, 1851. Parliament loses the supreme command of the army.
    (b) January 12 to April 11, 1851. It is worsted in its attempts to regain administrative power. The Party of Order loses its independent parliamentary majority. Its coalition with the republicans and the *Montagne.*
    (c) April 11, 1851, to October 9, 1851. Attempts at revision, fusion, prorogation. The Party of Order decomposes into its separate constituents. The breach between the bourgeois parliament and press and the mass of the bourgeoisie becomes definite.

(d)   October 9 to December 2, 1851. Open breach between par-
        liament and the executive power. Parliament performs its
        dying act and succumbs, left in the lurch by its own class,
        by the army, and by all the remaining classes. Passing of
        the parliamentary regime and the bourgeois rule. Victory of
        Bonaparte. Parody of restoration of the empire.[7]

I suppose that it is possible to interpret these passages in the light of
the periodization strategy. The "victory of Bonaparte and parody of
restoration of empire" may be taken as E. The three periods may be
taken as three successive groups C_1, C_2, C_3 of the causes of E. Phenomena
like "parliament loses the supreme command of the army" or "The Party
of Order loses its independent parliamentary majority" may be interpreted
as concrete sub-causes or sub-sub-causes in the above-listed groups of
causes C_1, C_2, C_3. Of course, a lot depends here on interpretation and
intuitive expert judgment. For example, it seems to me – on the basis of
my intuitive judgment – that the elements in the above-given periodization
can be interpreted as causes having explanatory value. If somebody says
that this is not the case, then he has, of course, to look for other examples
to fit the periodization-of-causes strategy.

Finally, an example which may clarify the meaning of the *narrative*
strategy: the fifth chapter of Engels's *The Origin of the Family*, which
contains an explanatory account of the rise of the Athenian State. The
emergence of the Athenian State itself may be identified as E, and a number
of historically emerging causes identified as C_1, . . . ,C_n. These include
such phenomena as: the development of the division of labor between
agriculture and handicraft, trade and navigation, sales of the land, etc.;
the formation of the central administration in Athens in the Heroic Age;
the archonts became the heads of the state; the money system was rapidly
developing; many of the small peasant farms of Attica were ruined; laws
protecting the creditor against the debtor and sanctioning the exploitation
of the peasants by money owners were introduced; etc. Engels gives an
account of the main causal factors that gradually emerged one after another
(and some of which quickly disappeared again) and that played a decisive
causal role in the formation of the Athenian State. Engels's account here
puts a considerable emphasis on the time-dimension, on the developing and
changing nature of these causes, whereas the descriptive strategy in Marx's
The Class Struggles in France 1848 to 1850 is quite indifferent toward the
dynamic aspect, the time-dimension.

Especially important according to the narrative-of-causes strategy, is
that we can find in Engels's passages several statements about various

historical details that can be interpreted as mere non-causal conditions of
E. I would include in this group statements about mere conditions: for
example, descriptions of the concrete structure of agricultural production
(cereals, wine, oil) the exact size (400 members) of the Athenian Council
after Solon's reforms; the exact size of necessary crop production for
the members of each class of Athenian society; and similar pieces of
information.[8]

IV

Six strategies of causal explanation in history were identified in this article.
These were applied to some classical Marxist texts, but there are good
reasons to believe that similar strategies appear in non-Marxist and, indeed,
all historical studies.

Notes

1.   For example, in English: L. Addis, R. Atkinson, I. Berlin, R.
      Collingwood, A. Danto, A. Donagan, W. Dray, J. Farr, H. Fain,
      P. Gardiner, W. Gallie, E. Gellner, L. Goldstein, C. Hempel, Susan
      James, A. Louch, M. Mandelbaum, Rex Martin, Raymond Martin, P.
      Nowell-Smith, M. Oakeshott, K. Popper, J. Passmore, N. Rescher, M.
      Scriven, Q. Skinner, M. White, H. White, W. Walsh, J. Wisdom, G.
      H. von Wright, and others. For the development of English-speaking
      critical philosophy of history, see Andrus Pork [Park] *Narrativism
      ja analüütiline ajaloofilosoofia* [*Narrativism and the Analytical Phi-
      losophy of History*] (Tallinn: Eesti Raamat, 1979) and *Istoricheskoye
      obyasneniye* [*Historical Explanation*] (Tallinn, Eesti Raamat, 1981).
      Cf. also my "A Note on Schemes of Historical Explanation," *Philosophy
      of the Social Sciences* 12 (1982):409–14; "Assessing Relative Causal
      Importance in History," *History and Theory* 24 (1985):62–69; "Critical
      Philosophy of History in Soviet Thought," *History and Theory* 27
      (1988):135–45; and "The Role of Examples in Social Explanation,"
      Philosophy of the Social Sciences 19 (1989):41–54. See also, in
      Russian: I. Kon, "K sporam o logike istoricheskogo obyasneniya" ["On
      Discussions of the Logic of Historical Explanation"], in *Filosofskiye
      problemy istoricheskoi nauki* (Moscow: Nauka, 1969), 263–95; E.
      Loone, "Problema istoricheskogo obyasneniya" ["The Problem of
      Historical Explanation"], *Filosofskiye nauki* no. 6 (1975); A. I. Rakitov,
      Istoricheskoye poznaniye [*Historical Knowledge*] (Moscow: Politizdat,
      1982).

2. See Andrus Pork [Park] *Epistemological Independence and Explanation in the Social Studies* (Tallinn: Academy of Sciences, 1986), 6.

3. V. I. Lenin, *Polnoe sobranie sochinenii* [*Works*], 2nd edn (Moscow: Politizdat, 1957), 6:161–62.

4. F. Engels, *Anti-Dühring* (Moscow, Foreign Lang. Publ., 1954), 247–53.

5. K. Marx, "The Class Struggles in France 1848–1850," in K. Marx and F. Engels, *Selected Works* (Moscow: Foreign Lang. Publ., 1955), 1:139–44.

6. F. Engels, *Ludwig Feuerbach and the Outcome of Classical German Philosophy* (Moscow: Foreign Lang. Publ., 1946), 60.

7. K. Marx, *The Eighteenth Brumaire of Louis Bonaparte*, in *Selected Works*, 1:329–30.

8. F. Engels, *The Origin of the Family, Private Property and State* (Moscow: Foreign Lang. Publ., 1948), 155–70.

Index

The index entry shows the page(s) on which an author is cited, either in the text or in the notes of that page. The authors' names are shown as they are given in the text, not as they may appear in the notes (see "A Note on Transliteration from Cyrillic," p. viii).